RAPHAEL'S AST

Ephemeris of the

for 20

A Complete Aspectarian

Mean Obliquity of the Ecliptic, 2002, 23° 26′ 20″

INTRODUCTION

Greenwich Mean Time (G.M.T.) has been used as the basis for all tabulations and times. The tabular data are for Greenwich Mean Time 12h., except for the Moon tabulations headed 24h. All phenomena and aspect times are now in G.M.T. To obtain Local Mean Time of aspect, add the time equivalent of the longitude if East and subtract if West.

Both in the Aspectarian and the Phenomena the 24-hour clock replaces the old a.m./p.m. system.

The zodiacal sign entries are now incorporated in the Aspectarian as well as being given in a separate table.

BRITISH SUMMER TIME

British Summer Time begins on March 31 and ends on October 27. When *British Summer Time* (one hour in advance of G.M.T.) is used, subtract one hour from B.S.T. before entering this Ephemeris.

These dates are believed to be correct at the time of printing.

Printed in Great Britain

ISBN 0-572-02605-6

Published by

LONDON: W. FOULSHAM & CO. LTD.

BENNETTS CLOSE, SLOUGH, BERKS. ENGLAND

NEW YORK TORONTO CAPE TOWN SYDNEY

NEW MOON – Jan.13,13h.29m. (23°♑11′)

D M	D W	Sidereal Time	☉ Long.	☉ Dec.	☽ Long.	☽ Lat.	☽ Dec.	☽ Node	24h. ☽ Long.	24h. ☽ Dec.
		h m s	° ′ ″	° ′	° ′ ″	° ′	° ′	° ′	° ′ ″	° ′
1	T	18 43 53	10 ♑ 53 36	23 S 00	8 ♌ 23 01	3 N29	21 N31	26 ♊ 20	15 ♌ 40 18	19 N54
2	W	18 47 49	11 54 44	22 54	22 58 07	4 21	17 58	26 17	0 ♍ 15 42	15 46
3	Th	18 51 46	12 55 52	22 49	7 ♍ 32 19	4 58	13 20	26 14	14 47 19	10 44
4	F	18 55 42	13 57 01	22 42	22 00 09	5 14	7 59	26 11	29 10 20	5 N09
5	S	18 59 39	14 58 09	22 36	6 ♎ 17 29	5 12	2 N16	26 07	13 ♎ 21 19	0 S37
6	Su	19 03 35	15 59 18	22 29	20 21 39	4 50	3 S28	26 04	27 18 21	6 16
7	M	19 07 32	17 00 28	22 21	4 ♏ 11 25	4 12	8 58	26 01	11 ♏ 00 49	11 32
8	T	19 11 28	18 01 37	22 14	17 46 36	3 20	13 56	25 58	24 28 52	16 08
9	W	19 15 25	19 02 47	22 05	1 ♐ 07 41	2 18	18 08	25 55	7 ♐ 43 09	19 52
10	Th	19 19 22	20 03 56	21 56	14 15 23	1 N10	21 21	25 52	20 44 27	22 32
11	F	19 23 18	21 05 06	21 47	27 10 27	0 00	23 25	25 48	3 ♑ 33 28	23 59
12	S	19 27 15	22 06 15	21 38	9 ♑ 53 34	1 S10	24 14	25 45	16 10 49	24 09
13	Su	19 31 11	23 07 24	21 27	22 25 17	2 14	23 47	25 42	28 37 05	23 07
14	M	19 35 08	24 08 33	21 17	4 ♒ 46 18	3 12	22 10	25 39	10 ♒ 53 03	20 59
15	T	19 39 04	25 09 41	21 06	16 57 28	4 00	19 33	25 36	22 59 45	17 56
16	W	19 43 01	26 10 48	20 55	29 00 07	4 36	16 08	25 32	4 ♓ 58 49	14 10
17	Th	19 46 57	27 11 55	20 43	10 ♓ 56 09	5 00	12 05	25 29	16 52 27	9 54
18	F	19 50 54	28 13 01	20 31	22 48 07	5 11	7 37	25 26	28 43 34	5 16
19	S	19 54 51	29 ♑ 14 07	20 19	4 ♈ 39 18	5 09	2 S52	25 23	10 ♈ 35 48	0 S27
20	Su	19 58 47	0 ♒ 15 11	20 06	16 33 38	4 53	2 N00	25 20	22 33 21	4 N26
21	M	20 02 44	1 16 15	19 53	28 35 34	4 25	6 51	25 17	4 ♉ 40 53	9 13
22	T	20 06 40	2 17 17	19 39	10 ♉ 49 54	3 44	11 32	25 13	17 03 15	13 45
23	W	20 10 37	3 18 19	19 25	23 21 30	2 51	15 51	25 10	29 45 12	17 48
24	Th	20 14 33	4 19 20	19 11	6 ♊ 14 49	1 49	19 34	25 07	12 ♊ 50 48	21 07
25	F	20 18 30	5 20 20	18 56	19 33 26	0 S38	22 23	25 04	26 22 55	23 22
26	S	20 22 26	6 21 18	18 41	3 ♋ 19 18	0 N36	24 00	25 01	10 ♋ 22 27	24 16
27	Su	20 26 23	7 22 16	18 26	17 32 05	1 51	24 07	24 58	24 47 42	23 34
28	M	20 30 20	8 23 13	18 10	2 ♌ 08 36	3 00	22 37	24 54	9 ♌ 33 55	21 15
29	T	20 34 16	9 24 09	17 54	17 02 39	3 59	19 31	24 51	24 33 39	17 27
30	W	20 38 13	10 25 03	17 38	2 ♍ 05 42	4 41	15 06	24 48	9 ♍ 37 34	12 31
31	Th	20 42 09	11 ♒ 25 57	17 S 21	17 ♍ 08 03	5 N04	9 N45	24 ♊ 45	24 S 36 02	6 N51

D M	Mercury Lat.	Mercury Dec.		Venus Lat.	Venus Dec.		Mars Lat.	Mars Dec.		Jupiter Lat.	Jupiter Dec.
	° ′	° ′	° ′	° ′	° ′	° ′	° ′	° ′	° ′	° ′	° ′
1	2 S 01	22 S 52	22 S 30	0 S 25	23 S 38	23 S 35	0 S 41	5 S 40	5 S 22	0 00	23 N01
3	1 53	22 07	21 43	0 30	23 32	23 28	0 39	5 04	4 46	0 N 01	23 03
5	1 42	21 17	20 51	0 34	23 23	23 18	0 37	4 27	4 09	0 01	23 04
7	1 27	20 23	19 55	0 39	23 12	23 05	0 34	3 51	3 32	0 01	23 06
9	1 09	19 26	18 57	0 43	22 57	22 49	0 32	3 14	2 56	0 01	23 07
11	0 46	18 28	17 59	0 47	22 40	22 30	0 30	2 37	2 19	0 02	23 09
13	0 S 20	17 31	17 03	0 51	22 20	22 09	0 28	2 00	1 42	0 02	23 10
15	0 N 10	16 37	16 13	0 55	21 57	21 45	0 26	1 24	1 05	0 02	23 11
17	0 44	15 50	15 30	0 58	21 32	21 18	0 23	0 47	0 S 28	0 02	23 12
19	1 20	15 13	15 00	1 02	21 04	20 49	0 21	0 S 10	0 N 08	0 03	23 14
21	1 56	14 49	14 42	1 05	20 33	20 17	0 19	0 N 27	0 45	0 03	23 15
23	2 31	14 39	14 40	1 08	20 00	19 43	0 17	1 03	1 21	0 03	23 16
25	3 00	14 44	14 51	1 11	19 25	19 06	0 15	1 40	1 58	0 04	23 17
27	3 22	15 00	15 12	1 14	18 47	18 28	0 13	2 16	2 34	0 04	23 18
29	3 34	15 26	15 S 40	1 16	18 08	17 S 47	0 11	2 52	3 N 10	0 04	23 19
31	3 N 36	15 S 56		1 S 18	17 S 26		0 S 09	3 N 28		0 N 04	23 N 20

FIRST QUARTER – Jan.21,17h.46m. (1°♉31′)

D M	☿ Long.	♀ Long.	♂ Long.	♃ Long.	♄ Long.	♅ Long.	♆ Long.	♇ Long.	☉	☿	♀	♂	♃	♄	♅	♆	♇
	° ′	° ′	° ′	° ′	° ′	° ′	° ′	° ′	Lunar Aspects								
1	26♑21	7♑47	17♓15	10♋36	9♊18	22♒29	7♒28	16♐03				⚼	⚺	⚹		☍	
2	27 53	9 03	17 59	10R 28	9R 14	22 32	7 30	16 05	⚼		⚼		∠		☍		△
3	29♑24	10 18	18 43	10 20	9 10	22 35	7 32	16 07	△		△		⚹	□			
4	0♒53	11 34	19 27	10 12	9 07	22 37	7 34	16 10		⚼		☍				⚼	□
5	2 21	12 49	20 10	10 04	9 03	22 40	7 36	16 12		△			□	△	⚼	△	
6	3 46	14 05	20 54	9 55	9 00	22 43	7 38	16 14	□		□			⚼	△		⚹
7	5 09	15 20	21 38	9 47	8 56	22 46	7 40	16 16		□		⚼	△			□	∠
8	6 29	16 36	22 22	9 39	8 53	22 49	7 43	16 18	⚹		⚹	△			□		⚺
9	7 45	17 51	23 06	9 32	8 50	22 52	7 45	16 20	∠		∠		⚼				
10	8 57	19 07	23 50	9 24	8 47	22 55	7 47	16 22	⚺	⚹	⚺			☍		⚹	☌
11	10 04	20 22	24 34	9 16	8 44	22 58	7 49	16 24		∠		□			⚹	∠	
12	11 06	21 38	25 17	9 08	8 41	23 01	7 51	16 26		⚺			☍		∠	⚺	
13	12 01	22 53	26 01	9 00	8 38	23 04	7 54	16 28	☌		☌	⚹		⚼	⚺		⚺
14	12 48	24 09	26 45	8 53	8 35	23 08	7 56	16 30						△		☌	∠
15	13 28	25 24	27 29	8 45	8 33	23 11	7 58	16 32		☌		∠					⚹
16	13 58	26 40	28 13	8 38	8 30	23 14	8 00	16 34	⚺		⚺	⚺	⚼		☌		
17	14 19	27 55	28 56	8 30	8 28	23 17	8 03	16 35	∠	⚺	∠		△	□		⚺	□
18	14 28	29♑11	29♓40	8 23	8 25	23 20	8 05	16 37							⚺	∠	
19	14R 27	0♒26	0♈24	8 16	8 23	23 24	8 07	16 39	⚹	∠	⚹	☌	□	⚹	∠	⚹	
20	14 14	1 42	1 08	8 09	8 21	23 27	8 09	16 41		⚹							△
21	13 49	2 57	1 51	8 02	8 19	23 30	8 12	16 43	□		□	⚺		∠	⚹		⚼
22	13 13	4 12	2 35	7 55	8 17	23 33	8 14	16 45		□			⚹	⚺		□	
23	12 26	5 28	3 19	7 48	8 15	23 37	8 16	16 46				∠	∠		□		
24	11 30	6 43	4 02	7 42	8 14	23 40	8 18	16 48	△	△	△	⚹	⚺	●		△	
25	10 26	7 59	4 46	7 35	8 12	23 43	8 21	16 50	⚼	⚼	⚼				△	⚼	☍
26	9 16	9 14	5 29	7 29	8 11	23 47	8 23	16 51				□	●	⚺	⚼		
27	8 02	10 29	6 13	7 23	8 09	23 50	8 25	16 53						∠			
28	6 46	11 45	6 57	7 17	8 08	23 53	8 28	16 55	☍	☍		△	⚺	⚹		☍	⚼
29	5 31	13 00	7 40	7 11	8 07	23 57	8 30	16 56			☍	⚼	∠		☍		△
30	4 19	14 15	8 23	7 05	8 06	24 00	8 32	16 58					⚹	□			
31	3♒11	15♒31	9♈07	7♋00	8♊05	24♒04	8♒34	16♐59		⚼						⚼	□

D M	Saturn Lat.	Saturn Dec.	Uranus Lat.	Uranus Dec.	Neptune Lat.	Neptune Dec.	Pluto Lat.	Pluto Dec.
	° ′	° ′	° ′	° ′	° ′	° ′	° ′	° ′
1	1S48	20N04	0S42	14S41	0N06	18S18	9N46	13S00
3	1 48	20 03	0 42	14 39	0 06	18 17	9 46	13 00
5	1 47	20 02	0 42	14 37	0 06	18 16	9 46	13 00
7	1 47	20 02	0 42	14 35	0 06	18 15	9 46	13 01
9	1 47	20 01	0 42	14 33	0 06	18 14	9 46	13 01
11	1 46	20 01	0 42	14 31	0 06	18 13	9 46	13 01
13	1 46	20 00	0 42	14 29	0 06	18 12	9 47	13 01
15	1 45	20 00	0 42	14 27	0 06	18 11	9 47	13 01
17	1 45	19 59	0 42	14 25	0 06	18 09	9 47	13 02
19	1 44	19 59	0 42	14 23	0 06	18 08	9 47	13 02
21	1 44	19 59	0 42	14 21	0 06	18 07	9 48	13 02
23	1 43	19 59	0 42	14 18	0 06	18 06	9 48	13 02
25	1 43	19 59	0 42	14 16	0 06	18 05	9 48	13 02
27	1 42	19 59	0 42	14 14	0 06	18 04	9 48	13 02
29	1 42	19 59	0 42	14 12	0 06	18 03	9 49	13 02
31	1S41	19N59	0S42	14S09	0N06	18S01	9N49	13S02

Mutual Aspects

1 ☉☍♃. ♀∠♅. ♀⚺♆. ☉∥☿. ☉#♃.
☿#♃.
2 ♀⚻♄. 3 ♀☍♃.
4 ☿∠♇.
5 ☉±♄.
6 ☉⚺♇.
7 ☉⊥♅. ♀±♄.
8 ♀⊥♅. ♀⚺♇. ♂∠♆. ☿#♄. ♀#♃.
9 ☿☌♆. ♂⚺♅.
10 ☿∠♂. ☿⚻♃. ☿△♄.
12 ☉⊥♇. ☿∥♆.
13 ☉⚼♄. ☉⚺♅. ♀⚺♅. ♀⊥♇.
14 ☉☌♀. ♀⚼♄. ♂Q♄.
18 ☿∠♂. ☿±♃. ♂⊥♅. ♃⚺♄. ♃⚼♅.
☿Stat.
19 ♀⚹♂.
20 ☿±♃. ♀∠♇. ♃⚻♆.
21 ☉∠♇. ☉#♄.
23 ☉⚹♂. ♄△♆. ♀#♄.
25 ♀⚻♃. ♀△♄. ♀☌♆.
26 ☿☌♀.
27 ☉☌☿. ☉⚻♃. ☿△♄. ☿☌♆.
28 ☉△♄. ☉☌♆. ☿⚹♂. ☿⚻♃. ♂□♃.
☉∥♆.
29 ♀±♃. ♀∥♆.
30 ♂⚹♄. ♂⚹♆.
31 ♂∠♅.

NEW MOON–Feb.12,07h.41m. (23°♒25′)

D M	D W	Sidereal Time	☉ Long.	☉ Dec.	☽ Long.	☽ Lat.	☽ Dec.	☽ Node	24h. ☽ Long.	24h. ☽ Dec.
		h m s	° ′ ″	° ′	° ′ ″	° ′	° ′	° ′	° ′ ″	° ′
1	F	20 46 06	12 ♒ 26 50	17 S 04	2 ♎ 00 31	5 N06	3 N53	24 ♊ 42	9 ♎ 20 42	0 N54
2	S	20 50 02	13 27 42	16 47	16 35 54	4 49	2 S 05	24 38	23 45 41	5 S 00
3	Su	20 53 59	14 28 34	16 29	0 ♏ 49 46	4 13	7 48	24 35	7 ♏ 48 01	10 29
4	M	20 57 55	15 29 24	16 12	14 40 29	3 24	13 00	24 32	21 27 19	15 19
5	T	21 01 52	16 30 14	15 53	28 08 44	2 24	17 24	24 29	4 ♐ 45 05	19 15
6	W	21 05 49	17 31 03	15 35	11 ♐ 16 43	1 18	20 50	24 26	17 44 01	22 08
7	Th	21 09 45	18 31 51	15 16	24 07 21	0 N10	23 08	24 23	0 ♑ 27 07	23 50
8	F	21 13 42	19 32 38	14 57	6 ♑ 43 41	0 S 57	24 13	24 19	12 57 22	24 18
9	S	21 17 38	20 33 24	14 38	19 08 29	2 01	24 04	24 16	25 17 18	23 32
10	Su	21 21 35	21 34 09	14 19	1 ♒ 24 04	2 58	22 44	24 13	7 ♒ 28 57	21 40
11	M	21 25 31	22 34 53	13 59	13 32 11	3 46	20 22	24 10	19 33 53	18 50
12	T	21 29 28	23 35 35	13 39	25 34 13	4 23	17 07	24 07	1 ♓ 33 20	15 14
13	W	21 33 24	24 36 16	13 19	7 ♓ 31 22	4 49	13 13	24 03	13 28 29	11 04
14	Th	21 37 21	25 36 55	12 59	19 24 52	5 02	8 49	24 00	25 20 43	6 29
15	F	21 41 18	26 37 33	12 38	1 ♈ 16 16	5 01	4 S 06	23 57	7 ♈ 11 49	1 S 41
16	S	21 45 14	27 38 09	12 18	13 07 41	4 48	0 N46	23 54	19 04 14	3 N12
17	Su	21 49 11	28 38 43	11 57	25 01 53	4 22	5 37	23 51	1 ♉ 01 05	8 00
18	M	21 53 07	29 ♒ 39 16	11 36	7 ♉ 02 22	3 44	10 20	23 48	13 06 15	12 34
19	T	21 57 04	0 ♓ 39 47	11 14	19 13 19	2 56	14 42	23 44	25 24 11	16 43
20	W	22 01 00	1 40 16	10 53	1 ♊ 39 27	1 58	18 34	23 41	7 ♊ 59 46	20 13
21	Th	22 04 57	2 40 44	10 31	14 25 41	0 S 53	21 39	23 38	20 57 48	22 49
22	F	22 08 53	3 41 09	10 09	27 36 36	0 N16	23 41	23 35	4 ♋ 22 30	24 14
23	S	22 12 50	4 41 33	9 47	11 ♋ 15 47	1 28	24 25	23 32	18 16 35	24 13
24	Su	22 16 47	5 41 54	9 25	25 24 51	2 36	23 37	23 29	2 ♌ 40 19	22 36
25	M	22 20 43	6 42 14	9 03	10 ♌ 02 31	3 36	21 12	23 25	17 30 41	19 25
26	T	22 24 40	7 42 32	8 41	25 03 52	4 23	17 18	23 22	2 ♍ 40 53	14 52
27	W	22 28 36	8 42 48	8 18	10 ♍ 20 22	4 52	12 12	23 19	18 00 53	9 20
28	Th	22 32 33	9 ♓ 43 02	7 S 56	25 ♍ 40 55	5 N01	6 N19	23 ♊ 16	3 ♎ 19 01	3 N13

D M	Mercury Lat.	Mercury Dec.		Venus Lat.	Venus Dec.		Mars Lat.	Mars Dec.		Jupiter Lat.	Jupiter Dec.
	° ′	° ′	° ′	° ′	° ′	° ′	° ′	° ′	° ′	° ′	° ′
1	3 N34	16 S 12	16 S 28	1 S 19	17 S 04	16 S 42	0 S 08	3 N46	4 N 04	0 N 04	23 N20
3	3 24	16 44	17 00	1 21	16 20	15 57	0 06	4 22	4 40	0 05	23 21
5	3 07	17 14	17 28	1 23	15 33	15 09	0 05	4 58	5 15	0 05	23 21
7	2 47	17 41	17 53	1 24	14 45	14 20	0 03	5 33	5 50	0 05	23 22
9	2 24	18 04	18 14	1 25	13 55	13 30	0 S 01	6 08	6 25	0 05	23 23
11	2 00	18 23	18 30	1 26	13 04	12 38	0 N 01	6 43	7 00	0 06	23 23
13	1 36	18 36	18 41	1 27	12 11	11 44	0 03	7 17	7 34	0 06	23 24
15	1 13	18 45	18 47	1 27	11 17	10 50	0 04	7 51	8 08	0 06	23 24
17	0 50	18 48	18 48	1 28	10 22	9 54	0 06	8 25	8 42	0 06	23 25
19	0 28	18 46	18 43	1 27	9 25	8 57	0 08	8 59	9 16	0 07	23 25
21	0 N07	18 39	18 33	1 27	8 28	7 59	0 09	9 32	9 49	0 07	23 26
23	0 S 13	18 26	18 18	1 26	7 30	7 01	0 11	10 05	10 21	0 07	23 26
25	0 31	18 08	17 57	1 25	6 31	6 01	0 12	10 37	10 53	0 07	23 26
27	0 49	17 45	17 31	1 24	5 31	5 01	0 14	11 09	11 25	0 07	23 27
29	1 04	17 16	17 S 00	1 23	4 31	4 S 01	0 15	11 41	11 N 57	0 08	23 27
31	1 S 18	16 S 43		1 S 21	3 S 30		0 N 17	12 N12		0 N 08	23 N27

FIRST QUARTER–Feb.20,12h.02m. (1°♊40′)

D M	☿ Long.	♀ Long.	♂ Long.	♃ Long.	♄ Long.	♅ Long.	♆ Long.	♇ Long.	☉	☿	♀	♂	♃	♄	♅	♆	♇
	° ′	° ′	° ′	° ′	° ′	° ′	° ′	° ′									
1	2♒09	16♒46	9♈50	6♋55	8♊04	24♒07	8♒37	17♐01	⚼	△	⚼		□	△	⚼	△	
2	1R 14	18 01	10 34	6R 49	8R 04	24 10	8 39	17 02	△		△	☍		⚼			⚹
3	0♒27	19 16	11 17	6 44	8 03	24 14	8 41	17 04		□			△		△		∠
4	29♑49	20 32	12 00	6 39	8 03	24 17	8 43	17 05	□		□					□	⚺
5	29 19	21 47	12 44	6 35	8 02	24 21	8 46	17 07		⚹		⚼	⚼		□		
6	28 57	23 02	13 27	6 30	8 02	24 24	8 48	17 08		∠		△		☍		⚹	☌
7	28 44	24 17	14 10	6 26	8 02	24 28	8 50	17 09	⚹	⚺	⚹				⚹	∠	
8	28 38	25 33	14 54	6 21	8D 02	24 31	8 52	17 11	∠		∠		☍		∠	⚺	
9	28D 40	26 48	15 37	6 17	8 02	24 35	8 55	17 12	⚺			□		⚼	⚺		⚺
10	28 49	28 03	16 20	6 14	8 02	24 38	8 57	17 13		☌	⚺						∠
11	29 04	29♒18	17 03	6 10	8 03	24 41	8 59	17 15				⚹		△		☌	⚹
12	29 26	0♓34	17 46	6 06	8 03	24 45	9 01	17 16	☌	⚺	☌		⚼		☌		
13	29♑53	1 49	18 29	6 03	8 04	24 48	9 04	17 17				∠	△	□		⚺	
14	0♒26	3 04	19 12	6 00	8 04	24 52	9 06	17 18		∠		⚺			⚺	∠	□
15	1 03	4 19	19 55	5 57	8 05	24 55	9 08	17 19	⚺	⚹	⚺		□				
16	1 44	5 34	20 39	5 54	8 06	24 59	9 10	17 20	∠					⚹	∠	⚹	△
17	2 30	6 49	21 21	5 52	8 07	25 02	9 12	17 21	⚹		∠	☌		∠	⚹		
18	3 19	8 04	22 04	5 50	8 08	25 06	9 15	17 22		□	⚹		⚹	⚺		□	⚼
19	4 11	9 19	22 47	5 48	8 09	25 09	9 17	17 23				⚺	∠		□		
20	5 07	10 34	23 30	5 46	8 11	25 13	9 19	17 24	□	△			⚺				
21	6 05	11 49	24 13	5 44	8 12	25 16	9 21	17 25			□	∠		●		△	☍
22	7 07	13 04	24 56	5 42	8 14	25 20	9 23	17 26	△	⚼		⚹			△	⚼	
23	8 10	14 19	25 39	5 41	8 15	25 23	9 25	17 27			△		●	⚺	⚼		
24	9 17	15 34	26 21	5 40	8 17	25 26	9 27	17 28	⚼		⚼	□		∠			⚼
25	10 25	16 49	27 04	5 39	8 19	25 30	9 29	17 29		☍			⚺	⚹		☍	△
26	11 35	18 04	27 47	5 38	8 21	25 33	9 32	17 29				△	∠		☍		
27	12 47	19 19	28 29	5 38	8 23	25 37	9 34	17 30	☍			⚼	⚹	□			□
28	14♒01	20♓34	29♈12	5♋38	8♊25	25♒40	9♒36	17♐31		⚼	☍					⚼	

D M	Saturn Lat.	Saturn Dec.	Uranus Lat.	Uranus Dec.	Neptune Lat.	Neptune Dec.	Pluto Lat.	Pluto Dec.
	° ′	° ′	° ′	° ′	° ′	° ′	° ′	° ′
1	1S41	19N59	0S42	14S08	0N06	18S01	9N49	13S02
3	1 41	20 00	0 42	14 06	0 06	18 00	9 50	13 02
5	1 40	20 00	0 42	14 04	0 06	17 58	9 50	13 01
7	1 39	20 01	0 42	14 01	0 06	17 57	9 50	13 01
9	1 39	20 01	0 42	13 59	0 06	17 56	9 51	13 01
11	1 38	20 02	0 42	13 57	0 06	17 55	9 51	13 01
13	1 38	20 02	0 42	13 55	0 06	17 54	9 52	13 01
15	1 37	20 03	0 42	13 52	0 06	17 53	9 52	13 01
17	1 37	20 04	0 42	13 50	0 06	17 52	9 52	13 00
19	1 36	20 05	0 42	13 48	0 06	17 50	9 53	13 00
21	1 36	20 06	0 42	13 45	0 06	17 49	9 53	13 00
23	1 35	20 07	0 42	13 43	0 06	17 48	9 54	12 59
25	1 35	20 08	0 42	13 41	0 06	17 47	9 54	12 59
27	1 34	20 09	0 42	13 38	0 06	17 46	9 55	12 59
29	1 34	20 10	0 42	13 36	0 06	17 45	9 55	12 58
31	1S33	20N12	0S42	13S34	0N06	17S44	9N56	12S58

Mutual Aspects

1 ☉±♃. ☿∠♇. ♀⚹♇. ☉∥♀.
2 ☿∥♀. 3 ☉∥☿.
4 ☿Q♂.
5 ♀⚼♃.
6 ☉⚹♇.
7 ♀☌♅.
8 ☿∥♆. ☿Stat. ♄Stat.
9 ♀∥♅. 10 ☉⚼♃.
11 ☿⚺♀. ♀Q♇. ♂△♇. ☉∥♅. ♀∥♇.
13 ☉☌♅. 14 ☉∥♇.
16 ♀∠♂. ♀△♃.
17 ☿∠♇. ♂Q♆.
18 ☉Q♇. ♀□♄.
19 ♀⚺♆.
20 ♂Q♃. ♂∠♄. ♀#♂.
21 ☿∇♃. 22 ☿⊥♀.
23 ☿△♄. ♂⚹♅. ☉#♂.
24 ☉△♃. ☿☌♆. ♀⊥♆.
26 ☿±♃. ♀□♇.
27 ☉□♄. ☿∥♆.
28 ☉⚺♆.

NEW MOON–Mar.14,02h.02m. (23° ♓ 19′)

D M	D W	Sidereal Time	☉ Long.	☉ Dec.	☽ Long.	☽ Lat.	☽ Dec.	☽ Node	24h. ☽ Long.	24h. ☽ Dec.
		h m s	° ′ ″	° ′	° ′ ″	° ′	° ′	° ′	° ′ ″	° ′
1	F	22 36 29	10 ♓ 43 15	7 S 33	10 ♎ 53 47	4 N48	0 N06	23 ♊ 13	18 ♎ 24 03	3 S 00
2	S	22 40 26	11 43 26	7 10	25 48 47	4 15	6 S 01	23 09	3 ♏ 07 14	8 55
3	Su	22 44 22	12 43 35	6 47	10 ♏ 18 52	3 27	11 39	23 06	17 23 23	14 11
4	M	22 48 19	13 43 43	6 24	24 20 42	2 27	16 29	23 03	1 ♐ 10 56	18 32
5	T	22 52 16	14 43 50	6 01	7 ♐ 54 19	1 21	20 18	23 00	14 31 14	21 46
6	W	22 56 12	15 43 55	5 38	21 02 07	0 N12	22 56	22 57	27 27 29	23 47
7	Th	23 00 09	16 43 58	5 14	3 ♑ 47 53	0 S 55	24 18	22 54	10 ♑ 03 53	24 30
8	F	23 04 05	17 44 00	4 51	16 16 01	1 58	24 24	22 50	22 24 49	23 59
9	S	23 08 02	18 44 00	4 27	28 30 46	2 54	23 18	22 47	4 ♒ 34 21	22 20
10	Su	23 11 58	19 43 59	4 04	10 ♒ 35 57	3 42	21 08	22 44	16 35 58	19 42
11	M	23 15 55	20 43 55	3 40	22 34 43	4 19	18 04	22 41	28 32 29	16 15
12	T	23 19 51	21 43 50	3 17	4 ♓ 29 31	4 44	14 16	22 38	10 ♓ 26 01	12 10
13	W	23 23 48	22 43 43	2 53	16 22 11	4 57	9 56	22 35	22 18 11	7 38
14	Th	23 27 45	23 43 34	2 29	28 14 10	4 57	5 15	22 31	4 ♈ 10 17	2 S 49
15	F	23 31 41	24 43 23	2 06	10 ♈ 06 43	4 45	0 S 22	22 28	16 03 38	2 N07
16	S	23 35 38	25 43 10	1 42	22 01 14	4 19	4 N34	22 25	27 59 46	6 59
17	Su	23 39 34	26 42 55	1 18	3 ♉ 59 30	3 42	9 22	22 22	10 ♉ 00 45	11 39
18	M	23 43 31	27 42 38	0 55	16 03 52	2 55	13 51	22 19	22 09 16	15 55
19	T	23 47 27	28 42 18	0 31	28 17 22	1 59	17 51	22 15	4 ♊ 28 41	19 35
20	W	23 51 24	29 ♓ 41 57	0 S 07	10 ♊ 43 43	0 S 56	21 08	22 12	17 03 01	22 25
21	Th	23 55 20	0 ♈ 41 33	0 N17	23 27 08	0 N11	23 27	22 09	29 56 36	24 11
22	F	23 59 17	1 41 07	0 40	6 ♋ 31 57	1 19	24 36	22 06	13 ♋ 13 38	24 39
23	S	0 03 14	2 40 38	1 04	20 02 02	2 25	24 20	22 03	26 57 27	23 39
24	Su	0 07 10	3 40 08	1 28	4 ♌ 00 01	3 25	22 34	22 00	11 ♌ 09 41	21 07
25	M	0 11 07	4 39 35	1 51	18 26 13	4 14	19 19	21 56	25 49 10	17 11
26	T	0 15 03	5 38 59	2 15	3 ♍ 17 48	4 47	14 45	21 53	10 ♍ 51 12	12 04
27	W	0 19 00	6 38 22	2 38	18 28 13	5 01	9 10	21 50	26 07 32	6 N08
28	Th	0 22 56	7 37 42	3 02	3 ♎ 47 44	4 54	2 N59	21 47	11 ♎ 27 19	0 S 12
29	F	0 26 53	8 37 00	3 25	19 04 49	4 25	3 S 23	21 44	26 38 53	6 29
30	S	0 30 49	9 36 16	3 48	4 ♏ 08 17	3 39	9 28	21 41	11 ♏ 32 00	12 17
31	Su	0 34 46	10 ♈ 35 30	4 N12	18 ♏ 49 16	2 N39	14 S 52	21 ♊ 37	25 ♏ 59 30	17 S 13

D M	Mercury Lat.	Mercury Dec.	Mercury Dec.	Venus Lat.	Venus Dec.	Venus Dec.	Mars Lat.	Mars Dec.	Mars Dec.	Jupiter Lat.	Jupiter Dec.
	° ′	° ′	° ′	° ′	° ′	° ′	° ′	° ′	° ′	° ′	° ′
1	1 S 04	17 S 16	17 S 00	1 S 23	4 S 31	4 S 01	0 N 15	11 N41	11 N 57	0 N 08	23 N27
3	1 18	16 43	16 24	1 21	3 30	3 00	0 17	12 12	12 27	0 08	23 27
5	1 31	16 04	15 42	1 19	2 29	1 58	0 18	12 43	12 58	0 08	23 27
7	1 42	15 20	14 56	1 17	1 28	0 S 57	0 20	13 13	13 28	0 08	23 27
9	1 52	14 30	14 04	1 15	0 S 26	0 N05	0 21	13 43	13 57	0 08	23 27
11	2 00	13 36	13 07	1 12	0 N36	1 07	0 23	14 12	14 26	0 09	23 27
13	2 07	12 37	12 05	1 09	1 37	2 08	0 24	14 41	14 55	0 09	23 27
15	2 12	11 33	10 59	1 06	2 39	3 10	0 25	15 09	15 23	0 09	23 27
17	2 15	10 24	9 47	1 03	3 40	4 11	0 27	15 36	15 50	0 09	23 27
19	2 16	9 10	8 31	0 59	4 41	5 12	0 28	16 03	16 17	0 09	23 27
21	2 16	7 51	7 10	0 55	5 42	6 12	0 29	16 30	16 43	0 10	23 27
23	2 14	6 28	5 44	0 52	6 42	7 12	0 30	16 56	17 08	0 10	23 27
25	2 09	5 00	4 14	0 47	7 42	8 12	0 32	17 21	17 33	0 10	23 27
27	2 03	3 27	2 40	0 43	8 41	9 10	0 33	17 45	17 58	0 10	23 26
29	1 55	1 51	1 S 01	0 39	9 39	10 N08	0 34	18 09	18 N 21	0 10	23 26
31	1 S 45	0 S 10		0 S 34	10 N36		0 N 35	18 N33		0 N 10	23 N26

FIRST QUARTER–Mar.22,02h.28m. (1° ♋ 17′)

FULL MOON–Mar.28,18h.25m. (7°♎54′)

D	☿	♀	♂	♃	♄	♅	♆	♇	Lunar Aspects								
M	Long.	Long.	Long.	Long.	Long.	Long.	Long.	Long.	☉	☿	♀	♂	♃	♄	♅	♆	♇
	° ′	° ′	° ′	° ′	° ′	° ′	° ′	° ′									
1	15♒17	21♓49	29♈55	5♋37	8♊28	25♒44	9♒38	17♐31		△			□	△	⚼	△	✱
2	16 35	23 04	0♉37	5D 37	8 30	25 47	9 40	17 32	⚼			☍		⚼	△		∠
3	17 54	24 18	1 20	5 38	8 33	25 50	9 42	17 33	△		⚼		△			□	
4	19 14	25 33	2 02	5 38	8 35	25 54	9 44	17 33		□	△		⚼		□		⊻
5	20 36	26 48	2 44	5 39	8 38	25 57	9 46	17 34						☍		✱	
6	21 59	28 03	3 27	5 40	8 41	26 00	9 48	17 34	□	✱		⚼			✱	∠	☌
7	23 24	29♓17	4 09	5 41	8 44	26 04	9 49	17 35		∠	□	△	☍			⊻	
8	24 50	0♈32	4 51	5 42	8 47	26 07	9 51	17 35	✱						∠		⊻
9	26 18	1 47	5 34	5 44	8 50	26 10	9 53	17 36	∠	⊻	✱			⚼	⊻		∠
10	27 46	3 01	6 16	5 45	8 53	26 13	9 55	17 36				□		△		☌	
11	29♒16	4 16	6 58	5 47	8 57	26 17	9 57	17 36	⊻		∠		⚼		☌		✱
12	0♓47	5 31	7 40	5 49	9 00	26 20	9 59	17 37		☌	⊻	✱	△	□		⊻	
13	2 20	6 45	8 23	5 51	9 04	26 23	10 01	17 37									□
14	3 53	8 00	9 05	5 54	9 07	26 26	10 02	17 37	☌			∠			⊻	∠	
15	5 28	9 14	9 47	5 56	9 11	26 29	10 04	17 37		⊻	☌	⊻	□	✱	∠	✱	
16	7 04	10 29	10 29	5 59	9 15	26 33	10 06	17 37	⊻	∠				∠	✱		△
17	8 42	11 43	11 11	6 02	9 19	26 36	10 08	17 37		✱			✱	⊻			⚼
18	10 20	12 58	11 53	6 05	9 23	26 39	10 09	17 38	∠		⊻	☌	∠			□	
19	12 00	14 12	12 35	6 08	9 27	26 42	10 11	17 38	✱		∠				□		
20	13 41	15 26	13 16	6 12	9 31	26 45	10 13	17 38		□	✱	⊻	⊻	●		△	
21	15 23	16 41	13 58	6 16	9 35	26 48	10 14	17R 38				∠			△	⚼	☍
22	17 06	17 55	14 40	6 20	9 40	26 51	10 16	17 38	□				●	⊻	⚼		
23	18 51	19 09	15 22	6 24	9 44	26 54	10 17	17 38		△	□	✱		∠			
24	20 37	20 24	16 04	6 28	9 49	26 57	10 19	17 37	△	⚼			⊻	✱		☍	⚼
25	22 25	21 38	16 45	6 32	9 53	27 00	10 20	17 37	⚼		△	□	∠				△
26	24 13	22 52	17 27	6 37	9 58	27 03	10 22	17 37			⚼		✱	□	☍		
27	26 03	24 06	18 09	6 42	10 03	27 06	10 23	17 37				△				⚼	□
28	27 54	25 20	18 50	6 46	10 08	27 08	10 25	17 37	☍	☍		⚼	□	△		△	
29	29♓47	26 34	19 32	6 52	10 13	27 11	10 26	17 36						⚼	⚼		✱
30	1♈41	27 48	20 13	6 57	10 18	27 14	10 28	17 36			☍		△		△	□	∠
31	3♈36	29♈02	20♉55	7♋02	10♊23	27♒17	10♒29	17♐36		⚼		☍	⚼				⊻

D	Saturn		Uranus		Neptune		Pluto	
M	Lat.	Dec.	Lat.	Dec.	Lat.	Dec.	Lat.	Dec.
	° ′	° ′	° ′	° ′	° ′	° ′	° ′	° ′
1	1S34	20N10	0S42	13S36	0N06	17S45	9N55	12S58
3	1 33	20 12	0 42	13 34	0 06	17 44	9 56	12 58
5	1 33	20 13	0 42	13 32	0 06	17 43	9 56	12 58
7	1 32	20 14	0 42	13 29	0 06	17 42	9 57	12 57
9	1 32	20 16	0 42	13 27	0 06	17 41	9 57	12 57
11	1 31	20 17	0 42	13 25	0 06	17 40	9 58	12 56
13	1 31	20 19	0 42	13 23	0 06	17 39	9 58	12 56
15	1 30	20 20	0 42	13 21	0 06	17 38	9 59	12 56
17	1 30	20 22	0 42	13 19	0 06	17 37	9 59	12 55
19	1 30	20 23	0 42	13 16	0 06	17 36	10 00	12 55
21	1 29	20 25	0 42	13 14	0 06	17 35	10 00	12 54
23	1 29	20 27	0 42	13 12	0 05	17 35	10 01	12 54
25	1 28	20 29	0 42	13 10	0 05	17 34	10 01	12 53
27	1 28	20 31	0 42	13 09	0 05	17 33	10 01	12 53
29	1 27	20 32	0 42	13 07	0 05	17 32	10 02	12 52
31	1S27	20N34	0S42	13S05	0N05	17S31	10N02	12S52

Mutual Aspects

1 ♃Stat.
3 ☿✱♇. ♀∠♆.
4 ♀⊻♅.
5 ☿Q♂. ☿⚼♃. ♀⊥♂. ♀Q♄. ♂⊥♄.
♂⚼♇.
6 ☉⊥♆. ☿⊥♀. ♂♯♇.
8 ☉□♇. ♂♯♅.
9 ☿☌♅. ♀⊥♅. ♂✱♃.
10 ☿♯♂.
11 ☿Q♇. ☿∥♅.
12 ♀□♃. ☿∥♇.
13 ♂Q♅.
14 ♂⊻♄. ☉♯♀.
15 ☉∠♂. ☉∠♆. ☿△♃. ♀✱♄. ♂□♆.
16 ♀⊻♂. ♀✱♆.
17 ☉⊻♅. ☿□♄. ♀∠♅.
18 ☉Q♄. ☿⊻♆. ♂±♇.
20 ☿✱♂. ♇Stat.
22 ☿⊥♆. ☿□♇. ♀△♇.
23 ☉⊥♅. ☿♯♀.
24 ☿⊻♀.
26 ♀Q♆. ♂∇♇. ♂♯♆.
27 ☉□♃. ☿∠♆.
28 ☿Q♄. ☿⊻♅. ♀Q♃. ♀∠♄. ☉♯☿.
30 ♀✱♅.
31 ☉✱♄. ☉✱♆. ☿⊥♅.

LAST QUARTER–Mar. 6,01h.24m. (15°♐17′)

NEW MOON–Apr.12,19h.21m. (22°♈42′)

D M	D W	Sidereal Time	☉ Long.	☉ Dec.	☽ Long.	☽ Lat.	☽ Dec.	☽ Node	24h. ☽ Long.	24h. ☽ Dec.
		h m s	° ′ ″	° ′	° ′ ″	° ′	° ′	° ′	° ′ ″	° ′
1	M	0 38 43	11 ♈ 34 43	4 N35	3 ♐ 02 23	1 N30	19 S 17	21 ♊ 34	9 ♐ 57 48	21 S 02
2	T	0 42 39	12 33 54	4 58	16 45 51	0 N19	22 28	21 31	23 26 46	23 33
3	W	0 46 36	13 33 03	5 21	0 ♑ 00 55	0 S51	24 18	21 28	6 ♑ 28 46	24 42
4	Th	0 50 32	14 32 10	5 44	12 50 51	1 57	24 45	21 25	19 07 44	24 30
5	F	0 54 29	15 31 15	6 07	25 20 03	2 55	23 56	21 21	1 ♒ 28 23	23 05
6	S	0 58 25	16 30 19	6 29	7 ♒ 33 20	3 44	21 59	21 18	13 35 29	20 38
7	Su	1 02 22	17 29 21	6 52	19 35 22	4 22	19 05	21 15	25 33 31	17 20
8	M	1 06 18	18 28 21	7 14	1 ♓ 30 24	4 48	15 25	21 12	7 ♓ 26 25	13 21
9	T	1 10 15	19 27 19	7 37	13 21 59	5 01	11 10	21 09	19 17 25	8 53
10	W	1 14 12	20 26 16	7 59	25 13 01	5 02	6 31	21 06	1 ♈ 09 02	4 S 05
11	Th	1 18 08	21 25 10	8 21	7 ♈ 05 43	4 50	1 S 37	21 02	13 03 15	0 N53
12	F	1 22 05	22 24 02	8 43	19 01 49	4 24	3 N22	20 59	25 01 35	5 51
13	S	1 26 01	23 22 53	9 05	1 ♉ 02 42	3 47	8 17	20 56	7 ♉ 05 20	10 39
14	Su	1 29 58	24 21 42	9 27	13 09 40	2 59	12 56	20 53	19 15 52	15 06
15	M	1 33 54	25 20 28	9 48	25 24 10	2 03	17 08	20 50	1 ♊ 34 49	18 59
16	T	1 37 51	26 19 12	10 10	7 ♊ 48 03	0 S59	20 38	20 47	14 04 12	22 03
17	W	1 41 47	27 17 55	10 31	20 23 36	0 N08	23 13	20 43	26 46 35	24 06
18	Th	1 45 44	28 16 35	10 52	3 ♋ 13 32	1 16	24 40	20 40	9 ♋ 44 49	24 54
19	F	1 49 41	29 ♈ 15 13	11 13	16 20 49	2 22	24 47	20 37	23 01 54	24 19
20	S	1 53 37	0 ♉ 13 49	11 33	29 48 20	3 22	23 29	20 34	6 ♌ 40 22	22 17
21	Su	1 57 34	1 12 22	11 54	13 ♌ 38 10	4 12	20 45	20 31	20 41 44	18 53
22	M	2 01 30	2 10 54	12 14	27 50 59	4 48	16 43	20 27	5 ♍ 05 38	14 17
23	T	2 05 27	3 09 23	12 34	12 ♍ 25 13	5 06	11 37	20 24	19 49 08	8 45
24	W	2 09 23	4 07 50	12 54	27 16 34	5 05	5 N45	20 21	4 ♎ 46 34	2 N38
25	Th	2 13 20	5 06 14	13 13	12 ♎ 18 02	4 43	0 S31	20 18	19 49 49	3 S41
26	F	2 17 16	6 04 37	13 33	27 20 40	4 01	6 47	20 15	4 ♏ 49 26	9 46
27	S	2 21 13	7 02 58	13 52	12 ♏ 14 58	3 03	12 36	20 12	19 36 16	15 14
28	Su	2 25 10	8 01 17	14 11	26 52 27	1 54	17 37	20 08	4 ♐ 02 51	19 42
29	M	2 29 06	8 59 35	14 30	11 ♐ 06 55	0 N39	21 28	20 05	18 04 22	22 53
30	T	2 33 03	9 ♉ 57 51	14 N48	24 ♐ 55 03	0 S36	23 S56	20 ♊ 02	1 ♑ 38 57	24 S37

D M	Mercury Lat.	Mercury Dec.		Venus Lat.	Venus Dec.		Mars Lat.	Mars Dec.		Jupiter Lat.	Jupiter Dec.
	° ′	° ′	° ′	° ′	° ′	° ′	° ′	° ′	° ′	° ′	° ′
1	1 S39	0 N41	1 N 34	0 S 32	11 N04	11 N32	0 N 36	18 N44	18 N 55	0 N 10	23 N25
3	1 26	2 27	3 21	0 27	12 00	12 28	0 37	19 07	19 17	0 11	23 25
5	1 11	4 15	5 10	0 22	12 55	13 21	0 38	19 28	19 39	0 11	23 24
7	0 53	6 06	7 01	0 17	13 48	14 14	0 39	19 49	19 59	0 11	23 24
9	0 35	7 57	8 53	0 12	14 40	15 05	0 40	20 09	20 19	0 11	23 23
11	0 S14	9 49	10 44	0 07	15 30	15 55	0 41	20 29	20 38	0 11	23 22
13	0 N07	11 38	12 32	0 S 01	16 19	16 43	0 42	20 48	20 57	0 11	23 22
15	0 29	13 25	14 17	0 N 04	17 07	17 30	0 43	21 06	21 15	0 12	23 21
17	0 51	15 07	15 55	0 09	17 52	18 15	0 44	21 23	21 32	0 12	23 20
19	1 13	16 42	17 27	0 15	18 36	18 57	0 45	21 40	21 48	0 12	23 19
21	1 33	18 09	18 49	0 20	19 18	19 38	0 45	21 56	22 03	0 12	23 18
23	1 51	19 27	20 03	0 26	19 58	20 17	0 46	22 11	22 18	0 12	23 17
25	2 07	20 36	21 06	0 31	20 36	20 54	0 47	22 25	22 32	0 12	23 16
27	2 20	21 34	21 59	0 37	21 11	21 28	0 48	22 39	22 45	0 12	23 14
29	2 30	22 22	22 N 42	0 42	21 44	22 N00	0 49	22 51	22 N 57	0 13	23 13
31	2 N36	23 N00		0 N 47	22 N15		0 N 50	23 N03		0 N 13	23 N12

FIRST QUARTER–Apr.20,12h.48m. (0°♌16′)

FULL MOON–Apr.27,03h.00m. (6°♏41′)

D M	☿ Long.	♀ Long.	♂ Long.	♃ Long.	♄ Long.	♅ Long.	♆ Long.	♇ Long.	☉	☿	♀	♂	♃	♄	♅	♆	♇
	° ′	° ′	° ′	° ′	° ′	° ′	° ′	° ′									
1	5♈33	0♉16	21♉36	7♋08	10♊28	27♒20	10♒30	17♐35	⚼	△					□		
2	7 31	1 30	22 17	7 13	10 33	27 22	10 32	17R 35	△		⚼			☍		⚹	☌
3	9 30	2 44	22 59	7 19	10 39	27 25	10 33	17 34			△				⚹	∠	
4	11 30	3 58	23 40	7 25	10 44	27 28	10 34	17 34	□	□		⚼	☍		∠	⚺	⚺
5	13 32	5 12	24 21	7 32	10 49	27 30	10 35	17 34				△		⚼	⚺		
6	15 34	6 26	25 03	7 38	10 55	27 33	10 37	17 33			□			△		☌	∠
7	17 38	7 40	25 44	7 44	11 01	27 35	10 38	17 32	⚹	⚹			⚼				⚹
8	19 42	8 53	26 25	7 51	11 06	27 38	10 39	17 32	∠	∠		□			☌		
9	21 47	10 07	27 06	7 58	11 12	27 40	10 40	17 31			⚹		△	□		⚺	□
10	23 52	11 21	27 47	8 05	11 18	27 43	10 41	17 31	⚺	⚺	∠	⚹			⚺	∠	
11	25 58	12 35	28 28	8 12	11 24	27 45	10 42	17 30					□	⚹	∠	⚹	
12	28♈04	13 48	29 09	8 19	11 30	27 47	10 43	17 29	☌		⚺	∠					△
13	0♉10	15 02	29♉50	8 26	11 36	27 50	10 44	17 28		☌		⚺		∠	⚹		⚼
14	2 15	16 15	0♊31	8 34	11 42	27 52	10 45	17 28			☌		⚹	⚺		□	
15	4 19	17 29	1 12	8 41	11 48	27 54	10 46	17 27	⚺			☌	∠		□		
16	6 22	18 42	1 53	8 49	11 54	27 56	10 47	17 26	∠	⚺			⚺	●		△	
17	8 23	19 56	2 34	8 57	12 01	27 59	10 48	17 25		∠	⚺					⚼	☍
18	10 23	21 09	3 15	9 05	12 07	28 01	10 49	17 24	⚹		∠	⚺	☌		△		
19	12 21	22 23	3 56	9 13	12 13	28 03	10 49	17 23		⚹	⚹	∠		⚺	⚼		
20	14 16	23 36	4 36	9 22	12 20	28 05	10 50	17 22	□			⚹		∠			⚼
21	16 08	24 49	5 17	9 30	12 26	28 07	10 51	17 21		□			⚺	⚹		☍	△
22	17 57	26 02	5 58	9 39	12 33	28 09	10 52	17 20	△		□		∠		☍		
23	19 43	27 16	6 39	9 47	12 39	28 11	10 52	17 19	⚼			□	⚹	□			□
24	21 25	28 29	7 19	9 56	12 46	28 13	10 53	17 18		△	△					⚼	
25	23 04	29♉42	8 00	10 05	12 53	28 14	10 54	17 17		⚼	⚼	△	□	△	⚼	△	⚹
26	24 39	0♊55	8 40	10 14	12 59	28 16	10 54	17 16				⚼		⚼	△		∠
27	26 09	2 08	9 21	10 23	13 06	28 18	10 55	17 15	☍				△			□	⚺
28	27 35	3 21	10 01	10 32	13 13	28 20	10 55	17 14		☍	☍		⚼		□		
29	28♉57	4 34	10 42	10 41	13 20	28 21	10 56	17 13				☍		☍		⚹	☌
30	0♊15	5♊47	11♊22	10♋51	13♊27	28♒23	10♒56	17♐12	⚼						⚹	∠	

D M	Saturn Lat.	Saturn Dec.	Uranus Lat.	Uranus Dec.	Neptune Lat.	Neptune Dec.	Pluto Lat.	Pluto Dec.
	° ′	° ′	° ′	° ′	° ′	° ′	° ′	° ′
1	1S27	20N35	0S42	13S04	0N05	17S31	10N03	12S52
3	1 26	20 37	0 42	13 02	0 05	17 30	10 03	12 51
5	1 26	20 39	0 43	13 00	0 05	17 30	10 03	12 50
7	1 26	20 41	0 43	12 59	0 05	17 29	10 04	12 50
9	1 25	20 43	0 43	12 57	0 05	17 29	10 04	12 49
11	1 25	20 45	0 43	12 55	0 05	17 28	10 05	12 49
13	1 24	20 47	0 43	12 54	0 05	17 27	10 05	12 48
15	1 24	20 49	0 43	12 52	0 05	17 27	10 05	12 48
17	1 24	20 51	0 43	12 51	0 05	17 26	10 06	12 47
19	1 23	20 53	0 43	12 49	0 05	17 26	10 06	12 47
21	1 23	20 55	0 43	12 48	0 05	17 26	10 06	12 47
23	1 23	20 57	0 43	12 47	0 05	17 25	10 07	12 46
25	1 22	20 59	0 43	12 46	0 05	17 25	10 07	12 46
27	1 22	21 01	0 43	12 44	0 05	17 25	10 07	12 45
29	1 22	21 03	0 43	12 43	0 05	17 24	10 07	12 45
31	1S22	21N05	0S43	12S42	0N05	17S24	10N08	12S44

Mutual Aspects

2 ☉∠♅. ☿∠♂. ☿□♃. ♂∠♃. ♄△♆.
3 ♀⚼♇.
4 ☿⚹♄. ☿∠♅. ☿⚹♆.
5 ♀⊥♄. ♀#♅. ♀#♇.
7 ☉☌☿. ☉△♇. ☿△♇. ♀⚹♃.
8 ☉∥☿.
9 ☿⊥♂. ☿Q♆. ♀Q♅. ♀□♆.
10 ♀⚺♄. ♀±♇. ♂□♅.
11 ☿Q♃. ☿∠♄.
12 ☉Q♆. ☿⚹♅.
13 ☿⚺♂. ♂∥♄.
14 ☿⚼♇. ☿#♅. ☿#♇.
15 ☉⊥♂. ♀⚻♇.
16 ☿⊥♄. ♀#♆.
17 ☉Q♃. ☉∠♄. ☿⚹♃.
18 ☉⚹♅. ☿Q♅. ☿□♆. ♂⊥♃.
19 ☿⚺♄. ☿±♇.
20 ☿#♆. 21 ♀∠♃.
22 ☉⚼♇. ☿⚻♇.
24 ♀□♅. ☉#♅. ☉#♇.
25 ☿∥♀. ♅∥♇.
26 ☿∠♃. ☿∥♄. ♀∥♄.
27 ☉⊥♄.
29 ☿□♅. ♀⊥♃. ♂⚺♃. ♂△♆.
30 ☉Q♅.

LAST QUARTER–Apr. 4,15h.29m. (14°♑41′)

NEW MOON–May 12,10h.45m. (21° ♉ 32′)

D M	D W	Sidereal Time	☉ Long.	☉ Dec.	☽ Long.	☽ Lat.	☽ Dec.	☽ Node	24h. ☽ Long.	24h. ☽ Dec.
		h m s	° ′ ″	° ′	° ′ ″	° ′	° ′	° ′	° ′ ″	° ′
1	W	2 36 59	10 ♉ 56 06	15 N06	8 ♑ 16 16	1 S 46	24 S 57	19 ♊ 59	14 ♑ 47 17	24 S 55
2	Th	2 40 56	11 54 19	15 24	21 12 21	2 49	24 33	19 56	27 31 58	23 52
3	F	2 44 52	12 52 30	15 42	3 ♒ 46 37	3 42	22 54	19 52	9 ♒ 56 54	21 40
4	S	2 48 49	13 50 40	16 00	16 03 21	4 24	20 13	19 49	22 06 36	18 33
5	Su	2 52 45	14 48 49	16 17	28 07 14	4 52	16 42	19 46	4 ♓ 05 48	14 42
6	M	2 56 42	15 46 56	16 34	10 ♓ 02 53	5 08	12 33	19 43	15 59 02	10 18
7	T	3 00 38	16 45 01	16 51	21 54 43	5 11	7 58	19 40	27 50 25	5 33
8	W	3 04 35	17 43 05	17 07	3 ♈ 46 35	5 00	3 S 06	19 37	9 ♈ 43 35	0 S 36
9	Th	3 08 32	18 41 08	17 23	15 41 46	4 37	1 N55	19 33	21 41 28	4 N26
10	F	3 12 28	19 39 09	17 39	27 42 56	4 01	6 55	19 30	3 ♉ 46 25	9 21
11	S	3 16 25	20 37 09	17 54	9 ♉ 52 07	3 13	11 43	19 27	16 00 12	13 59
12	Su	3 20 21	21 35 07	18 10	22 10 49	2 16	16 07	19 24	28 24 06	18 06
13	M	3 24 18	22 33 04	18 25	4 ♊ 40 11	1 12	19 54	19 21	10 ♊ 59 09	21 28
14	T	3 28 14	23 30 59	18 39	17 21 07	0 S 03	22 47	19 18	23 46 11	23 50
15	W	3 32 11	24 28 53	18 53	0 ♋ 14 28	1 N07	24 34	19 14	6 ♋ 46 04	24 58
16	Th	3 36 07	25 26 45	19 07	13 21 07	2 16	25 01	19 11	19 59 42	24 43
17	F	3 40 04	26 24 36	19 21	26 41 56	3 18	24 03	19 08	3 ♌ 27 54	23 02
18	S	3 44 01	27 22 24	19 34	10 ♌ 17 42	4 10	21 40	19 05	17 11 21	19 59
19	Su	3 47 57	28 20 11	19 47	24 08 50	4 48	18 00	19 02	1 ♍ 10 06	15 45
20	M	3 51 54	29 ♉ 17 57	20 00	8 ♍ 14 59	5 11	13 16	18 58	15 23 17	10 36
21	T	3 55 50	0 ♊ 15 40	20 12	22 34 40	5 14	7 45	18 55	29 48 44	4 N47
22	W	3 59 47	1 13 22	20 24	7 ♎ 04 58	4 58	1 N45	18 52	14 ♎ 22 45	1 S20
23	Th	4 03 43	2 11 02	20 36	21 41 25	4 22	4 S24	18 49	29 00 13	7 25
24	F	4 07 40	3 08 41	20 47	6 ♏ 18 22	3 30	10 19	18 46	13 ♏ 35 04	13 05
25	S	4 11 36	4 06 19	20 58	20 49 31	2 24	15 39	18 43	28 00 59	17 58
26	Su	4 15 33	5 03 55	21 09	5 ♐ 08 46	1 N10	20 01	18 39	12 ♐ 12 16	21 45
27	M	4 19 30	6 01 30	21 19	19 11 00	0 S08	23 07	18 36	26 04 33	24 08
28	T	4 23 26	6 59 04	21 29	2 ♑ 52 40	1 22	24 47	18 33	9 ♑ 35 13	25 03
29	W	4 27 23	7 56 37	21 38	16 12 09	2 31	24 57	18 30	22 43 33	24 30
30	Th	4 31 19	8 54 09	21 47	29 09 36	3 29	23 44	18 27	5 ♒ 30 35	22 41
31	F	4 35 16	9 ♊ 51 40	21 N56	11 ♒ 46 49	4 S 16	21 S 21	18 ♊ 24	17 ♒ 58 44	19 S 48

D M	Mercury Lat.	Mercury Dec.		Venus Lat.	Venus Dec.		Mars Lat.	Mars Dec.		Jupiter Lat.	Jupiter Dec.
	° ′	° ′	° ′	° ′	° ′	° ′	° ′	° ′	° ′	° ′	° ′
1	2 N36	23 N00	23 N 16	0 N 47	22 N15	22 N30	0 N 50	23 N03	23 N 09	0 N 13	23 N12
3	2 39	23 29	23 40	0 52	22 44	22 57	0 50	23 14	23 20	0 13	23 10
5	2 37	23 48	23 55	0 58	23 10	23 22	0 51	23 25	23 30	0 13	23 09
7	2 31	23 59	24 01	1 03	23 33	23 44	0 52	23 34	23 39	0 13	23 07
9	2 21	24 01	23 59	1 08	23 54	24 03	0 53	23 43	23 47	0 13	23 05
11	2 06	23 55	23 49	1 12	24 12	24 20	0 53	23 51	23 54	0 13	23 03
13	1 47	23 41	23 31	1 17	24 27	24 33	0 54	23 58	24 01	0 14	23 01
15	1 24	23 20	23 07	1 21	24 39	24 44	0 55	24 04	24 07	0 14	22 59
17	0 57	22 52	22 36	1 26	24 49	24 53	0 55	24 10	24 12	0 14	22 57
19	0 N27	22 18	22 00	1 30	24 56	24 58	0 56	24 14	24 16	0 14	22 55
21	0 S06	21 40	21 19	1 34	25 00	25 01	0 56	24 18	24 20	0 14	22 53
23	0 41	20 57	20 35	1 37	25 01	25 00	0 57	24 21	24 22	0 14	22 51
25	1 16	20 12	19 49	1 41	24 59	24 57	0 58	24 23	24 24	0 14	22 48
27	1 51	19 27	19 05	1 44	24 54	24 51	0 58	24 24	24 25	0 15	22 46
29	2 23	18 43	18 N 22	1 47	24 47	24 N42	0 59	24 25	24 N 25	0 15	22 43
31	2 S52	18 N03		1 N 49	24 N37		0 N 59	24 N25		0 N 15	22 N40

FIRST QUARTER–May 19,19h.42m. (28° ♌ 39′)

FULL MOON–May 26,11h.51m. (5°♐04′)

EPHEMERIS]				MAY 2002													11
D	☿	♀	♂	♃	♄	♅	♆	♇	Lunar Aspects								
M	Long.	Long.	Long.	Long.	Long.	Long.	Long.	Long.	☉	☿	♀	♂	♃	♄	♅	♆	♇
	° ′	° ′	° ′	° ′	° ′	° ′	° ′	° ′									
1	1♊28	7♊00	12♊02	11♋00	13♊34	28♒24	10♒57	17♐11	△				☍		∠	⚺	
2	2 36	8 12	12 43	11 10	13 41	28 26	10 57	17R 09		⚼	⚼						⚺
3	3 40	9 25	13 23	11 20	13 48	28 28	10 57	17 08		△		⚼		⚼	⚺		∠
4	4 39	10 38	14 03	11 30	13 55	28 29	10 58	17 07	□		△	△		△		☌	✱
5	5 33	11 51	14 43	11 40	14 02	28 30	10 58	17 06					⚼		☌		
6	6 22	13 03	15 24	11 50	14 09	28 32	10 58	17 04		□	□	□	△	□		⚺	
7	7 07	14 16	16 04	12 00	14 16	28 33	10 58	17 03	✱							∠	□
8	7 46	15 29	16 44	12 10	14 24	28 34	10 58	17 02	∠	✱					⚺		
9	8 20	16 41	17 24	12 20	14 31	28 35	10 59	17 00	⚺		✱	✱	□	✱	∠	✱	△
10	8 49	17 53	18 04	12 31	14 38	28 37	10 59	16 59		∠	∠	∠		∠	✱		⚼
11	9 14	19 06	18 44	12 41	14 46	28 38	10 59	16 58		⚺			✱	⚺		□	
12	9 32	20 18	19 24	12 52	14 53	28 39	10 59	16 56	☌		⚺	⚺	∠				
13	9 46	21 31	20 04	13 03	15 00	28 40	10 59	16 55		☌					□	△	
14	9 55	22 43	20 44	13 14	15 08	28 41	10R 59	16 53			●	●	⚺	●			☍
15	9 59	23 55	21 24	13 24	15 15	28 42	10 59	16 52	⚺						△	⚼	
16	9R 58	25 07	22 04	13 35	15 23	28 43	10 59	16 50	∠	⚺			☌	⚺	⚼		
17	9 52	26 20	22 44	13 46	15 30	28 43	10 59	16 49	✱	∠	⚺	⚺		∠			⚼
18	9 42	27 32	23 24	13 57	15 38	28 44	10 58	16 47		✱	∠	∠	⚺	✱		☍	△
19	9 27	28 44	24 04	14 09	15 45	28 45	10 58	16 46	□		✱	✱	∠		☍		
20	9 09	29♊56	24 43	14 20	15 53	28 46	10 58	16 44		□			✱				
21	8 47	1♋08	25 23	14 31	16 01	28 46	10 58	16 43				□		□		⚼	□
22	8 21	2 19	26 03	14 43	16 08	28 47	10 58	16 41	△	△	□				⚼	△	
23	7 53	3 31	26 43	14 54	16 16	28 47	10 57	16 40	⚼	⚼		△	□	△	△		✱
24	7 23	4 43	27 22	15 06	16 23	28 48	10 57	16 38			△	⚼		⚼		□	∠
25	6 50	5 55	28 02	15 17	16 31	28 48	10 57	16 37			⚼		△				⚺
26	6 17	7 06	28 41	15 29	16 39	28 49	10 56	16 35	☍	☍			⚼		□	✱	
27	5 43	8 18	29♊21	15 41	16 47	28 49	10 56	16 34						☍		∠	☌
28	5 09	9 29	0♋00	15 53	16 54	28 49	10 55	16 32				☍			✱		
29	4 36	10 41	0 40	16 04	17 02	28 50	10 55	16 30		⚼	☍		☍		∠	⚺	⚺
30	4 04	11 52	1 19	16 16	17 10	28 50	10 54	16 29	⚼	△				⚼	⚺		∠
31	3♊33	13♋04	1♋59	16♋28	17♊17	28♒50	10♒54	16♐27	△			⚼		△		☌	✱

D	Saturn		Uranus		Neptune		Pluto	
M	Lat.	Dec.	Lat.	Dec.	Lat.	Dec.	Lat.	Dec.
	° ′	° ′	° ′	° ′	° ′	° ′	° ′	° ′
1	1S22	21N05	0S43	12S42	0N05	17S24	10N08	12S44
3	1 21	21 07	0 43	12 41	0 05	17 24	10 08	12 44
5	1 21	21 09	0 44	12 40	0 05	17 24	10 08	12 43
7	1 21	21 11	0 44	12 40	0 05	17 24	10 08	12 43
9	1 20	21 13	0 44	12 39	0 05	17 24	10 08	12 43
11	1 20	21 14	0 44	12 38	0 05	17 24	10 09	12 42
13	1 20	21 16	0 44	12 37	0 05	17 24	10 09	12 42
15	1 20	21 18	0 44	12 37	0 05	17 24	10 09	12 41
17	1 19	21 20	0 44	12 36	0 05	17 24	10 09	12 41
19	1 19	21 22	0 44	12 36	0 05	17 24	10 09	12 41
21	1 19	21 24	0 44	12 35	0 05	17 24	10 09	12 40
23	1 19	21 25	0 44	12 35	0 05	17 24	10 09	12 40
25	1 19	21 27	0 44	12 35	0 05	17 24	10 09	12 40
27	1 18	21 29	0 44	12 35	0 05	17 25	10 09	12 40
29	1 18	21 31	0 44	12 35	0 05	17 25	10 09	12 39
31	1S18	21N32	0S45	12S35	0N05	17S25	10N09	12S39

Mutual Aspects

1 ☉✱♃. ☉□♆. ☉±♇. ♃⊼♆. ☿∥♂.
2 ☿∥♃. ♂∥♃.
4 ☉⚺♄. ♀△♆. ♂☌♄.
5 ☉⚺♂. ☿⊥♃. ♀⚺♃. ♀∥♃.
7 ☉⊼♇. ♀☌♄. ♀∥♂.
8 ♂☍♇.
9 ♀☍♇. ☉#♆.
10 ♀☌♂. ☿∥♀.
11 ☿∥♂. 13 ♆Stat.
15 ☿Stat.
17 ☉⚺♀. ♀⚼♆. ♃⚼♅. ☿∥♃.
19 ☉□♅. ♀△♅. ♅Q♇.
20 ☉∠♃. 21 ☿⊥♃.
22 ♂⚼♆. ☿∥♄.
24 ♀±♆. ☉∥☿.
26 ☿⚺♀. ♂△♅. ♄☍♇.
27 ☉☌☿. 28 ☉∥♄.
29 ☿⊥♀. ♀⊼♆.
31 ♃⊼♇.

LAST QUARTER–May 4,07h.16m. (13°♒39′)

NEW MOON – June 10, 23h.46m. (19° ♊ 54′)

D M	D W	Sidereal Time	☉ Long.	☉ Dec.	☽ Long.	☽ Lat.	☽ Dec.	☽ Node	24h. ☽ Long.	24h. ☽ Dec.
		h m s	° ′ ″	° ′	° ′ ″	° ′	° ′	° ′	° ′ ″	° ′
1	S	4 39 12	10 ♊ 49 11	22 N04	24 ♒ 06 48	4 S 50	18 S 02	18 ♊ 20	0 ♓ 11 31	16 S 06
2	Su	4 43 09	11 46 40	22 12	6 ♓ 13 25	5 10	14 02	18 17	12 13 05	11 50
3	M	4 47 05	12 44 09	22 19	18 11 04	5 17	9 32	18 14	24 07 56	7 09
4	T	4 51 02	13 41 37	22 27	0 ♈ 04 16	5 10	4 S 42	18 11	6 ♈ 00 38	2 S 13
5	W	4 54 59	14 39 04	22 33	11 57 33	4 49	0 N 17	18 08	17 55 33	2 N 48
6	Th	4 58 55	15 36 31	22 40	23 55 08	4 16	5 18	18 04	29 56 43	7 47
7	F	5 02 52	16 33 56	22 46	6 ♉ 00 44	3 32	10 12	18 01	12 ♉ 07 34	12 32
8	S	5 06 48	17 31 22	22 51	18 17 31	2 37	14 46	17 58	24 30 52	16 52
9	Su	5 10 45	18 28 46	22 56	0 ♊ 47 49	1 33	18 48	17 55	7 ♊ 08 32	20 32
10	M	5 14 41	19 26 10	23 01	13 33 08	0 S 24	22 02	17 52	20 01 40	23 16
11	T	5 18 38	20 23 33	23 05	26 34 07	0 N 48	24 12	17 49	3 ♋ 10 26	24 48
12	W	5 22 34	21 20 56	23 09	9 ♋ 50 32	1 59	25 03	17 45	16 34 15	24 56
13	Th	5 26 31	22 18 18	23 13	23 21 25	3 04	24 27	17 42	0 ♌ 11 49	23 35
14	F	5 30 28	23 15 38	23 16	7 ♌ 05 13	4 00	22 22	17 39	14 01 21	20 49
15	S	5 34 24	24 12 58	23 19	20 59 58	4 43	18 57	17 36	28 00 46	16 49
16	Su	5 38 21	25 10 17	23 21	5 ♍ 03 29	5 09	14 26	17 33	12 ♍ 07 48	11 51
17	M	5 42 17	26 07 35	23 23	19 13 25	5 16	9 07	17 30	26 20 03	6 15
18	T	5 46 14	27 04 52	23 24	3 ♎ 27 23	5 05	3 N 17	17 26	10 ♎ 35 05	0 N 17
19	W	5 50 10	28 02 09	23 25	17 42 51	4 35	2 S 43	17 23	24 50 18	5 S 42
20	Th	5 54 07	28 59 24	23 26	1 ♏ 57 08	3 47	8 35	17 20	9 ♏ 02 57	11 22
21	F	5 58 03	29 ♊ 56 39	23 26	16 07 23	2 47	14 00	17 17	23 10 03	16 26
22	S	6 02 00	0 ♋ 53 53	23 26	0 ♐ 10 35	1 36	18 37	17 14	7 ♐ 08 36	20 32
23	Su	6 05 57	1 51 07	23 26	14 03 44	0 N 21	22 08	17 10	20 55 37	23 25
24	M	6 09 53	2 48 20	23 25	27 43 59	0 S 54	24 19	17 07	4 ♑ 28 32	24 52
25	T	6 13 50	3 45 33	23 23	11 ♑ 09 03	2 05	25 03	17 04	17 45 21	24 52
26	W	6 17 46	4 42 46	23 21	24 17 22	3 08	24 20	17 01	0 ♒ 45 03	23 29
27	Th	6 21 43	5 39 58	23 19	7 ♒ 08 25	3 59	22 20	16 58	13 27 36	20 56
28	F	6 25 39	6 37 10	23 16	19 42 45	4 38	19 18	16 55	25 54 08	17 28
29	S	6 29 36	7 34 22	23 13	2 ♓ 02 03	5 03	15 28	16 51	8 ♓ 06 53	13 19
30	Su	6 33 32	8 ♋ 31 35	23 N10	14 ♓ 09 01	5 S 14	11 S 04	16 ♊ 48	20 ♓ 08 57	8 S 43

D M	Mercury Lat.	Mercury Dec.		Venus Lat.	Venus Dec.		Mars Lat.	Mars Dec.		Jupiter Lat.	Jupiter Dec.
	° ′	° ′	° ′	° ′	° ′	° ′	° ′	° ′	° ′	° ′	° ′
1	3 S 05	17 N45	17 N 28	1 N 51	24 N31	24 N24	1 N 00	24 N24	24 N 24	0 N 15	22 N39
3	3 28	17 13	17 00	1 53	24 16	24 08	1 00	24 23	24 22	0 15	22 36
5	3 46	16 49	16 40	1 55	23 59	23 50	1 00	24 21	24 19	0 15	22 33
7	3 58	16 33	16 28	1 56	23 40	23 29	1 01	24 17	24 16	0 15	22 30
9	4 06	16 25	16 24	1 58	23 17	23 05	1 01	24 14	24 11	0 16	22 27
11	4 10	16 25	16 28	1 58	22 52	22 39	1 02	24 09	24 06	0 16	22 23
13	4 08	16 33	16 40	1 59	22 25	22 11	1 02	24 04	24 01	0 16	22 20
15	4 03	16 48	16 58	1 59	21 56	21 40	1 03	23 57	23 54	0 16	22 16
17	3 54	17 10	17 23	1 59	21 24	21 07	1 03	23 50	23 47	0 16	22 13
19	3 42	17 37	17 53	1 59	20 50	20 32	1 03	23 43	23 39	0 16	22 09
21	3 27	18 09	18 26	1 58	20 13	19 54	1 04	23 34	23 30	0 16	22 05
23	3 09	18 45	19 04	1 56	19 35	19 15	1 04	23 25	23 20	0 17	22 02
25	2 50	19 23	19 43	1 55	18 55	18 34	1 05	23 15	23 10	0 17	21 58
27	2 28	20 03	20 23	1 53	18 13	17 51	1 05	23 05	22 59	0 17	21 54
29	2 05	20 43	21 N 03	1 50	17 29	17 N06	1 05	22 53	22 N 48	0 17	21 49
31	1 S 42	21 N22		1 N 47	16 N44		1 N 05	22 N41		0 N 17	21 N45

FIRST QUARTER – June 18, 00h.29m. (26° ♍ 37′)

FULL MOON–June24,21h.42m. (3°♑11′)

EPHEMERIS]				JUNE 2002													13
D	☿	♀	♂	♃	♄	♅	♆	♇	Lunar Aspects								
M	Long.	Long.	Long.	Long.	Long.	Long.	Long.	Long.	☉	☿	♀	♂	♃	♄	♅	♆	♇
	° ′	° ′	° ′	° ′	° ′	° ′	° ′	° ′									
1	3♊05	14♋15	2♋38	16♋40	17♊25	28♒50	10♒53	16♐26			⚼				☌		
2	2R 39	15 26	3 18	16 53	17 33	28 50	10R 53	16R 24		□		△	⚼			⚺	
3	2 17	16 37	3 57	17 05	17 41	28R 50	10 52	16 22	□		△		△	□			□
4	1 58	17 48	4 37	17 17	17 49	28 50	10 51	16 21		⚹		□			⚺	∠	
5	1 43	18 59	5 16	17 29	17 56	28 50	10 50	16 19	⚹	∠			□		∠	⚹	△
6	1 31	20 10	5 55	17 42	18 04	28 50	10 50	16 18			□			⚹	⚹		
7	1 24	21 21	6 34	17 54	18 12	28 50	10 49	16 16	∠	⚺		⚹		∠		□	⚼
8	1 21	22 32	7 14	18 06	18 20	28 49	10 48	16 14	⚺		⚹	∠	⚹	⚺			
9	1D 23	23 43	7 53	18 19	18 28	28 49	10 47	16 13		☌			∠		□		
10	1 29	24 54	8 32	18 31	18 35	28 49	10 47	16 11	●		∠	⚺	⚺	☌		△	☍
11	1 40	26 04	9 11	18 44	18 43	28 48	10 46	16 10		⚺	⚺				△	⚼	
12	1 55	27 15	9 51	18 57	18 51	28 48	10 45	16 08				●			⚼		
13	2 15	28 25	10 30	19 09	18 59	28 47	10 44	16 06	⚺	∠	☌		☌	⚺			
14	2 39	29♋36	11 09	19 22	19 07	28 47	10 43	16 05	∠	⚹		⚺		∠		☍	⚼
15	3 07	0♌46	11 48	19 35	19 14	28 46	10 42	16 03	⚹			∠	⚺	⚹			△
16	3 40	1 56	12 27	19 48	19 22	28 46	10 41	16 02		□	⚺		∠		☍		
17	4 17	3 07	13 06	20 00	19 30	28 45	10 40	16 00			∠	⚹	⚹	□		⚼	□
18	4 59	4 17	13 45	20 13	19 38	28 44	10 39	15 58	□	△	⚹						
19	5 44	5 27	14 24	20 26	19 45	28 44	10 38	15 57		⚼		□	□	△	⚼	△	⚹
20	6 34	6 37	15 03	20 39	19 53	28 43	10 37	15 55	△		□			⚼	△		∠
21	7 28	7 46	15 42	20 52	20 01	28 42	10 36	15 54	⚼			△	△			□	⚺
22	8 25	8 56	16 21	21 05	20 09	28 41	10 34	15 52				⚼	⚼		□		
23	9 27	10 06	17 00	21 18	20 16	28 40	10 33	15 51		☍	△			☍		⚹	☌
24	10 32	11 15	17 39	21 31	20 24	28 39	10 32	15 49	☍		⚼				⚹	∠	
25	11 41	12 25	18 18	21 44	20 32	28 38	10 31	15 48							∠	⚺	⚺
26	12 54	13 34	18 57	21 57	20 39	28 37	10 30	15 46		⚼		☍	☍		⚺		
27	14 10	14 43	19 35	22 10	20 47	28 36	10 28	15 45						⚼		☌	∠
28	15 31	15 53	20 14	22 23	20 55	28 35	10 27	15 43	⚼	△	☍			△			⚹
29	16 54	17 02	20 53	22 37	21 02	28 34	10 26	15 42	△			⚼	⚼		☌		
30	18♊21	18♌11	21♋32	22♋50	21♊10	28♒32	10♒25	15♐40		□						⚺	□

D	Saturn		Uranus		Neptune		Pluto	
M	Lat.	Dec.	Lat.	Dec.	Lat.	Dec.	Lat.	Dec.
	° ′	° ′	° ′	° ′	° ′	° ′	° ′	° ′
1	1S18	21N33	0S45	12S35	0N05	17S25	10N09	12S39
3	1 18	21 35	0 45	12 35	0 05	17 26	10 08	12 39
5	1 18	21 36	0 45	12 35	0 05	17 26	10 08	12 39
7	1 17	21 38	0 45	12 35	0 05	17 27	10 08	12 39
9	1 17	21 39	0 45	12 35	0 05	17 27	10 08	12 39
11	1 17	21 41	0 45	12 36	0 05	17 27	10 08	12 39
13	1 17	21 42	0 45	12 36	0 05	17 28	10 07	12 38
15	1 17	21 44	0 45	12 36	0 05	17 29	10 07	12 38
17	1 17	21 45	0 45	12 37	0 05	17 29	10 07	12 38
19	1 17	21 46	0 45	12 37	0 05	17 30	10 07	12 38
21	1 17	21 47	0 45	12 38	0 05	17 30	10 06	12 39
23	1 16	21 49	0 45	12 39	0 05	17 31	10 06	12 39
25	1 16	21 50	0 46	12 40	0 05	17 32	10 05	12 39
27	1 16	21 51	0 46	12 40	0 05	17 32	10 05	12 39
29	1 16	21 52	0 46	12 41	0 05	17 33	10 05	12 39
31	1S16	21N53	0S46	12S42	0N05	17S34	10N04	12S39

Mutual Aspects

1 ☉⊥♃. ☉△♆. ☿⚺♂. ♀⚼♅.
2 ☿⋕♆. ♀∥♂.
3 ☿∠♀. ☿∠♃. ♀☌♃. ♀∇♇. ♅Stat.
4 ♀⚺♄. ♂±♆.
5 ☉∥♃. 7 ☉☍♇.
8 ☿⊥♂. ♀±♅. ♀±♇. ☿Stat.
9 ☉⚺♃. ☉☌♄.
10 ♀⊥♄. ☉∥♀.
11 ♃⚺♄. 12 ☉⊥♀.
13 ♀∇♅. ♂∇♆. ♀∥♃.
15 ♀⚼♇. 16 ♀∥♄.
17 ☉⚼♆.
18 ☿∠♃. ♀∠♄. ♂⚼♅. ☿⋕♆.
20 ☉△♅. ☿⚹♀.
21 ♂∇♇. 22 ♅∥♇.
23 ♀☍♆. ☉∥♂.
24 ☿△♆. ☿∥♀.
25 ♃±♇.
26 ☉±♆. ☿⊥♂.
28 ☿☍♇. ♀△♇. ♃∥♄.
29 ☿⚹♀. ☿⊥♃. ♂⚺♄. ♃±♅. ♀⋕♆.
30 ♂±♇.

LAST QUARTER–June 3,00h.05m. (12°♓16′)

NEW MOON–July10,10h.26m. (18°♋00′)

D M	D W	Sidereal Time	☉ Long.	☉ Dec.	☽ Long.	☽ Lat.	☽ Dec.	☽ Node	24h. ☽ Long.	24h. ☽ Dec.
		h m s	° ′ ″	° ′	° ′ ″	° ′	° ′	° ′	° ′ ″	° ′
1	M	6 37 29	9 ♋ 28 47	23 N06	26 ♓ 07 10	5 S 11	6 S 18	16 ♊ 45	2 ♈ 04 13	3 S 50
2	T	6 41 26	10 25 59	23 02	8 ♈ 00 40	4 55	1 S 20	16 42	13 57 06	1 N 10
3	W	6 45 22	11 23 12	22 57	19 54 05	4 26	3 N 40	16 39	25 52 15	6 09
4	Th	6 49 19	12 20 25	22 52	1 ♉ 52 10	3 46	8 36	16 36	7 ♉ 54 25	10 58
5	F	6 53 15	13 17 38	22 47	13 59 32	2 55	13 16	16 32	20 08 05	15 26
6	S	6 57 12	14 14 51	22 41	26 20 30	1 55	17 29	16 29	2 ♊ 37 13	19 21
7	Su	7 01 08	15 12 05	22 34	8 ♊ 58 36	0 S 48	21 01	16 26	15 24 56	22 26
8	M	7 05 05	16 09 18	22 28	21 56 25	0 N 23	23 35	16 23	28 33 08	24 25
9	T	7 09 01	17 06 33	22 21	5 ♋ 15 05	1 35	24 55	16 20	12 ♋ 02 09	25 02
10	W	7 12 58	18 03 47	22 13	18 54 07	2 42	24 47	16 16	25 50 38	24 08
11	Th	7 16 55	19 01 02	22 05	2 ♌ 51 16	3 42	23 07	16 13	9 ♌ 55 31	21 43
12	F	7 20 51	19 58 16	21 57	17 02 46	4 29	19 59	16 10	24 12 21	17 57
13	S	7 24 48	20 55 31	21 49	1 ♍ 23 38	4 59	15 38	16 07	8 ♍ 35 56	13 06
14	Su	7 28 44	21 52 45	21 40	15 48 34	5 11	10 22	16 04	23 00 57	7 31
15	M	7 32 41	22 50 00	21 30	0 ♎ 12 31	5 03	4 N 33	16 01	7 ♎ 22 47	1 N 33
16	T	7 36 37	23 47 15	21 21	14 31 20	4 37	1 S 28	15 57	21 37 51	4 S 27
17	W	7 40 34	24 44 30	21 11	28 42 05	3 54	7 22	15 54	5 ♏ 43 51	10 11
18	Th	7 44 30	25 41 44	21 00	12 ♏ 42 59	2 57	12 51	15 51	19 39 26	15 20
19	F	7 48 27	26 39 00	20 50	26 33 07	1 50	17 36	15 48	3 ♐ 24 00	19 37
20	S	7 52 24	27 36 15	20 38	10 ♐ 12 04	0 N 39	21 21	15 45	16 57 18	22 46
21	Su	7 56 20	28 33 31	20 27	23 39 38	0 S 34	23 51	15 41	0 ♑ 19 03	24 36
22	M	8 00 17	29 ♋ 30 47	20 15	6 ♑ 55 30	1 44	24 59	15 38	13 28 55	25 01
23	T	8 04 13	0 ♌ 28 03	20 03	19 59 15	2 47	24 42	15 35	26 26 26	24 04
24	W	8 08 10	1 25 20	19 51	2 ♒ 50 27	3 41	23 06	15 32	9 ♒ 11 15	21 52
25	Th	8 12 06	2 22 37	19 38	15 28 51	4 22	20 22	15 29	21 43 17	18 39
26	F	8 16 03	3 19 56	19 25	27 54 38	4 51	16 44	15 26	4 ♓ 03 02	14 40
27	S	8 19 59	4 17 14	19 11	10 ♓ 08 39	5 05	12 28	15 22	16 11 43	10 09
28	Su	8 23 56	5 14 34	18 57	22 12 31	5 06	7 46	15 19	28 11 25	5 19
29	M	8 27 53	6 11 55	18 43	4 ♈ 08 47	4 53	2 S 50	15 16	10 ♈ 05 05	0 S 19
30	T	8 31 49	7 09 16	18 29	16 00 49	4 27	2 N 11	15 13	21 56 29	4 N 40
31	W	8 35 46	8 ♌ 06 39	18 N 14	27 ♈ 52 42	3 S 51	7 N 08	15 ♊ 10	3 ♉ 50 02	9 N 32

D M	Mercury Lat.	Mercury Dec.		Venus Lat.	Venus Dec.		Mars Lat.	Mars Dec.		Jupiter Lat.	Jupiter Dec.
	° ′	° ′	° ′	° ′	° ′	° ′	° ′	° ′	° ′	° ′	° ′
1	1 S 42	21 N 22	21 N 41	1 N 47	16 N 44	16 N 20	1 N 05	22 N 41	22 N 35	0 N 17	21 N 45
3	1 17	21 59	22 16	1 44	15 57	15 32	1 06	22 29	22 22	0 17	21 41
5	0 52	22 32	22 46	1 40	15 08	14 43	1 06	22 15	22 09	0 18	21 36
7	0 27	22 59	23 10	1 36	14 18	13 53	1 06	22 01	21 54	0 18	21 32
9	0 S 03	23 19	23 26	1 32	13 27	13 01	1 07	21 47	21 39	0 18	21 27
11	0 N 19	23 31	23 34	1 27	12 35	12 08	1 07	21 32	21 24	0 18	21 23
13	0 40	23 33	23 31	1 21	11 41	11 14	1 07	21 16	21 07	0 18	21 18
15	0 58	23 25	23 17	1 16	10 47	10 19	1 07	20 59	20 51	0 18	21 13
17	1 14	23 06	22 52	1 09	9 52	9 24	1 07	20 42	20 33	0 19	21 08
19	1 27	22 35	22 17	1 03	8 55	8 27	1 08	20 24	20 15	0 19	21 03
21	1 36	21 55	21 32	0 56	7 59	7 30	1 08	20 06	19 57	0 19	20 58
23	1 43	21 06	20 38	0 48	7 01	6 32	1 08	19 47	19 38	0 19	20 53
25	1 47	20 08	19 37	0 40	6 03	5 34	1 08	19 28	19 18	0 19	20 48
27	1 47	19 04	18 29	0 32	5 05	4 35	1 08	19 08	18 58	0 19	20 43
29	1 45	17 53	17 N 17	0 23	4 06	3 N 36	1 08	18 48	18 N 37	0 20	20 37
31	1 N 41	16 N 39		0 N 14	3 N 07		1 N 08	18 N 27		0 N 20	20 N 32

FIRST QUARTER–July17,04h.47m. (24°♎27′)

FULL MOON–July24,09h.07m. (1°♒18′)

D	☿	♀	♂	♃	♄	♅	♆	♇	Lunar Aspects								
M	Long.	Long.	Long.	Long.	Long.	Long.	Long.	Long.	☉	☿	♀	♂	♃	♄	♅	♆	♇
	° ′	° ′	° ′	° ′	° ′	° ′	° ′	° ′									
1	19♊52	19♌19	22♋11	23♋03	21♊17	28♒31	10♒23	15♐39				△	△	□	⚺	∠	
2	21 26	20 28	22 49	23 16	21 25	28R 30	10R 22	15R 37	□		⚼				∠	⚹	
3	23 04	21 37	23 28	23 30	21 32	28 28	10 21	15 36		⚹	△	□	□	⚹			△
4	24 45	22 45	24 07	23 43	21 40	28 27	10 19	15 35						∠	⚹		⚼
5	26 29	23 54	24 45	23 56	21 47	28 26	10 18	15 33	⚹	∠						□	
6	28♊16	25 02	25 24	24 09	21 55	28 24	10 16	15 32	∠	⚺	□	⚹	⚹	⚺	□		
7	0♋07	26 10	26 03	24 23	22 02	28 23	10 15	15 31				∠	∠			△	
8	2 00	27 18	26 41	24 36	22 10	28 21	10 14	15 29	⚺		⚹	⚺	⚺	☌	△	⚼	☍
9	3 56	28 26	27 20	24 49	22 17	28 19	10 12	15 28		☌							
10	5 54	29♌34	27 59	25 03	22 24	28 18	10 11	15 27	☌		∠		☌	⚺	⚼		
11	7 55	0♍42	28 37	25 16	22 31	28 16	10 09	15 25		⚺	⚺	☌		∠			⚼
12	9 57	1 49	29 16	25 30	22 39	28 15	10 08	15 24	⚺					⚹		☍	△
13	12 02	2 57	29♋55	25 43	22 46	28 13	10 06	15 23	∠	∠	☌	⚺	⚺		☍		
14	14 07	4 04	0♌33	25 56	22 53	28 11	10 05	15 22	⚹	⚹		∠	∠	□			□
15	16 14	5 11	1 12	26 10	23 00	28 09	10 03	15 20			⚺	⚹	⚹			⚼	
16	18 22	6 18	1 50	26 23	23 07	28 07	10 02	15 19		□					⚼	△	⚹
17	20 30	7 25	2 29	26 37	23 14	28 06	10 00	15 18	□		∠	□	□	△	△		∠
18	22 39	8 32	3 07	26 50	23 21	28 04	9 58	15 17			⚹			⚼		□	⚺
19	24 48	9 39	3 46	27 03	23 28	28 02	9 57	15 16	△	△			△		□		
20	26 56	10 45	4 24	27 17	23 35	28 00	9 55	15 15	⚼	⚼	□	△	⚼			⚹	☌
21	29♋03	11 51	5 03	27 30	23 42	27 58	9 54	15 14				⚼		☍	⚹	∠	
22	1♌10	12 57	5 41	27 44	23 49	27 56	9 52	15 13							∠	⚺	
23	3 16	14 03	6 20	27 57	23 56	27 54	9 50	15 12			△						⚺
24	5 21	15 09	6 58	28 10	24 03	27 52	9 49	15 11	☍	☍	⚼	☍	☍	⚼	⚺		∠
25	7 25	16 14	7 36	28 24	24 09	27 50	9 47	15 10								☌	⚹
26	9 27	17 20	8 15	28 37	24 16	27 48	9 46	15 09						△	☌		
27	11 28	18 25	8 53	28 50	24 23	27 46	9 44	15 08					⚼			⚺	□
28	13 27	19 30	9 32	29 04	24 29	27 43	9 42	15 07	⚼		☍	⚼		□	⚺	∠	
29	15 25	20 35	10 10	29 17	24 36	27 41	9 41	15 06	△	⚼			△			⚹	
30	17 21	21 39	10 48	29 30	24 42	27 39	9 39	15 05		△		△			∠		△
31	19♌16	22♍43	11♌27	29♋44	24♊49	27♒37	9♒38	15♐04					□	⚹	⚹		⚼

D	Saturn		Uranus		Neptune		Pluto	
M	Lat.	Dec.	Lat.	Dec.	Lat.	Dec.	Lat.	Dec.
	° ′	° ′	° ′	° ′	° ′	° ′	° ′	° ′
1	1S16	21N53	0S46	12S42	0N05	17S34	10N04	12S39
3	1 16	21 54	0 46	12 43	0 05	17 34	10 04	12 39
5	1 16	21 55	0 46	12 44	0 05	17 35	10 03	12 40
7	1 16	21 56	0 46	12 45	0 05	17 36	10 03	12 40
9	1 16	21 57	0 46	12 47	0 05	17 37	10 02	12 40
11	1 16	21 58	0 46	12 48	0 05	17 38	10 02	12 40
13	1 16	21 59	0 46	12 49	0 04	17 38	10 01	12 41
15	1 16	22 00	0 46	12 50	0 04	17 39	10 00	12 41
17	1 16	22 00	0 46	12 52	0 04	17 40	10 00	12 41
19	1 16	22 01	0 46	12 53	0 04	17 41	9 59	12 42
21	1 16	22 02	0 46	12 54	0 04	17 42	9 58	12 42
23	1 16	22 02	0 46	12 56	0 04	17 43	9 58	12 43
25	1 16	22 03	0 46	12 57	0 04	17 44	9 57	12 43
27	1 16	22 03	0 46	12 59	0 04	17 45	9 56	12 44
29	1 16	22 04	0 46	13 00	0 04	17 45	9 56	12 44
31	1S16	22N04	0S46	13S02	0N04	17S46	9N55	12S45

Mutual Aspects

2 ☉▽♆. ☿☌♄. ♂±♅. ☿∥♃.
3 ☿⚺♂. ☿⚺♃. ♀⚹♄. ♂☌♃. ☿∥♄.
4 ☿⚼♆. ☿∥♂.
5 ☉⚼♅. ♀⚺♃.
6 ☿△♅. ☉∥☿.
7 ☉▽♇. ♀⚺♂.
8 ♂∥♄.
9 ☿±♆. ♀☍♅.
10 ♂▽♅.
11 ♂⊥♄. ♀#♅. ♀#♇.
12 ☿▽♆. ♀⊥♃. ☉∥♄.
13 ☉±♇. ♂∥♃.
14 ☉±♅. ☿⚼♅. ♂⚼♇.
15 ☉⚺♄. ☿▽♇. ♀Q♄.
17 ☿±♇. ☉∥♃.
18 ☿⚺♄. ☿±♅.
19 ☿∠♀. ☿⊥♂. ♀▽♆.
20 ☉☌♃. ☉▽♅. ☿☌♃. ☿▽♅.
21 ☉☌☿. ☿⊥♄. ☿∥♄.
22 ☉⊥♄. ☿⚼♇. ♀∠♃.
23 ☉⚼♇. ♃▽♅.
24 ♀□♇. ☿∥♃.
25 ☿☌♂. ☿±♆.
26 ☿∠♄. ☿☍♆.
27 ☉∥☿. ☿∥♂.
28 ☿⊥♀. ♂∠♄. ♂☍♆. ☉∥♂.
29 ☿△♇. ☿#♆.
30 ♄⚼♆.

LAST QUARTER–July 2,17h.19m. (10°♈39′)

NEW MOON–Aug. 8,19h.15m. (16° ♌ 04′)

D M	D W	Sidereal Time	☉ Long.	☉ Dec.	☽ Long.	☽ Lat.	☽ Dec.	☽ Node	24h. ☽ Long.	24h. ☽ Dec.
		h m s	° ′ ″	° ′	° ′ ″	° ′	° ′	° ′	° ′ ″	° ′
1	Th	8 39 42	9 ♌ 04 03	17 N59	9 ♉ 49 08	3 S 04	11 N51	15 ♊ 07	15 ♉ 50 38	14 N05
2	F	8 43 39	10 01 28	17 44	21 55 09	2 08	16 11	15 03	28 03 20	18 09
3	S	8 47 35	10 58 54	17 29	4 ♊ 15 48	1 S 05	19 56	15 00	10 ♊ 33 07	21 31
4	Su	8 51 32	11 56 21	17 13	16 55 49	0 N03	22 51	14 57	23 24 20	23 54
5	M	8 55 28	12 53 50	16 57	29 59 03	1 12	24 38	14 54	6 ♋ 40 11	25 02
6	T	8 59 25	13 51 20	16 40	13 ♋ 27 51	2 19	25 04	14 51	20 22 01	24 43
7	W	9 03 22	14 48 51	16 23	27 22 29	3 21	23 58	14 47	4 ♌ 28 51	22 49
8	Th	9 07 18	15 46 23	16 07	11 ♌ 40 34	4 11	21 18	14 44	18 56 54	19 25
9	F	9 11 15	16 43 56	15 49	26 17 00	4 46	17 14	14 41	3 ♍ 39 54	14 46
10	S	9 15 11	17 41 30	15 32	11 ♍ 04 31	5 02	12 04	14 38	18 29 49	9 12
11	Su	9 19 08	18 39 05	15 14	25 54 42	4 59	6 N12	14 35	3 ♎ 18 13	3 N07
12	M	9 23 04	19 36 40	14 56	10 ♎ 39 27	4 35	0 00	14 32	17 57 40	3 S 05
13	T	9 27 01	20 34 17	14 38	25 12 14	3 54	6 S 07	14 28	2 ♏ 22 44	9 02
14	W	9 30 57	21 31 55	14 20	9 ♏ 28 50	2 59	11 49	14 25	16 30 24	14 25
15	Th	9 34 54	22 29 34	14 01	23 27 22	1 54	16 48	14 22	0 ♐ 19 48	18 55
16	F	9 38 51	23 27 13	13 42	7 ♐ 07 51	0 N44	20 46	14 19	13 51 42	22 19
17	S	9 42 47	24 24 54	13 23	20 31 33	0 S 27	23 33	14 16	27 07 40	24 26
18	Su	9 46 44	25 22 36	13 04	3 ♑ 40 16	1 35	24 58	14 13	10 ♑ 09 36	25 10
19	M	9 50 40	26 20 18	12 44	16 35 50	2 37	25 00	14 09	22 59 11	24 31
20	T	9 54 37	27 18 02	12 25	29 19 46	3 30	23 43	14 06	5 ♒ 37 44	22 37
21	W	9 58 33	28 15 48	12 05	11 ♒ 53 10	4 12	21 15	14 03	18 06 10	19 39
22	Th	10 02 30	29 ♌ 13 34	11 45	24 16 48	4 41	17 51	14 00	0 ♓ 25 09	15 52
23	F	10 06 26	0 ♍ 11 22	11 24	6 ♓ 31 17	4 57	13 43	13 57	12 35 18	11 27
24	S	10 10 23	1 09 11	11 04	18 37 19	5 00	9 06	13 53	24 37 30	6 39
25	Su	10 14 20	2 07 02	10 43	0 ♈ 36 03	4 49	4 S 10	13 50	6 ♈ 33 10	1 S 40
26	M	10 18 16	3 04 54	10 22	12 29 11	4 25	0 N52	13 47	18 24 23	3 N23
27	T	10 22 13	4 02 48	10 02	24 19 12	3 50	5 52	13 44	0 ♉ 14 03	8 18
28	W	10 26 09	5 00 44	9 40	6 ♉ 09 26	3 05	10 40	13 41	12 05 52	12 56
29	Th	10 30 06	5 58 42	9 19	18 03 57	2 12	15 06	13 38	24 04 16	17 08
30	F	10 34 02	6 56 41	8 58	0 ♊ 07 29	1 12	19 00	13 34	6 ♊ 14 15	20 41
31	S	10 37 59	7 ♍ 54 42	8 N36	12 ♊ 25 13	0 S 07	22 N10	13 ♊ 31	18 ♊ 41 03	23 N23

D M	Mercury Lat.	Mercury Dec.	Mercury Dec.	Venus Lat.	Venus Dec.	Venus Dec.	Mars Lat.	Mars Dec.	Mars Dec.	Jupiter Lat.	Jupiter Dec.
	° ′	° ′	° ′	° ′	° ′	° ′	° ′	° ′	° ′	° ′	° ′
1	1 N38	16 N00	15 N 20	0 N 10	2 N37	2 N07	1 N 08	18 N16	18 N 05	0 N 20	20 N29
3	1 31	14 40	13 59	0 00	1 37	1 08	1 09	17 54	17 43	0 20	20 24
5	1 21	13 18	12 36	0 S 10	0 N38	0 N08	1 09	17 32	17 21	0 20	20 18
7	1 10	11 54	11 12	0 20	0 S 22	0 S 51	1 09	17 10	16 58	0 21	20 13
9	0 58	10 29	9 46	0 31	1 21	1 51	1 09	16 47	16 35	0 21	20 07
11	0 44	9 04	8 21	0 42	2 20	2 50	1 09	16 23	16 11	0 21	20 01
13	0 29	7 38	6 56	0 53	3 19	3 49	1 09	15 59	15 47	0 21	19 56
15	0 N13	6 13	5 31	1 05	4 18	4 47	1 09	15 35	15 22	0 21	19 50
17	0 S 03	4 49	4 08	1 17	5 16	5 45	1 09	15 10	14 58	0 22	19 44
19	0 21	3 27	2 46	1 30	6 14	6 43	1 09	14 45	14 32	0 22	19 38
21	0 39	2 05	1 26	1 42	7 11	7 39	1 09	14 20	14 07	0 22	19 32
23	0 57	0 N46	0 N 08	1 55	8 08	8 36	1 09	13 54	13 41	0 22	19 27
25	1 16	0 S 30	1 S 08	2 08	9 03	9 31	1 09	13 28	13 14	0 23	19 21
27	1 35	1 44	2 20	2 22	9 58	10 25	1 09	13 01	12 48	0 23	19 15
29	1 54	2 55	3 S 29	2 35	10 52	11 S 19	1 09	12 34	12 N 21	0 23	19 09
31	2 S 13	4 S 01		2 S 49	11 S 45		1 N 09	12 N07		0 N 23	19 N03

FIRST QUARTER–Aug.15,10h.12m. (22° ♏ 25′)

FULL MOON – Aug.22,22h.29m. (29°♒39′)

EPHEMERIS]				AUGUST 2002													17
D	☿	♀	♂	♃	♄	♅	♆	♇	Lunar Aspects								
M	Long.	Long.	Long.	Long.	Long.	Long.	Long.	Long.	☉	☿	♀	♂	♃	♄	♅	♆	♇
	° ′	° ′	° ′	° ′	° ′	° ′	° ′	° ′									
1	21♌09	23♍48	12♌05	29♋57	24♊55	27♒35	9♒36	15♐04	□		⚼	□		∠		□	
2	23 00	24 51	12 43	0♌10	25 01	27R 32	9R 34	15R 03		□	△			⚺	□		
3	24 50	25 55	13 22	0 24	25 08	27 30	9 33	15 02					⚹			△	
4	26 38	26 59	14 00	0 37	25 14	27 28	9 31	15 02	⚹			⚹	∠				☍
5	28♌24	28 02	14 38	0 50	25 20	27 26	9 29	15 01	∠	⚹	□	∠	⚺	☌	△	⚼	
6	0♍09	29♍05	15 17	1 03	25 26	27 23	9 28	15 00	⚺	∠		⚺			⚼		
7	1 53	0♎07	15 55	1 17	25 32	27 21	9 26	15 00		⚺	⚹		☌	⚺			⚼
8	3 34	1 10	16 33	1 30	25 38	27 19	9 25	14 59	☌		∠	☌		∠		☍	△
9	5 15	2 12	17 11	1 43	25 44	27 16	9 23	14 59			⚺		⚺	⚹	☍		
10	6 53	3 14	17 50	1 56	25 50	27 14	9 21	14 58	⚺	☌		⚺	∠				□
11	8 30	4 16	18 28	2 09	25 56	27 12	9 20	14 58					⚹	□		⚼	
12	10 06	5 17	19 06	2 22	26 01	27 09	9 18	14 57	∠	⚺	☌	∠			⚼	△	⚹
13	11 40	6 18	19 45	2 35	26 07	27 07	9 16	14 57	⚹	∠		⚹		△	△		∠
14	13 12	7 19	20 23	2 48	26 12	27 05	9 15	14 56		⚹	⚺		□	⚼		□	⚺
15	14 43	8 19	21 01	3 01	26 18	27 02	9 13	14 56	□		∠	□			□		
16	16 12	9 19	21 39	3 14	26 23	27 00	9 12	14 56			⚹		△			⚹	
17	17 40	10 19	22 18	3 27	26 29	26 57	9 10	14 55	△	□		△	⚼	☍	⚹	∠	☌
18	19 06	11 18	22 56	3 40	26 34	26 55	9 09	14 55				⚼				⚺	
19	20 30	12 18	23 34	3 53	26 39	26 53	9 07	14 55	⚼	△	□				∠		⚺
20	21 53	13 16	24 12	4 06	26 44	26 50	9 06	14 55					☍		⚺		∠
21	23 14	14 14	24 50	4 18	26 49	26 48	9 04	14 54		⚼	△			⚼		☌	⚹
22	24 33	15 12	25 29	4 31	26 54	26 45	9 02	14 54	☍			☍		△	☌		
23	25 51	16 10	26 07	4 44	26 59	26 43	9 01	14 54			⚼					⚺	
24	27 07	17 07	26 45	4 56	27 04	26 41	9 00	14 54					⚼			∠	□
25	28 21	18 03	27 23	5 09	27 09	26 38	8 58	14 54		☍			△	□	⚺		
26	29♍33	18 59	28 01	5 22	27 13	26 36	8 57	14D 54				⚼			∠	⚹	△
27	0♎43	19 55	28 39	5 34	27 18	26 34	8 55	14 54	⚼		☍	△		⚹	⚹		⚼
28	1 51	20 50	29 18	5 47	27 22	26 31	8 54	14 54	△				□			□	
29	2 57	21 44	29♌56	5 59	27 27	26 29	8 52	14 54		⚼				∠			
30	4 00	22 38	0♍34	6 11	27 31	26 26	8 51	14 54		△		□		⚺	□		
31	5♎01	23♎32	1♍12	6♌24	27♊35	26♒24	8♒50	14♐54	□		⚼		⚹			△	☍

D	Saturn		Uranus		Neptune		Pluto	
M	Lat.	Dec.	Lat.	Dec.	Lat.	Dec.	Lat.	Dec.
	° ′	° ′	° ′	° ′	° ′	° ′	° ′	° ′
1	1S16	22N05	0S46	13S02	0N04	17S47	9N55	12S45
3	1 16	22 05	0 47	13 04	0 04	17 48	9 54	12 46
5	1 16	22 06	0 47	13 06	0 04	17 49	9 53	12 46
7	1 16	22 06	0 47	13 07	0 04	17 49	9 52	12 47
9	1 16	22 06	0 47	13 09	0 04	17 50	9 52	12 47
11	1 16	22 07	0 47	13 11	0 04	17 51	9 51	12 48
13	1 16	22 07	0 47	13 12	0 04	17 52	9 50	12 49
15	1 16	22 07	0 47	13 14	0 04	17 53	9 49	12 50
17	1 16	22 07	0 47	13 15	0 04	17 54	9 48	12 50
19	1 16	22 08	0 47	13 17	0 04	17 55	9 48	12 51
21	1 16	22 08	0 47	13 19	0 04	17 55	9 47	12 52
23	1 16	22 08	0 47	13 20	0 04	17 56	9 46	12 53
25	1 17	22 08	0 47	13 22	0 04	17 57	9 45	12 53
27	1 17	22 08	0 47	13 24	0 04	17 58	9 44	12 54
29	1 17	22 08	0 47	13 25	0 04	17 59	9 44	12 55
31	1S17	22N08	0S47	13S27	0N04	17S59	9N43	12S56

Mutual Aspects

1 ♃⚼♇.
2 ☉∠♄. ☉☍♆. ♀□♄. ♀⚼♆. ☉∥♆.
3 ☿⚹♄.
4 ☉∠♀. ☿⚺♀. ☿☍♅. ♀∇♅. ♂∥♆.
5 ☿∥♅.
6 ♂△♇. ☿∥♇.
7 ☉△♇. ☿⚺♃.
8 ♀⚹♃.
9 ♀∠♂. ♃⊥♄.
10 ☉☌♂. ♀±♅. ♀Q♇.
11 ☿⊥♃. ☿Q♄.
12 ☿∇♆.
15 ☿±♆. ♀□♇.
16 ♀△♆.
17 ☉∥♅. ☿∥♀.
18 ☿∠♃. ♅Q♇.
19 ☉⚹♄. ♀⚼♅. ☉∥♇.
20 ☉☍♅. 21 ♄△♅.
22 ☿⚼♆. ♀⚹♇.
23 ☿⚺♂.
24 ☿□♄. ☿∇♅. ♀Q♃. ♂☍♅.
25 ♂⚹♄. ♂∥♅.
26 ♇Stat.
27 ☉∥♀. ♂∥♇.
29 ☉⚺♃. ☿±♅. ☿Q♇.

LAST QUARTER – Aug. 1,10h.22m. (9°♉00′) & Aug.31,02h.31m. (7°♊32′)

NEW MOON–Sep. 7,03h.10m. (14°♍20′)

D M	D W	Sidereal Time	☉ Long.	☉ Dec.	☽ Long.	☽ Lat.	☽ Dec.	☽ Node	24h. ☽ Long.	24h. ☽ Dec.
		h m s	° ′ ″	° ′	° ′ ″	° ′	° ′	° ′	° ′ ″	° ′
1	Su	10 41 55	8 ♍ 52 46	8 N14	25 ♊ 02 23	0 N59	24 N20	13 ♊ 28	1 ♋ 29 48	24 N58
2	M	10 45 52	9 50 51	7 53	8 ♋ 03 47	2 04	25 16	13 25	14 44 46	25 12
3	T	10 49 49	10 48 58	7 31	21 33 02	3 05	24 46	13 22	28 28 43	23 56
4	W	10 53 45	11 47 07	7 09	5 ♌ 31 45	3 57	22 43	13 19	12 ♌ 41 53	21 07
5	Th	10 57 42	12 45 18	6 46	19 58 38	4 36	19 11	13 15	27 21 18	16 54
6	F	11 01 38	13 43 31	6 24	4 ♍ 48 57	4 57	14 21	13 12	12 ♍ 20 30	11 33
7	S	11 05 35	14 41 45	6 02	19 54 42	4 58	8 34	13 09	27 30 12	5 N26
8	Su	11 09 31	15 40 01	5 39	5 ♎ 05 39	4 38	2 N14	13 06	12 ♎ 39 44	1 S00
9	M	11 13 28	16 38 19	5 16	20 11 11	3 59	4 S12	13 03	27 38 58	7 19
10	T	11 17 24	17 36 38	4 54	5 ♏ 02 10	3 04	10 18	12 59	12 ♏ 20 06	13 07
11	W	11 21 21	18 34 59	4 31	19 32 17	1 59	15 43	12 56	26 38 26	18 03
12	Th	11 25 18	19 33 22	4 08	3 ♐ 38 27	0 N47	20 06	12 53	10 ♐ 32 22	21 51
13	F	11 29 14	20 31 46	3 45	17 20 22	0 S25	23 15	12 50	24 02 44	24 18
14	S	11 33 11	21 30 12	3 22	0 ♑ 39 48	1 34	25 00	12 47	7 ♑ 11 56	25 21
15	Su	11 37 07	22 28 39	2 59	13 39 35	2 36	25 20	12 44	20 03 07	24 59
16	M	11 41 04	23 27 08	2 36	26 22 58	3 29	24 18	12 40	2 ♒ 39 29	23 20
17	T	11 45 00	24 25 39	2 13	8 ♒ 53 02	4 11	22 05	12 37	15 03 56	20 35
18	W	11 48 57	25 24 11	1 50	21 12 27	4 41	18 52	12 34	27 18 51	16 57
19	Th	11 52 53	26 22 45	1 26	3 ♓ 23 19	4 57	14 53	12 31	9 ♓ 26 04	12 40
20	F	11 56 50	27 21 20	1 03	15 27 15	5 00	10 20	12 28	21 27 02	7 56
21	S	12 00 47	28 19 58	0 40	27 25 34	4 49	5 27	12 25	3 ♈ 22 59	2 S56
22	Su	12 04 43	29 ♍ 18 37	0 N16	9 ♈ 19 29	4 26	0 S23	12 21	15 15 13	2 N09
23	M	12 08 40	0 ♎ 17 19	0 S07	21 10 25	3 52	4 N41	12 18	27 05 18	7 10
24	T	12 12 36	1 16 02	0 30	3 ♉ 00 12	3 07	9 35	12 15	8 ♉ 55 23	11 55
25	W	12 16 33	2 14 48	0 54	14 51 16	2 14	14 10	12 12	20 48 15	16 16
26	Th	12 20 29	3 13 36	1 17	26 46 47	1 15	18 14	12 09	2 ♊ 47 23	20 01
27	F	12 24 26	4 12 26	1 40	8 ♊ 50 35	0 S11	21 36	12 05	14 56 58	22 57
28	S	12 28 22	5 11 18	2 04	21 07 09	0 N54	24 03	12 02	27 21 43	24 51
29	Su	12 32 19	6 10 13	2 27	3 ♋ 41 19	1 58	25 22	11 59	10 ♋ 06 31	25 32
30	M	12 36 16	7 ♎ 09 10	2 S50	16 ♋ 37 53	2 N58	25 N21	11 ♊ 56	23 ♋ 15 55	24 N49

D M	Mercury Lat.	Mercury Dec.		Venus Lat.	Venus Dec.		Mars Lat.	Mars Dec.		Jupiter Lat.	Jupiter Dec.
	° ′	° ′	° ′	° ′	° ′	° ′	° ′	° ′	° ′	° ′	° ′
1	2 S 22	4 S 33	5 S 04	2 S 56	12 S 12	12 S 37	1 N 09	11 N 53	11 N 40	0 N 23	19 N 00
3	2 40	5 33	6 01	3 10	13 03	13 28	1 09	11 26	11 12	0 24	18 54
5	2 57	6 27	6 52	3 24	13 53	14 18	1 09	10 58	10 44	0 24	18 48
7	3 14	7 14	7 35	3 39	14 42	15 06	1 08	10 30	10 16	0 24	18 42
9	3 29	7 54	8 11	3 53	15 30	15 53	1 08	10 02	9 47	0 24	18 36
11	3 42	8 25	8 37	4 08	16 16	16 38	1 08	9 33	9 19	0 25	18 31
13	3 53	8 46	8 52	4 22	17 00	17 22	1 08	9 04	8 50	0 25	18 25
15	4 00	8 54	8 53	4 37	17 43	18 04	1 08	8 35	8 21	0 25	18 19
17	4 03	8 48	8 39	4 51	18 24	18 44	1 08	8 06	7 51	0 25	18 13
19	4 00	8 26	8 09	5 05	19 03	19 22	1 08	7 36	7 22	0 26	18 08
21	3 52	7 48	7 22	5 19	19 40	19 58	1 07	7 07	6 52	0 26	18 02
23	3 36	6 53	6 19	5 33	20 15	20 31	1 07	6 37	6 22	0 26	17 56
25	3 12	5 42	5 03	5 46	20 47	21 02	1 07	6 07	5 52	0 27	17 51
27	2 41	4 21	3 39	5 59	21 17	21 31	1 07	5 37	5 22	0 27	17 45
29	2 04	2 56	2 S 14	6 12	21 44	21 S 57	1 07	5 07	4 N 52	0 27	17 40
31	1 S 24	1 S 34		6 S 23	22 S 08		1 N 06	4 N 37		0 N 28	17 N 35

FIRST QUARTER–Sep.13,18h.08m. (20°♐47′)

FULL MOON–Sep.21,13h.59m. (28°♓25′)

D M	☿ Long.	♀ Long.	♂ Long.	♃ Long.	♄ Long.	♅ Long.	♆ Long.	♇ Long.	☉	☿	♀	♂	♃	♄	♅	♆	♇
	Lunar Aspects																
	° ′	° ′	° ′	° ′	° ′	° ′	° ′	° ′									
1	6♎00	24♎25	1♍50	6♌36	27♊40	26♒22	8♒48	14♐55			△		∠	☌	△	⚼	
2	6 55	25 17	2 29	6 48	27 44	26R 19	8R 47	14 55	⚹	□		⚹	⚺		⚼		
3	7 48	26 09	3 07	7 00	27 48	26 17	8 45	14 55	∠		□	∠		⚺			
4	8 38	27 00	3 45	7 12	27 51	26 15	8 44	14 55	⚺	⚹		⚺	☌			☍	⚼
5	9 25	27 51	4 23	7 25	27 55	26 13	8 43	14 56		∠				∠	☍		△
6	10 08	28 40	5 01	7 37	27 59	26 10	8 42	14 56		⚺	⚹	☌	⚺	⚹			
7	10 47	29♎30	5 39	7 48	28 03	26 08	8 40	14 56	☌		∠		∠			⚼	□
8	11 23	0♏18	6 18	8 00	28 06	26 06	8 39	14 57		☌	⚺	⚺	⚹	□	⚼	△	
9	11 54	1 06	6 56	8 12	28 10	26 04	8 38	14 57	⚺			∠			△		⚹
10	12 20	1 52	7 34	8 24	28 13	26 02	8 37	14 58	∠		☌	⚹	□	△		□	∠
11	12 42	2 38	8 12	8 36	28 16	25 59	8 36	14 58	⚹	⚺				⚼	□		⚺
12	12 58	3 24	8 50	8 47	28 19	25 57	8 34	14 59		∠	⚺	□	△			⚹	
13	13 09	4 08	9 28	8 59	28 22	25 55	8 33	14 59	□	⚹	∠					∠	☌
14	13 14	4 51	10 07	9 10	28 25	25 53	8 32	15 00			⚹		⚼	☍	⚹		
15	13R 13	5 33	10 45	9 21	28 28	25 51	8 31	15 01		□		△			∠	⚺	⚺
16	13 06	6 15	11 23	9 33	28 31	25 49	8 30	15 01	△			⚼			⚺		∠
17	12 51	6 55	12 01	9 44	28 33	25 47	8 29	15 02	⚼	△	□		☍	⚼		☌	⚹
18	12 30	7 34	12 39	9 55	28 36	25 45	8 28	15 03		⚼					☌		
19	12 01	8 12	13 17	10 06	28 38	25 43	8 27	15 03			△			△		⚺	
20	11 26	8 49	13 56	10 17	28 41	25 41	8 26	15 04				☍					□
21	10 44	9 25	14 34	10 28	28 43	25 39	8 25	15 05	☍		⚼		⚼	□	⚺	∠	
22	9 56	9 59	15 12	10 39	28 45	25 37	8 24	15 06		☍			△		∠	⚹	△
23	9 01	10 32	15 50	10 50	28 47	25 35	8 24	15 07							⚹		
24	8 02	11 04	16 28	11 00	28 49	25 34	8 23	15 08				⚼		⚹		□	⚼
25	6 59	11 34	17 06	11 11	28 51	25 32	8 22	15 09	⚼		☍	△	□	∠			
26	5 53	12 03	17 45	11 21	28 53	25 30	8 21	15 10		⚼				⚺	□		
27	4 47	12 30	18 23	11 32	28 54	25 28	8 20	15 11	△	△			⚹			△	
28	3 40	12 56	19 01	11 42	28 56	25 27	8 20	15 12				□	∠		△	⚼	☍
29	2 36	13 19	19 39	11 52	28 57	25 25	8 19	15 13	□	□	⚼			☌			
30	1♎37	13♏42	20♍17	12♌02	28♊58	25♒23	8♒18	15♐14			△	⚹	⚺		⚼		

D M	Saturn Lat.	Saturn Dec.	Uranus Lat.	Uranus Dec.	Neptune Lat.	Neptune Dec.	Pluto Lat.	Pluto Dec.
	° ′	° ′	° ′	° ′	° ′	° ′	° ′	° ′
1	1S17	22N08	0S47	13S28	0N04	18S00	9N42	12S56
3	1 17	22 08	0 47	13 29	0 04	18 00	9 41	12 57
5	1 17	22 08	0 47	13 31	0 04	18 01	9 41	12 58
7	1 17	22 08	0 47	13 32	0 04	18 02	9 40	12 59
9	1 17	22 08	0 47	13 34	0 04	18 03	9 39	13 00
11	1 17	22 08	0 47	13 35	0 04	18 03	9 38	13 01
13	1 17	22 08	0 46	13 37	0 04	18 04	9 37	13 02
15	1 18	22 08	0 46	13 38	0 04	18 04	9 36	13 03
17	1 18	22 08	0 46	13 39	0 04	18 05	9 36	13 04
19	1 18	22 08	0 46	13 41	0 04	18 05	9 35	13 05
21	1 18	22 08	0 46	13 42	0 04	18 06	9 34	13 06
23	1 18	22 08	0 46	13 43	0 04	18 06	9 33	13 07
25	1 18	22 08	0 46	13 44	0 04	18 07	9 32	13 08
27	1 18	22 08	0 46	13 45	0 04	18 07	9 32	13 09
29	1 18	22 08	0 46	13 46	0 04	18 08	9 31	13 10
31	1S19	22N08	0S46	13S47	0N04	18S08	9N30	13S11

Mutual Aspects

1 ☉∇♆. ♀#♂.
2 ☉Q♄. ☿⚹♃.
3 ♀△♅. ♀∥♇.
4 ☿△♆. ♀∥♅.
5 ♀△♄. ☉#☿.
6 ☉∠♀. ☉⊥♃.
7 ☉±♆. ☉□♇.
8 ☿⚼♅. ♀∠♇.
11 ♃☍♆.
12 ♂⚺♃. ♂∇♆.
14 ☿#♂. ☿Stat.
15 ♂Q♄.
16 ☉⚼♆. ♀∥♆.
17 ☉∠♃. ♀#♃.
18 ☉∇♅. ☿⚺♂.
19 ♀□♆.
20 ♀⊥♇. ♃#♆.
21 ☉□♄. ☿⚹♃. ☿⚼♅. ♂±♆.
22 ☿⚺♀. ♂□♇.
24 ☉±♅. ☿△♆. ♀□♃. ☿#♂.
25 ♂⊥♃.
26 ☉Q♇. ☿⊥♀.
27 ☉☌☿.
28 ☿Q♇.
29 ☉∥☿.
30 ☿±♅.

LAST QUARTER–Sep.29,17h.03m. (6°♋23′)

NEW MOON–Oct. 6,11h.18m. (13°♎02′)

D M	D W	Sidereal Time	☉ Long.	☉ Dec.	☽ Long.	☽ Lat.	☽ Dec.	☽ Node	24h. ☽ Long.	24h. ☽ Dec.
		h m s	° ′ ″	° ′	° ′ ″	° ′	° ′	° ′	° ′ ″	° ′
1	T	12 40 12	8 ♎ 08 09	3 S 14	0 ♌ 01 01	3 N51	23 N54	11 ♊ 53	6 ♌ 53 27	22 N38
2	W	12 44 09	9 07 11	3 37	13 53 21	4 32	21 00	11 50	21 00 40	19 01
3	Th	12 48 05	10 06 14	4 00	28 15 07	4 57	16 44	11 46	5 ♍ 36 14	14 09
4	F	12 52 02	11 05 20	4 23	13 ♍ 03 16	5 04	11 20	11 43	20 35 17	8 19
5	S	12 55 58	12 04 29	4 46	28 11 08	4 50	5 N09	11 40	5 ♎ 49 31	1 N54
6	Su	12 59 55	13 03 39	5 09	13 ♎ 29 01	4 15	1 S24	11 37	21 08 13	4 S41
7	M	13 03 51	14 02 51	5 32	28 45 42	3 22	7 53	11 34	6 ♏ 20 10	10 57
8	T	13 07 48	15 02 05	5 55	13 ♏ 50 27	2 16	13 50	11 30	21 15 36	16 29
9	W	13 11 45	16 01 21	6 18	28 34 49	1 N01	18 51	11 27	5 ♐ 47 36	20 54
10	Th	13 15 41	17 00 40	6 41	12 ♐ 53 37	0 S15	22 36	11 24	19 52 43	23 56
11	F	13 19 38	17 59 59	7 04	26 44 57	1 29	24 53	11 21	3 ♑ 30 31	25 26
12	S	13 23 34	18 59 21	7 26	10 ♑ 09 41	2 35	25 37	11 18	16 42 51	25 26
13	Su	13 27 31	19 58 45	7 49	23 10 28	3 31	24 55	11 15	29 33 00	24 04
14	M	13 31 27	20 58 10	8 11	5 ♒ 50 57	4 15	22 56	11 11	12 ♒ 04 50	21 31
15	T	13 35 24	21 57 36	8 33	18 15 09	4 46	19 53	11 08	24 22 21	18 03
16	W	13 39 20	22 57 05	8 55	0 ♓ 26 53	5 04	16 03	11 05	6 ♓ 29 11	13 53
17	Th	13 43 17	23 56 35	9 17	12 29 37	5 07	11 36	11 02	18 28 32	9 13
18	F	13 47 14	24 56 07	9 39	24 26 16	4 58	6 46	10 59	0 ♈ 23 04	4 S15
19	S	13 51 10	25 55 41	10 01	6 ♈ 19 13	4 35	1 S42	10 56	12 14 56	0 N52
20	Su	13 55 07	26 55 17	10 23	18 10 27	4 01	3 N25	10 52	24 05 58	5 57
21	M	13 59 03	27 54 55	10 44	0 ♉ 01 42	3 16	8 26	10 49	5 ♉ 57 52	10 50
22	T	14 03 00	28 54 35	11 05	11 54 40	2 22	13 09	10 46	17 52 21	15 21
23	W	14 06 56	29 ♎ 54 17	11 26	23 51 10	1 22	17 25	10 43	29 51 24	19 18
24	Th	14 10 53	0 ♏ 54 01	11 47	5 ♊ 53 22	0 S17	21 00	10 40	11 ♊ 57 26	22 29
25	F	14 14 49	1 53 48	12 08	18 03 56	0 N49	23 43	10 36	24 13 19	24 40
26	S	14 18 46	2 53 36	12 29	0 ♋ 25 59	1 54	25 20	10 33	6 ♋ 42 24	25 41
27	Su	14 22 43	3 53 27	12 49	13 03 02	2 55	25 42	10 30	19 28 21	25 22
28	M	14 26 39	4 53 20	13 09	25 58 48	3 48	24 41	10 27	2 ♌ 34 47	23 40
29	T	14 30 36	5 53 15	13 29	9 ♌ 16 43	4 31	22 18	10 24	16 04 51	20 36
30	W	14 34 32	6 53 12	13 49	22 59 24	5 01	18 35	10 21	0 ♍ 00 26	16 17
31	Th	14 38 29	7 ♏ 53 11	14 S08	7 ♍ 07 52	5 N13	13 N44	10 ♊ 17	14 ♍ 21 28	10 N57

D M	Mercury Lat.	Mercury Dec.		Venus Lat.	Venus Dec.		Mars Lat.	Mars Dec.		Jupiter Lat.	Jupiter Dec.
	° ′	° ′	° ′	° ′	° ′	° ′	° ′	° ′	° ′	° ′	° ′
1	1 S24	1 S34	0 S 57	6 S 23	22 S08	22 S 19	1 N 06	4 N37	4 N 22	0 N 28	17 N35
3	0 43	0 S23	0 N 07	6 34	22 29	22 39	1 06	4 06	3 51	0 28	17 29
5	0 S05	0 N32	0 52	6 44	22 47	22 55	1 06	3 36	3 21	0 28	17 24
7	0 N30	1 06	1 16	6 53	23 01	23 07	1 06	3 05	2 50	0 28	17 19
9	0 59	1 19	1 18	7 00	23 11	23 15	1 05	2 35	2 20	0 29	17 14
11	1 23	1 11	1 00	7 06	23 17	23 18	1 05	2 04	1 49	0 29	17 09
13	1 40	0 44	0 N 25	7 09	23 18	23 17	1 05	1 33	1 18	0 29	17 05
15	1 52	0 N02	0 S 25	7 11	23 14	23 11	1 05	1 03	0 47	0 30	17 00
17	1 59	0 S54	1 26	7 10	23 05	22 59	1 04	0 32	0 N 17	0 30	16 56
19	2 02	1 59	2 35	7 07	22 51	22 41	1 04	0 N01	0 S 14	0 31	16 51
21	2 01	3 12	3 50	7 00	22 30	22 18	1 03	0 S29	0 45	0 31	16 47
23	1 57	4 30	5 09	6 51	22 04	21 49	1 03	1 00	1 15	0 31	16 43
25	1 51	5 50	6 31	6 38	21 33	21 16	1 03	1 31	1 46	0 32	16 39
27	1 43	7 12	7 53	6 22	20 57	20 37	1 02	2 01	2 17	0 32	16 35
29	1 33	8 34	9 S 15	6 03	20 16	19 S 54	1 02	2 32	2 S 47	0 32	16 32
31	1 N22	9 S56		5 S 42	19 S31		1 N 02	3 S03		0 N 33	16 N28

FIRST QUARTER–Oct.13,05h.33m. (19°♑43′)

FULL MOON – Oct.21,07h.20m. (27°♈43′)

D M	☿ Long. ° ′	♀ Long. ° ′	♂ Long. ° ′	♃ Long. ° ′	♄ Long. ° ′	♅ Long. ° ′	♆ Long. ° ′	♇ Long. ° ′
1	0♎42	14♏02	20♍56	12♌12	29♊00	25♒22	8♒18	15♐15
2	29♍55	14 21	21 34	12 22	29 01	25R 20	8R 17	15 16
3	29R 17	14 37	22 12	12 32	29 02	25 19	8 17	15 18
4	28 47	14 52	22 50	12 42	29 02	25 17	8 16	15 19
5	28 28	15 05	23 29	12 51	29 03	25 16	8 15	15 20
6	28 20	15 16	24 07	13 01	29 04	25 15	8 15	15 21
7	28D 22	15 24	24 45	13 10	29 04	25 13	8 15	15 23
8	28 34	15 31	25 23	13 19	29 05	25 12	8 14	15 24
9	28 57	15 35	26 02	13 29	29 05	25 11	8 14	15 25
10	29♍30	15 36	26 40	13 38	29 05	25 10	8 13	15 27
11	0♎11	15R 36	27 18	13 47	29 05	25 08	8 13	15 28
12	1 01	15 33	27 56	13 55	29R 05	25 07	8 13	15 30
13	1 59	15 28	28 35	14 04	29 05	25 06	8 13	15 31
14	3 04	15 20	29 13	14 13	29 05	25 05	8 12	15 33
15	4 15	15 10	29♍51	14 21	29 04	25 04	8 12	15 34
16	5 31	14 57	0♎29	14 29	29 04	25 03	8 12	15 36
17	6 52	14 42	1 08	14 37	29 03	25 02	8 12	15 37
18	8 16	14 25	1 46	14 46	29 02	25 02	8 12	15 39
19	9 44	14 05	2 24	14 53	29 02	25 01	8 12	15 40
20	11 15	13 43	3 02	15 01	29 01	25 00	8 12	15 42
21	12 48	13 19	3 41	15 09	29 00	24 59	8D 12	15 44
22	14 23	12 53	4 19	15 16	28 58	24 59	8 12	15 45
23	16 00	12 25	4 57	15 24	28 57	24 58	8 12	15 47
24	17 38	11 55	5 36	15 31	28 56	24 57	8 12	15 49
25	19 16	11 24	6 14	15 38	28 54	24 57	8 12	15 51
26	20 55	10 51	6 52	15 45	28 53	24 56	8 12	15 52
27	22 35	10 17	7 31	15 52	28 51	24 56	8 13	15 54
28	24 15	9 42	8 09	15 59	28 49	24 56	8 13	15 56
29	25 55	9 06	8 47	16 05	28 47	24 55	8 13	15 58
30	27 35	8 30	9 26	16 11	28 45	24 55	8 13	16 00
31	29♎15	7♏54	10♎04	16♌18	28♊43	24♒55	8♒14	16♐02

D	Lunar Aspects ☉	☿	♀	♂	♃	♄	♅	♆	♇
1		✱		∠		⊻			⚼
2	✱	∠	□		☌	∠		☍	△
3	∠	⊻		⊻		✱	☍		
4	⊻		✱		⊻				□
5		☌	∠	☌	∠	□		⚼	
6	☌		⊻		✱		⚼	△	✱
7		⊻		⊻		△	△		∠
8	⊻	∠	☌	∠	□	⚼		□	⊻
9	∠	✱		✱			□		
10	✱		⊻		△			✱	☌
11		□	∠	□	⚼	☍	✱	∠	
12			✱				∠	⊻	⊻
13	□			△			⊻		
14		△						☌	∠
15	△	⚼	□	⚼	☍	⚼			✱
16						△	☌		
17	⚼		△					⊻	□
18			⚼		⚼	□	⊻	∠	
19		☍		☍			∠	✱	
20					△				△
21	☍					✱	✱		⚼
22			☍		□	∠		□	
23				⚼		⊻	□		
24		⚼		△				△	
25	⚼	△			✱			⚼	☍
26	△		⚼		∠	☌	△		
27			△	□	⊻		⚼		
28		□				⊻			⚼
29	□		□	✱		∠		☍	△
30		✱		∠	☌	✱	☍		
31	✱		✱	⊻					

D M	Saturn Lat. ° ′	Saturn Dec. ° ′	Uranus Lat. ° ′	Uranus Dec. ° ′	Neptune Lat. ° ′	Neptune Dec. ° ′	Pluto Lat. ° ′	Pluto Dec. ° ′
1	1S19	22N08	0S46	13S47	0N04	18S08	9N30	13S11
3	1 19	22 08	0 46	13 48	0 04	18 08	9 29	13 12
5	1 19	22 07	0 46	13 49	0 03	18 09	9 29	13 13
7	1 19	22 07	0 46	13 50	0 03	18 09	9 28	13 14
9	1 19	22 07	0 46	13 51	0 03	18 09	9 27	13 15
11	1 19	22 07	0 46	13 52	0 03	18 09	9 26	13 16
13	1 19	22 07	0 46	13 52	0 03	18 10	9 26	13 17
15	1 19	22 07	0 46	13 53	0 03	18 10	9 25	13 18
17	1 19	22 07	0 46	13 54	0 03	18 10	9 24	13 19
19	1 20	22 07	0 46	13 54	0 03	18 10	9 24	13 19
21	1 20	22 07	0 46	13 54	0 03	18 10	9 23	13 20
23	1 20	22 06	0 45	13 55	0 03	18 10	9 22	13 21
25	1 20	22 06	0 45	13 55	0 03	18 10	9 22	13 22
27	1 20	22 06	0 45	13 55	0 03	18 10	9 21	13 23
29	1 20	22 06	0 45	13 56	0 03	18 10	9 21	13 24
31	1S20	22N06	0S45	13S56	0N03	18S09	9N20	13S25

Mutual Aspects

1 ☉⊥♀. ☉△♆. ♀⚼♄. ♀#♄.
3 ☉⚼♅. ☿∠♀. ☿□♄. ☉#♂.
5 ♂⚼♆.
6 ☉✱♃. ☿Stat.
7 ♀⊻♇.
8 ☉✱♇. ♂▽♅.
9 ☉⊻♀. ☿□♄.
10 ♀Stat.
11 ☿∠♀. ♄Stat.
12 ☿±♅.
13 ♀⊻♇. ♃∠♄.
14 ☿Q♇. ♂∠♃. ♂□♄.
15 ♀∠♂.
17 ♀□♃. ♂±♅. ☿#♂.
18 ☉△♅. ☿⊥♀. ☿△♆.
19 ☿⚼♅. ♀⚼♄.
20 ☉Q♃. ♆Stat.
21 ☿⊻♀. ♂Q♇.
22 ☉△♄.
23 ☿✱♃. ☿✱♇. ♀#♄.
24 ☉∠♇. ♀⊥♂.
27 ♃△♇.
28 ☿△♅. ♀⊥♇. ♂△♆.
29 ♀⊻♂. ☉∥♇.
30 ☿Q♃. ♀□♆. ☉∥♅.
31 ☉☌♀. ☉□♆. ☿△♄. ♂⚼♅.

LAST QUARTER – Oct.29,05h.28m. (5°♌37′)

NEW MOON–Nov. 4,20h.34m. (12°♏15′)

D M	D W	Sidereal Time	☉ Long.	☉ Dec.	☽ Long.	☽ Lat.	☽ Dec.	☽ Node	24h. ☽ Long.	24h. ☽ Dec.
		h m s	° ′ ″	° ′	° ′ ″	° ′	° ′	° ′	° ′ ″	° ′
1	F	14 42 25	8 ♏ 53 13	14 S 28	21 ♍ 40 48	5 N05	7 N58	10 ♊ 14	29 ♍ 05 15	4 N51
2	S	14 46 22	9 53 17	14 47	6 ♎ 34 00	4 38	1 N38	10 11	14 ♎ 06 05	1 S 37
3	Su	14 50 18	10 53 22	15 06	21 40 23	3 50	4 S 53	10 08	29 15 41	8 05
4	M	14 54 15	11 53 30	15 24	6 ♏ 50 44	2 46	11 11	10 05	14 ♏ 24 16	14 05
5	T	14 58 12	12 53 40	15 43	21 55 07	1 31	16 46	10 02	29 22 08	19 11
6	W	15 02 08	13 53 51	16 01	6 ♐ 44 25	0 N11	21 15	9 58	14 ♐ 01 10	22 58
7	Th	15 06 05	14 54 04	16 18	21 11 46	1 S 08	24 17	9 55	28 15 49	25 11
8	F	15 10 01	15 54 19	16 36	5 ♑ 13 05	2 21	25 41	9 52	12 ♑ 03 31	25 46
9	S	15 13 58	16 54 35	16 53	18 47 11	3 23	25 28	9 49	25 24 18	24 49
10	Su	15 17 54	17 54 53	17 10	1 ♒ 55 12	4 12	23 50	9 46	8 ♒ 20 17	22 33
11	M	15 21 51	18 55 12	17 27	14 40 01	4 48	21 01	9 42	20 54 54	19 16
12	T	15 25 47	19 55 33	17 43	27 05 28	5 09	17 19	9 39	3 ♓ 12 18	15 12
13	W	15 29 44	20 55 54	17 59	9 ♓ 15 55	5 16	12 58	9 36	15 16 53	10 37
14	Th	15 33 41	21 56 18	18 15	21 15 43	5 08	8 11	9 33	27 12 56	5 41
15	F	15 37 37	22 56 42	18 31	3 ♈ 09 00	4 48	3 S 09	9 30	9 ♈ 04 23	0 S 35
16	S	15 41 34	23 57 08	18 46	14 59 28	4 15	1 N59	9 27	20 54 40	4 N32
17	Su	15 45 30	24 57 36	19 00	26 50 19	3 31	7 04	9 23	2 ♉ 46 45	9 32
18	M	15 49 27	25 58 05	19 15	8 ♉ 44 14	2 38	11 55	9 20	14 43 02	14 12
19	T	15 53 23	26 58 35	19 29	20 43 24	1 38	16 22	9 17	26 45 33	18 22
20	W	15 57 20	27 59 07	19 43	2 ♊ 49 41	0 S 32	20 12	9 14	8 ♊ 56 00	21 49
21	Th	16 01 16	28 ♏ 59 41	19 56	15 04 41	0 N36	23 12	9 11	21 15 54	24 18
22	F	16 05 13	0 ♐ 00 16	20 09	27 29 51	1 43	25 08	9 08	3 ♋ 46 44	25 38
23	S	16 09 10	1 00 53	20 22	10 ♋ 06 44	2 46	25 49	9 04	16 30 02	25 39
24	Su	16 13 06	2 01 31	20 34	22 56 53	3 42	25 08	9 01	29 27 26	24 17
25	M	16 17 03	3 02 11	20 46	6 ♌ 01 56	4 28	23 05	8 58	12 ♌ 40 34	21 34
26	T	16 20 59	4 02 52	20 57	19 23 29	5 00	19 45	8 55	26 10 50	17 39
27	W	16 24 56	5 03 36	21 09	3 ♍ 02 44	5 16	15 18	8 52	9 ♍ 59 12	12 43
28	Th	16 28 52	6 04 20	21 19	17 00 13	5 14	9 57	8 48	24 05 39	7 02
29	F	16 32 49	7 05 06	21 30	1 ♎ 15 17	4 53	3 N59	8 45	8 ♎ 28 47	0 N52
30	S	16 36 45	8 ♐ 05 54	21 S 40	15 ♎ 45 44	4 N14	2 S 18	8 ♊ 42	23 ♎ 05 32	5 S 27

D M	Mercury Lat.	Mercury Dec.		Venus Lat.	Venus Dec.		Mars Lat.	Mars Dec.		Jupiter Lat.	Jupiter Dec.
	° ′	° ′	° ′	° ′	° ′	° ′	° ′	° ′	° ′	° ′	° ′
1	1 N16	10 S 37	11 S 17	5 S 30	19 S 08	18 S 44	1 N 01	3 S 18	3 S 33	0 N 33	16 N27
3	1 04	11 56	12 35	5 04	18 19	17 55	1 01	3 48	4 03	0 33	16 24
5	0 51	13 14	13 52	4 36	17 30	17 05	1 00	4 18	4 34	0 34	16 21
7	0 38	14 29	15 05	4 07	16 40	16 16	1 00	4 49	5 04	0 34	16 18
9	0 24	15 41	16 16	3 37	15 52	15 28	1 00	5 19	5 34	0 35	16 15
11	0 N11	16 50	17 23	3 06	15 05	14 43	0 59	5 49	6 03	0 35	16 13
13	0 S 03	17 56	18 27	2 36	14 22	14 01	0 59	6 18	6 33	0 35	16 11
15	0 16	18 58	19 28	2 05	13 42	13 23	0 58	6 48	7 03	0 36	16 09
17	0 29	19 56	20 24	1 36	13 06	12 49	0 58	7 17	7 32	0 36	16 07
19	0 42	20 51	21 17	1 07	12 34	12 20	0 57	7 46	8 01	0 37	16 06
21	0 55	21 41	22 05	0 40	12 07	11 55	0 56	8 15	8 30	0 37	16 05
23	1 07	22 27	22 49	0 S 14	11 45	11 36	0 56	8 44	8 59	0 38	16 04
25	1 18	23 09	23 28	0 N 10	11 28	11 21	0 55	9 13	9 27	0 38	16 03
27	1 29	23 46	24 02	0 33	11 15	11 10	0 55	9 41	9 55	0 39	16 02
29	1 39	24 18	24 S 32	0 54	11 06	11 S 03	0 54	10 09	10 S 23	0 39	16 02
31	1 S 48	24 S 45		1 N 14	11 S 02		0 N 53	10 S 37		0 N 39	16 N02

FIRST QUARTER–Nov.11,20h.52m. (19°♒17′)

FULL MOON–Nov.20,01h.34m. (27° ♉ 33′)

D M	☿ Long.	♀ Long.	♂ Long.	♃ Long.	♄ Long.	♅ Long.	♆ Long.	♇ Long.	☉	☿	♀	♂	♃	♄	♅	♆	♇
	° ′	° ′	° ′	° ′	° ′	° ′	° ′	° ′	Lunar Aspects								
1	0♏55	7♏17	10♎42	16♌24	28♊41	24♒55	8♒14	16♐04	∠	∠	∠		⊻	□		⚼	□
2	2 35	6R 41	11 21	16 30	28R 39	24R 55	8 15	16 06	⊻	⊻	⊻	☌	∠		⚼	△	
3	4 15	6 05	11 59	16 35	28 36	24 55	8 15	16 08					✱	△	△		✱
4	5 54	5 30	12 37	16 41	28 34	24D 54	8 16	16 09	☌	☌	☌	⊻		⚼		□	∠
5	7 33	4 56	13 16	16 46	28 31	24 55	8 16	16 11				∠	□		□		⊻
6	9 11	4 23	13 54	16 52	28 28	24 55	8 17	16 13		⊻	⊻					✱	
7	10 49	3 51	14 33	16 57	28 26	24 55	8 17	16 15	⊻	∠	∠	✱	△		✱	∠	☌
8	12 27	3 21	15 11	17 02	28 23	24 55	8 18	16 18	∠		✱		⚼	☍	∠	⊻	
9	14 05	2 52	15 49	17 06	28 20	24 55	8 18	16 20	✱	✱		□			⊻		⊻
10	15 42	2 26	16 28	17 11	28 17	24 56	8 19	16 22			□					☌	∠
11	17 19	2 01	17 06	17 15	28 14	24 56	8 20	16 24	□	□		△	☍	⚼			✱
12	18 55	1 39	17 45	17 20	28 10	24 56	8 21	16 26			△	⚼		△	☌		
13	20 31	1 18	18 23	17 24	28 07	24 57	8 21	16 28								⊻	
14	22 07	1 00	19 02	17 28	28 04	24 57	8 22	16 30	△	△	⚼				⊻	∠	□
15	23 43	0 45	19 40	17 31	28 00	24 58	8 23	16 32	⚼				⚼	□		✱	
16	25 18	0 32	20 19	17 35	27 56	24 58	8 24	16 34		⚼		☍	△		∠		△
17	26 53	0 21	20 57	17 38	27 53	24 59	8 25	16 36			☍			✱	✱		⚼
18	28♏28	0 13	21 35	17 41	27 49	25 00	8 26	16 39						∠		□	
19	0♐02	0 07	22 14	17 44	27 45	25 00	8 27	16 41					□		□		
20	1 36	0 04	22 52	17 47	27 41	25 01	8 28	16 43	☍	☍		⚼		⊻		△	
21	3 10	0D 03	23 31	17 50	27 37	25 02	8 29	16 45			⚼		✱				☍
22	4 44	0 05	24 09	17 52	27 33	25 03	8 30	16 47			△	△	∠	☌	△	⚼	
23	6 18	0 09	24 48	17 54	27 29	25 04	8 31	16 50							⚼		
24	7 51	0 16	25 26	17 56	27 25	25 05	8 32	16 52	⚼	⚼		□	⊻	⊻			
25	9 25	0 24	26 05	17 58	27 21	25 06	8 33	16 54	△	△	□			∠		☍	⚼
26	10 58	0 35	26 43	18 00	27 17	25 07	8 35	16 56					☌		☍		△
27	12 31	0 49	27 22	18 01	27 12	25 08	8 36	16 59	□		✱	✱		✱			
28	14 04	1 04	28 00	18 03	27 08	25 10	8 37	17 01		□	∠	∠	⊻			⚼	□
29	15 37	1 21	28 39	18 04	27 03	25 11	8 38	17 03	✱		⊻	⊻	∠	□			
30	17♐10	1♏41	29♎18	18♌05	26♊59	25♒12	8♒40	17♐05		✱			✱		⚼	△	✱

D M	Saturn Lat.	Saturn Dec.	Uranus Lat.	Uranus Dec.	Neptune Lat.	Neptune Dec.	Pluto Lat.	Pluto Dec.
	° ′	° ′	° ′	° ′	° ′	° ′	° ′	° ′
1	1S20	22N06	0S45	13S56	0N03	18S09	9N20	13S26
3	1 20	22 06	0 45	13 56	0 03	18 09	9 19	13 27
5	1 20	22 06	0 45	13 56	0 03	18 09	9 19	13 27
7	1 20	22 06	0 45	13 55	0 03	18 09	9 18	13 28
9	1 20	22 06	0 45	13 55	0 03	18 08	9 18	13 29
11	1 20	22 05	0 45	13 55	0 03	18 08	9 17	13 30
13	1 20	22 05	0 45	13 55	0 03	18 08	9 17	13 31
15	1 20	22 05	0 45	13 54	0 03	18 07	9 16	13 32
17	1 20	22 05	0 45	13 54	0 03	18 07	9 16	13 33
19	1 20	22 05	0 44	13 53	0 03	18 06	9 16	13 33
21	1 20	22 05	0 44	13 52	0 03	18 06	9 15	13 34
23	1 20	22 05	0 44	13 52	0 03	18 05	9 15	13 35
25	1 20	22 05	0 44	13 51	0 03	18 05	9 15	13 36
27	1 20	22 05	0 44	13 50	0 03	18 04	9 14	13 36
29	1 20	22 04	0 44	13 49	0 03	18 03	9 14	13 37
31	1S20	22N04	0S44	13S48	0N03	18S03	9N14	13S38

Mutual Aspects

1 ☿∠♇. 2 ☉⊥♇.
3 ♀∥♆.
4 ☿☌♀. ♅Stat.
5 ☿□♆. ☿∥♇.
6 ☉⊻♂. ☉⚼♄. ☿∥♅.
7 ☿⊥♇. ☉#♃.
8 ☉⊻♇. ☉∥♀. ♀#♃.
9 ☉□♃. ☿⚼♄. ☿∥♀.
10 ☿⊻♇. ♂✱♇. ☿#♃.
11 ☿⊻♂. ☿□♃. ♂✱♃.
13 ♀∠♇. ☉∥☿. ☿∥♆.
14 ☉☌☿. ☉±♄. ☿±♄. ☉∥♆. ♀∥♅.
16 ☿□♅. ♀∥♇.
17 ☉□♅. ☿⊥♂. ☿Q♆.
18 ☉Q♆. ☿∇♄.
19 ☿⊻♀. 20 ☉∇♄.
21 ♀Stat.
22 ☉⊻♀. ☉⊥♂. ☿#♄.
23 ☿⊥♀. ♂△♅.
24 ☿✱♆.
27 ☿∠♂. ☿Q♅. ♂△♄.
29 ☉⊥♀.
30 ☿∠♀. ☿☌♇.

LAST QUARTER–Nov.27,15h.46m. (5°♍13′)

NEW MOON – Dec. 4, 07h.34m. (11° ♐ 58′)

D M	D W	Sidereal Time	☉ Long.	☉ Dec.	☽ Long.	☽ Lat.	☽ Dec.	☽ Node	24h. ☽ Long.	24h. ☽ Dec.
		h m s	° ′ ″	° ′	° ′ ″	° ′	° ′	° ′	° ′ ″	° ′
1	Su	16 40 42	9 ♐ 06 43	21 S 49	0 ♏ 27 33	3 N 17	8 S 33	8 ♊ 39	7 ♏ 51 00	11 S 33
2	M	16 44 39	10 07 34	21 58	15 15 03	2 07	14 23	8 36	22 38 48	17 01
3	T	16 48 35	11 08 26	22 07	0 ♐ 01 19	0 N 48	19 22	8 33	7 ♐ 21 42	21 25
4	W	16 52 32	12 09 20	22 15	14 39 05	0 S 33	23 06	8 29	21 52 38	24 24
5	Th	16 56 28	13 10 14	22 23	29 01 39	1 51	25 17	8 26	6 ♑ 05 33	25 44
6	F	17 00 25	14 11 09	22 30	13 ♑ 03 52	2 59	25 47	8 23	19 56 16	25 25
7	S	17 04 21	15 12 06	22 37	26 42 33	3 56	24 41	8 20	3 ♒ 22 42	23 36
8	Su	17 08 18	16 13 03	22 44	9 ♒ 56 46	4 38	22 13	8 17	16 24 57	20 35
9	M	17 12 14	17 14 01	22 50	22 47 32	5 05	18 43	8 14	29 04 55	16 40
10	T	17 16 11	18 14 59	22 55	5 ♓ 17 33	5 17	14 28	8 10	11 ♓ 25 55	12 09
11	W	17 20 08	19 15 58	23 00	17 30 35	5 13	9 44	8 07	23 32 08	7 15
12	Th	17 24 04	20 16 57	23 05	29 31 08	4 56	4 S 43	8 04	5 ♈ 28 12	2 S 10
13	F	17 28 01	21 17 57	23 09	11 ♈ 23 57	4 27	0 N 25	8 01	17 18 57	2 N 59
14	S	17 31 57	22 18 58	23 13	23 13 48	3 46	5 31	7 58	29 09 01	8 01
15	Su	17 35 54	23 19 59	23 16	5 ♉ 05 08	2 56	10 27	7 54	11 ♉ 02 39	12 48
16	M	17 39 50	24 21 01	23 19	17 01 59	1 57	15 03	7 51	23 03 33	17 09
17	T	17 43 47	25 22 03	23 22	29 07 42	0 S 53	19 06	7 48	5 ♊ 14 45	20 52
18	W	17 47 43	26 23 06	23 23	11 ♊ 24 56	0 N 15	22 24	7 45	17 38 27	23 41
19	Th	17 51 40	27 24 10	23 25	23 55 28	1 23	24 41	7 42	0 ♋ 16 04	25 23
20	F	17 55 37	28 25 14	23 26	6 ♋ 40 17	2 28	25 44	7 39	13 08 08	25 45
21	S	17 59 33	29 ♐ 26 18	23 26	19 39 34	3 27	25 25	7 35	26 14 29	24 43
22	Su	18 03 30	0 ♑ 27 24	23 26	2 ♌ 52 48	4 16	23 39	7 32	9 ♌ 34 22	22 16
23	M	18 07 26	1 28 29	23 26	16 19 04	4 51	20 34	7 29	23 06 42	18 35
24	T	18 11 23	2 29 36	23 25	29 57 08	5 11	16 20	7 26	6 ♍ 50 11	13 51
25	W	18 15 19	3 30 43	23 24	13 ♍ 45 43	5 13	11 12	7 23	20 43 33	8 23
26	Th	18 19 16	4 31 50	23 22	27 43 33	4 57	5 N 26	7 19	4 ♎ 45 32	2 N 25
27	F	18 23 12	5 32 59	23 19	11 ♎ 49 20	4 22	0 S 39	7 16	18 54 46	3 S 43
28	S	18 27 09	6 34 07	23 17	26 01 36	3 32	6 45	7 13	3 ♏ 09 36	9 43
29	Su	18 31 06	7 35 17	23 13	10 ♏ 18 28	2 28	12 34	7 10	17 27 51	15 14
30	M	18 35 02	8 36 27	23 10	24 37 23	1 N 15	17 43	7 07	1 ♐ 46 36	19 55
31	T	18 38 59	9 ♑ 37 37	23 S 05	8 ♐ 55 03	0 S 02	21 S 50	7 ♊ 04	16 ♐ 02 11	23 S 23

D M	Mercury Lat.	Mercury Dec.	Mercury Dec.	Venus Lat.	Venus Dec.	Venus Dec.	Mars Lat.	Mars Dec.	Mars Dec.	Jupiter Lat.	Jupiter Dec.
	° ′	° ′	° ′	° ′	° ′	° ′	° ′	° ′	° ′	° ′	° ′
1	1 S 48	24 S 45	24 S 57	1 N 14	11 S 02	11 S 01	0 N 53	10 S 37	10 S 51	0 N 39	16 N 02
3	1 56	25 07	25 16	1 32	11 01	11 02	0 53	11 05	11 18	0 40	16 02
5	2 03	25 23	25 29	1 48	11 04	11 07	0 52	11 32	11 45	0 40	16 03
7	2 09	25 34	25 38	2 04	11 11	11 15	0 51	11 59	12 12	0 41	16 03
9	2 13	25 39	25 40	2 17	11 20	11 26	0 51	12 25	12 38	0 41	16 04
11	2 16	25 39	25 36	2 30	11 32	11 39	0 50	12 51	13 04	0 42	16 05
13	2 17	25 32	25 27	2 41	11 47	11 55	0 49	13 17	13 30	0 42	16 07
15	2 17	25 20	25 12	2 51	12 04	12 13	0 48	13 43	13 55	0 43	16 08
17	2 14	25 02	24 51	3 00	12 22	12 32	0 48	14 08	14 20	0 43	16 10
19	2 08	24 38	24 24	3 07	12 43	12 54	0 47	14 33	14 45	0 44	16 12
21	2 00	24 09	23 52	3 14	13 05	13 16	0 46	14 57	15 09	0 44	16 15
23	1 48	23 35	23 16	3 20	13 28	13 40	0 45	15 21	15 33	0 44	16 17
25	1 32	22 57	22 37	3 24	13 52	14 04	0 44	15 45	15 56	0 45	16 20
27	1 13	22 16	21 55	3 28	14 17	14 30	0 43	16 08	16 19	0 45	16 23
29	0 49	21 34	21 S 14	3 31	14 42	14 S 55	0 42	16 30	16 S 41	0 46	16 26
31	0 S 20	20 S 53		3 N 33	15 S 08		0 N 41	16 S 52		0 N 46	16 N 30

FIRST QUARTER – Dec. 11, 15h.49m. (19° ♓ 26′)

FULL MOON – Dec.19,19h.10m. (27° ♊ 42′)

D M	☿ Long.	♀ Long.	♂ Long.	♃ Long.	♄ Long.	♅ Long.	♆ Long.	♇ Long.	☉	☿	♀	♂	♃	♄	♅	♆	♇
	° ′	° ′	° ′	° ′	° ′	° ′	° ′	° ′	Lunar Aspects								
1	18♐43	2♏02	29♎56	18♌05	26♊54	25♒13	8♒41	17♐08	∠	∠	☌	☌		△	△		∠
2	20 15	2 26	0♏35	18 06	26R 50	25 15	8 42	17 10	⊻	⊻			□	⚼		□	⊻
3	21 48	2 51	1 13	18 06	26 45	25 16	8 44	17 12			⊻	⊻			□		
4	23 20	3 18	1 52	18 06	26 40	25 18	8 45	17 15	●		∠	∠	△			⚹	☌
5	24 52	3 46	2 30	18R 06	26 36	25 19	8 47	17 17		●	⚹	⚹	⚼	☍	⚹	∠	
6	26 24	4 16	3 09	18 06	26 31	25 21	8 48	17 19	⊻						∠	⊻	⊻
7	27 56	4 48	3 48	18 05	26 26	25 23	8 50	17 21	∠	⊻					⊻		∠
8	29♐28	5 21	4 26	18 05	26 21	25 24	8 51	17 24		∠	□	□		⚼		☌	
9	1♑00	5 56	5 05	18 04	26 16	25 26	8 53	17 26	⚹				☍	△	☌		⚹
10	2 31	6 32	5 43	18 03	26 12	25 28	8 54	17 28		⚹	△	△				⊻	
11	4 02	7 09	6 22	18 01	26 07	25 30	8 56	17 31	□		⚼	⚼					□
12	5 32	7 48	7 00	18 00	26 02	25 31	8 58	17 33					⚼	□	⊻	∠	
13	7 02	8 28	7 39	17 58	25 57	25 33	8 59	17 35		□					∠	⚹	
14	8 32	9 09	8 18	17 56	25 52	25 35	9 01	17 37	△				△	⚹	⚹		△
15	10 00	9 51	8 56	17 54	25 47	25 37	9 03	17 40	⚼	△	☍	☍		∠		□	⚼
16	11 28	10 34	9 35	17 52	25 42	25 39	9 04	17 42					□				
17	12 55	11 19	10 14	17 50	25 37	25 41	9 06	17 44		⚼				⊻	□		
18	14 20	12 04	10 52	17 47	25 32	25 43	9 08	17 47								△	
19	15 44	12 51	11 31	17 44	25 27	25 46	9 10	17 49	☍		⚼	⚼	⚹	☌	△	⚼	☍
20	17 06	13 38	12 09	17 41	25 22	25 48	9 12	17 51				△	∠		⚼		
21	18 26	14 26	12 48	17 38	25 17	25 50	9 13	17 53		☍	△		⊻	⊻			
22	19 44	15 15	13 27	17 35	25 12	25 52	9 15	17 56								☍	⚼
23	20 59	16 05	14 05	17 31	25 07	25 55	9 17	17 58	⚼		□	□	☌	∠			△
24	22 10	16 56	14 44	17 27	25 03	25 57	9 19	18 00	△					⚹	☍		
25	23 18	17 48	15 23	17 23	24 58	25 59	9 21	18 02		⚼	⚹	⚹	⊻				□
26	24 21	18 40	16 01	17 19	24 53	26 02	9 23	18 05		△	∠	∠	∠	□		⚼	
27	25 18	19 33	16 40	17 15	24 48	26 04	9 25	18 07	□			⊻	⚹		⚼	△	⚹
28	26 10	20 27	17 19	17 10	24 43	26 07	9 27	18 09		□	⊻			△	△		
29	26 55	21 21	17 57	17 06	24 38	26 09	9 29	18 11	⚹				□	⚼		□	∠
30	27 32	22 17	18 36	17 01	24 34	26 12	9 31	18 13	∠	⚹	☌	●			□		⊻
31	28♑00	23♏12	19♏15	16♌56	24♊29	26♒14	9♒33	18♐16	⊻	∠						⚹	

D M	Saturn Lat.	Saturn Dec.	Uranus Lat.	Uranus Dec.	Neptune Lat.	Neptune Dec.	Pluto Lat.	Pluto Dec.
	° ′	° ′	° ′	° ′	° ′	° ′	° ′	° ′
1	1S20	22N04	0S44	13S48	0N03	18S03	9N14	13S38
3	1 20	22 04	0 44	13 47	0 03	18 02	9 13	13 38
5	1 20	22 04	0 44	13 46	0 03	18 01	9 13	13 39
7	1 20	22 04	0 44	13 45	0 03	18 01	9 13	13 40
9	1 19	22 04	0 44	13 44	0 03	18 00	9 13	13 40
11	1 19	22 04	0 44	13 43	0 03	17 59	9 13	13 41
13	1 19	22 04	0 44	13 41	0 03	17 58	9 12	13 41
15	1 19	22 03	0 44	13 40	0 03	17 57	9 12	13 42
17	1 19	22 03	0 44	13 38	0 03	17 56	9 12	13 42
19	1 19	22 03	0 44	13 37	0 03	17 55	9 12	13 43
21	1 18	22 03	0 43	13 35	0 03	17 54	9 12	13 43
23	1 18	22 03	0 43	13 34	0 02	17 54	9 12	13 44
25	1 18	22 03	0 43	13 32	0 02	17 53	9 12	13 44
27	1 18	22 03	0 43	13 30	0 02	17 52	9 12	13 45
29	1 17	22 03	0 43	13 29	0 02	17 50	9 12	13 45
31	1S17	22N02	0S43	13S27	0N02	17S49	9N12	13S45

Mutual Aspects

1 ☉⚹♆. ☿△♃. ♀∠♇. ♂Q♃.
3 ☉♯♄. ♀∥♂.
4 ☿∠♆. ♃Stat.
5 ☉Q♅. ☿⚹♅. ♂∠♇.
6 ☿☍♄. 9 ☉☌♇.
10 ☉△♃. ☿⚼♃. ☿⊥♆.
13 ♅∥♇.
14 ☿⚹♂. ☿⊻♆. ♀□♆.
15 ☿⚹♀. ☿∠♅. ♂□♆. ♂∥♅. ♂∥♇.
16 ☉∠♆. ☿±♃. ♀⚼♄. ♄△♅.
17 ☉∠♂. ☉☍♄. ☉⚹♅.
18 ♀⊥♇. ♂⚼♄. ♃△♇.
19 ♂⊥♇. 20 ☿∇♃.
21 ☉∠♀. ☿⊻♇.
22 ☿⊥♅. 23 ♀∥♅.
24 ☉⚼♃. ☉∥☿. ♀∥♇.
25 ☉⊥♆. ♀□♃. ♀⊻♇.
26 ☿⊥♇. ♀±♄.
27 ☿∇♄.
28 ☿⊻♅. ♂□♃. ☿♯♄.
29 ♂⊻♇. ♂♯♃.
30 ♂±♄. ♄⚼♆.
31 ☉⊻♆.

LAST QUARTER – Dec.27,00h.31m. (5° ♎ 04′)

JANUARY

D	☉	☽	☽Dec.	☿	♀	♂
	° ′ ″	° ′ ″	° ′	° ′	° ′	′
1	1 01 08	14 35 06	3 33	1 32	1 15	44
2	1 01 08	14 34 12	4 38	1 31	1 15	44
3	1 01 09	14 27 50	5 21	1 29	1 15	44
4	1 01 09	14 17 19	5 43	1 28	1 15	44
5	1 01 09	14 04 10	5 45	1 25	1 15	44
6	1 01 09	13 49 46	5 29	1 23	1 15	44
7	1 01 09	13 35 11	4 58	1 20	1 15	44
8	1 01 10	13 21 05	4 12	1 16	1 15	44
9	1 01 10	13 07 42	3 13	1 12	1 15	44
10	1 01 10	12 55 04	2 04	1 07	1 15	44
11	1 01 09	12 43 06	0 49	1 01	1 15	44
12	1 01 09	12 31 44	0 27	0 55	1 15	44
13	1 01 09	12 21 00	1 37	0 48	1 15	44
14	1 01 08	12 11 10	2 37	0 39	1 15	44
15	1 01 08	12 02 39	3 26	0 30	1 15	44
16	1 01 07	11 56 01	4 02	0 20	1 15	44
17	1 01 06	11 51 58	4 28	0 10	1 15	44
18	1 01 05	11 51 11	4 45	0 02	1 15	44
19	1 01 04	11 54 20	4 52	0 13	1 15	44
20	1 01 04	12 01 56	4 51	0 25	1 15	44
21	1 01 03	12 14 20	4 41	0 36	1 15	44
22	1 01 02	12 31 36	4 19	0 47	1 15	44
23	1 01 01	12 53 19	3 43	0 56	1 15	44
24	1 01 00	13 18 37	2 49	1 04	1 15	44
25	1 00 59	13 45 52	1 37	1 10	1 15	44
26	1 00 58	14 12 47	0 07	1 14	1 15	44
27	1 00 57	14 36 30	1 31	1 16	1 15	44
28	1 00 56	14 54 04	3 06	1 15	1 15	44
29	1 00 55	15 03 03	4 25	1 12	1 15	43
30	1 00 54	15 02 21	5 21	1 08	1 15	43
31	1 00 53	14 52 28	5 52	1 02	1 15	43

FEBRUARY

D	☉	☽	☽Dec.	☿	♀	♂
	° ′ ″	° ′ ″	° ′	° ′	° ′	′
1	1 00 52	14 35 23	5 58	0 55	1 15	43
2	1 00 51	14 13 52	5 43	0 47	1 15	43
3	1 00 51	13 50 43	5 11	0 39	1 15	43
4	1 00 50	13 28 15	4 25	0 30	1 15	43
5	1 00 49	13 07 59	3 26	0 22	1 15	43
6	1 00 48	12 50 38	2 18	0 13	1 15	43
7	1 00 47	12 36 20	1 05	0 06	1 15	43
8	1 00 46	12 24 48	0 09	0 02	1 15	43
9	1 00 45	12 15 34	1 20	0 09	1 15	43
10	1 00 44	12 08 07	2 22	0 16	1 15	43
11	1 00 42	12 02 02	3 14	0 22	1 15	43
12	1 00 41	11 57 09	3 55	0 27	1 15	43
13	1 00 39	11 53 30	4 24	0 32	1 15	43
14	1 00 38	11 51 25	4 43	0 37	1 15	43
15	1 00 36	11 51 25	4 52	0 41	1 15	43
16	1 00 34	11 54 12	4 52	0 45	1 15	43
17	1 00 33	12 00 29	4 42	0 49	1 15	43
18	1 00 31	12 10 57	4 23	0 53	1 15	43
19	1 00 29	12 26 08	3 51	0 56	1 15	43
20	1 00 27	12 46 14	3 05	0 59	1 15	43
21	1 00 26	13 10 55	2 03	1 01	1 15	43
22	1 00 24	13 39 11	0 44	1 04	1 15	43
23	1 00 22	14 09 04	0 48	1 06	1 15	43
24	1 00 20	14 37 40	2 25	1 08	1 15	43
25	1 00 18	15 01 21	3 54	1 10	1 15	43
26	1 00 16	15 16 30	5 06	1 12	1 15	43
27	1 00 14	15 20 33	5 53	1 14	1 15	43
28	1 00 13	15 12 52	6 13	1 16	1 15	43

MARCH

D	☉	☽	☽Dec.	☿	♀	♂
	° ′ ″	° ′ ″	° ′	° ′	° ′	′
1	1 00 11	14 54 59	6 07	1 17	1 15	43
2	1 00 09	14 30 05	5 38	1 19	1 15	42
3	1 00 08	14 01 51	4 50	1 21	1 15	42
4	1 00 07	13 33 37	3 49	1 22	1 15	42
5	1 00 05	13 07 47	2 38	1 23	1 15	42
6	1 00 03	12 45 47	1 22	1 25	1 15	42
7	1 00 02	12 28 08	0 06	1 26	1 15	42
8	1 00 00	12 14 45	1 06	1 27	1 15	42
9	0 59 58	12 05 11	2 10	1 29	1 15	42
10	0 59 57	11 58 46	3 04	1 30	1 15	42
11	0 59 55	11 54 48	3 47	1 31	1 15	42
12	0 59 53	11 52 40	4 20	1 32	1 15	42
13	0 59 51	11 51 59	4 42	1 34	1 15	42
14	0 59 49	11 52 33	4 53	1 35	1 15	42
15	0 59 47	11 54 31	4 55	1 36	1 14	42
16	0 59 45	11 58 16	4 48	1 37	1 14	42
17	0 59 43	12 04 22	4 29	1 38	1 14	42
18	0 59 41	12 13 30	4 00	1 40	1 14	42
19	0 59 38	12 26 21	3 17	1 41	1 14	42
20	0 59 36	12 43 25	2 20	1 42	1 14	42
21	0 59 34	13 04 49	1 08	1 43	1 14	42
22	0 59 32	13 30 06	0 15	1 45	1 14	42
23	0 59 29	13 57 59	1 46	1 46	1 14	42
24	0 59 27	14 26 12	3 15	1 47	1 14	42
25	0 59 25	14 51 34	4 34	1 49	1 14	42
26	0 59 22	15 10 25	5 35	1 50	1 14	42
27	0 59 20	15 19 31	6 11	1 51	1 14	42
28	0 59 18	15 17 05	6 22	1 53	1 14	42
29	0 59 16	15 03 28	6 05	1 54	1 14	41
30	0 59 14	14 40 59	5 25	1 55	1 14	41
31	0 59 13	14 13 07	4 25	1 57	1 14	41

APRIL

D	☉	☽	☽Dec.	☿	♀	♂
	° ′ ″	° ′ ″	° ′	° ′	° ′	′
1	0 59 11	13 43 29	3 11	1 58	1 14	41
2	0 59 09	13 15 04	1 50	1 59	1 14	41
3	0 59 07	12 49 56	0 28	2 00	1 14	41
4	0 59 06	12 29 12	0 49	2 01	1 14	41
5	0 59 04	12 13 17	1 57	2 03	1 14	41
6	0 59 02	12 02 03	2 54	2 03	1 14	41
7	0 59 00	11 55 01	3 40	2 04	1 14	41
8	0 58 58	11 51 35	4 15	2 05	1 14	41
9	0 58 56	11 51 02	4 39	2 05	1 14	41
10	0 58 54	11 52 43	4 54	2 06	1 14	41
11	0 58 52	11 56 06	4 59	2 06	1 14	41
12	0 58 51	12 00 53	4 55	2 06	1 14	41
13	0 58 49	12 06 58	4 39	2 05	1 14	41
14	0 58 47	12 14 31	4 11	2 04	1 14	41
15	0 58 44	12 23 53	3 30	2 03	1 13	41
16	0 58 42	12 35 33	2 35	2 02	1 13	41
17	0 58 40	12 49 56	1 27	2 00	1 13	41
18	0 58 38	13 07 18	0 07	1 58	1 13	41
19	0 58 36	13 27 30	1 19	1 55	1 13	41
20	0 58 34	13 49 50	2 44	1 52	1 13	41
21	0 58 31	14 12 49	4 02	1 49	1 13	41
22	0 58 29	14 34 14	5 06	1 46	1 13	41
23	0 58 27	14 51 21	5 52	1 42	1 13	41
24	0 58 25	15 01 28	6 16	1 39	1 13	41
25	0 58 23	15 02 38	6 15	1 35	1 13	41
26	0 58 21	14 54 18	5 50	1 31	1 13	40
27	0 58 19	14 37 29	5 00	1 26	1 13	40
28	0 58 18	14 14 28	3 51	1 22	1 13	40
29	0 58 16	13 48 07	2 28	1 18	1 13	40
30	0 58 14	13 21 14	1 01	1 13	1 13	40

MAY

D	☉ ° ′ ″	☽ ° ′ ″	☽Dec. ° ′	☿ ° ′	♀ ° ′	♂ ′
1	0 58 13	12 56 05	0 24	1 08	1 13	40
2	0 58 11	12 34 16	1 39	1 04	1 13	40
3	0 58 10	12 16 44	2 41	0 59	1 13	40
4	0 58 09	12 03 52	3 31	0 54	1 13	40
5	0 58 07	11 55 40	4 08	0 49	1 13	40
6	0 58 06	11 51 50	4 35	0 44	1 13	40
7	0 58 04	11 51 52	4 53	0 39	1 13	40
8	0 58 03	11 55 12	5 01	0 34	1 13	40
9	0 58 01	12 01 10	5 00	0 29	1 12	40
10	0 58 00	12 09 11	4 48	0 24	1 12	40
11	0 57 58	12 18 42	4 24	0 19	1 12	40
12	0 57 57	12 29 22	3 47	0 14	1 12	40
13	0 57 55	12 40 56	2 54	0 09	1 12	40
14	0 57 54	12 53 21	1 46	0 04	1 12	40
15	0 57 52	13 06 38	0 27	0 01	1 12	40
16	0 57 50	13 20 49	0 58	0 06	1 12	40
17	0 57 49	13 35 46	2 23	0 10	1 12	40
18	0 57 47	13 51 08	3 40	0 15	1 12	40
19	0 57 45	14 06 09	4 44	0 19	1 12	40
20	0 57 44	14 19 41	5 31	0 22	1 12	40
21	0 57 42	14 30 17	6 00	0 25	1 12	40
22	0 57 40	14 36 27	6 09	0 28	1 12	40
23	0 57 39	14 36 57	5 56	0 30	1 12	40
24	0 57 38	14 31 09	5 20	0 32	1 12	40
25	0 57 36	14 19 15	4 22	0 33	1 12	40
26	0 57 35	14 02 14	3 06	0 34	1 12	40
27	0 57 34	13 41 41	1 39	0 34	1 12	40
28	0 57 33	13 19 29	0 10	0 33	1 11	40
29	0 57 32	12 57 27	1 13	0 32	1 11	39
30	0 57 31	12 37 13	2 23	0 30	1 11	39
31	0 57 30	12 19 59	3 19	0 28	1 11	39

JUNE

D	☉ ° ′ ″	☽ ° ′ ″	☽Dec. ° ′	☿ ° ′	♀ ° ′	♂ ′
1	0 57 29	12 06 38	4 01	0 26	1 11	39
2	0 57 29	11 57 38	4 30	0 22	1 11	39
3	0 57 28	11 53 13	4 49	0 19	1 11	39
4	0 57 27	11 53 17	5 00	0 15	1 11	39
5	0 57 27	11 57 34	5 01	0 11	1 11	39
6	0 57 26	12 05 37	4 53	0 07	1 11	39
7	0 57 25	12 16 46	4 34	0 03	1 11	39
8	0 57 25	12 30 18	4 02	0 02	1 11	39
9	0 57 24	12 45 19	3 14	0 06	1 11	39
10	0 57 23	13 00 59	2 10	0 11	1 11	39
11	0 57 22	13 16 25	0 51	0 15	1 11	39
12	0 57 22	13 30 53	0 36	0 20	1 10	39
13	0 57 21	13 43 48	2 05	0 24	1 10	39
14	0 57 20	13 54 45	3 25	0 29	1 10	39
15	0 57 19	14 03 31	4 31	0 33	1 10	39
16	0 57 18	14 09 57	5 20	0 37	1 10	39
17	0 57 17	14 13 58	5 49	0 41	1 10	39
18	0 57 16	14 15 28	6 00	0 46	1 10	39
19	0 57 15	14 14 17	5 52	0 50	1 10	39
20	0 57 15	14 10 15	5 25	0 54	1 10	39
21	0 57 14	14 03 12	4 37	0 58	1 10	39
22	0 57 14	13 53 08	3 31	1 01	1 10	39
23	0 57 13	13 40 15	2 11	1 05	1 10	39
24	0 57 13	13 25 04	0 43	1 09	1 09	39
25	0 57 13	13 08 19	0 43	1 13	1 09	39
26	0 57 12	12 51 03	2 00	1 16	1 09	39
27	0 57 12	12 34 20	3 03	1 20	1 09	39
28	0 57 12	12 19 18	3 50	1 24	1 09	39
29	0 57 12	12 06 58	4 24	1 27	1 09	39
30	0 57 12	11 58 09	4 46	1 31	1 09	39

JULY

D	☉ ° ′ ″	☽ ° ′ ″	☽Dec. ° ′	☿ ° ′	♀ ° ′	♂ ′
1	0 57 12	11 53 30	4 58	1 34	1 09	39
2	0 57 13	11 53 25	5 01	1 38	1 09	39
3	0 57 13	11 58 04	4 55	1 41	1 09	39
4	0 57 13	12 07 23	4 40	1 44	1 08	39
5	0 57 13	12 20 57	4 13	1 47	1 08	39
6	0 57 14	12 38 07	3 32	1 50	1 08	39
7	0 57 14	12 57 48	2 34	1 53	1 08	39
8	0 57 14	13 18 40	1 20	1 56	1 08	39
9	0 57 14	13 39 02	0 08	1 58	1 08	39
10	0 57 15	13 57 10	1 40	2 01	1 08	39
11	0 57 15	14 11 29	3 08	2 03	1 08	39
12	0 57 15	14 20 53	4 21	2 04	1 07	39
13	0 57 15	14 24 56	5 16	2 06	1 07	39
14	0 57 15	14 23 57	5 49	2 07	1 07	39
15	0 57 15	14 18 49	6 01	2 08	1 07	39
16	0 57 15	14 10 45	5 54	2 08	1 07	39
17	0 57 15	14 00 54	5 28	2 09	1 07	39
18	0 57 15	13 50 08	4 45	2 09	1 07	38
19	0 57 15	13 38 58	3 45	2 08	1 06	38
20	0 57 16	13 27 33	2 31	2 08	1 06	38
21	0 57 16	13 15 52	1 08	2 07	1 06	38
22	0 57 16	13 03 45	0 17	2 06	1 06	38
23	0 57 17	12 51 12	1 36	2 05	1 06	38
24	0 57 17	12 38 24	2 44	2 04	1 06	38
25	0 57 18	12 25 47	3 38	2 02	1 05	38
26	0 57 19	12 14 00	4 16	2 01	1 05	38
27	0 57 20	12 03 52	4 42	1 59	1 05	38
28	0 57 21	11 56 16	4 56	1 58	1 05	38
29	0 57 22	11 52 01	5 01	1 56	1 05	38
30	0 57 23	11 51 53	4 57	1 55	1 04	38
31	0 57 24	11 56 26	4 44	1 53	1 04	38

AUGUST

D	☉ ° ′ ″	☽ ° ′ ″	☽Dec. ° ′	☿ ° ′	♀ ° ′	♂ ′
1	0 57 25	12 06 01	4 20	1 51	1 04	38
2	0 57 26	12 20 39	3 45	1 50	1 04	38
3	0 57 27	12 40 01	2 54	1 48	1 03	38
4	0 57 29	13 03 14	1 48	1 47	1 03	38
5	0 57 30	13 28 48	0 26	1 45	1 03	38
6	0 57 31	13 54 38	1 06	1 43	1 03	38
7	0 57 32	14 18 05	2 40	1 42	1 02	38
8	0 57 33	14 36 27	4 04	1 40	1 02	38
9	0 57 34	14 47 31	5 10	1 39	1 02	38
10	0 57 35	14 50 11	5 53	1 37	1 02	38
11	0 57 36	14 44 45	6 11	1 35	1 01	38
12	0 57 37	14 32 47	6 07	1 34	1 01	38
13	0 57 38	14 16 36	5 42	1 32	1 01	38
14	0 57 39	13 58 32	4 58	1 31	1 00	38
15	0 57 40	13 40 29	3 59	1 29	1 00	38
16	0 57 41	13 23 42	2 46	1 28	1 00	38
17	0 57 42	13 08 43	1 25	1 26	0 59	38
18	0 57 43	12 55 34	0 02	1 24	0 59	38
19	0 57 44	12 43 56	1 17	1 23	0 59	38
20	0 57 45	12 33 24	2 27	1 21	0 58	38
21	0 57 46	12 23 38	3 25	1 19	0 58	38
22	0 57 48	12 14 28	4 08	1 18	0 57	38
23	0 57 49	12 06 03	4 38	1 16	0 57	38
24	0 57 51	11 58 43	4 55	1 14	0 57	38
25	0 57 52	11 53 08	5 02	1 12	0 56	38
26	0 57 54	11 50 02	5 00	1 10	0 56	38
27	0 57 56	11 50 14	4 48	1 08	0 55	38
28	0 57 58	11 54 31	4 27	1 06	0 55	38
29	0 57 59	12 03 32	3 54	1 03	0 54	38
30	0 58 01	12 17 44	3 09	1 01	0 54	38
31	0 58 03	12 37 10	2 10	0 58	0 53	38

SEPTEMBER

D	☉	☽	☽Dec.	☿	♀	♂
	° ′ ″	° ′ ″	° ′	° ′	° ′	′
1	0 58 05	13 01 24	0 56	0 56	0 52	38
2	0 58 07	13 29 15	0 30	0 53	0 52	38
3	0 58 09	13 58 43	2 03	0 50	0 51	38
4	0 58 11	14 26 53	3 32	0 47	0 50	38
5	0 58 13	14 50 19	4 50	0 43	0 50	38
6	0 58 14	15 05 45	5 47	0 39	0 49	38
7	0 58 16	15 10 57	6 20	0 35	0 48	38
8	0 58 18	15 05 32	6 26	0 31	0 48	38
9	0 58 19	14 50 59	6 07	0 27	0 47	38
10	0 58 21	14 30 07	5 25	0 22	0 46	38
11	0 58 23	14 06 09	4 24	0 16	0 45	38
12	0 58 24	13 41 55	3 09	0 11	0 44	38
13	0 58 26	13 19 25	1 45	0 05	0 43	38
14	0 58 27	12 59 47	0 20	0 01	0 42	38
15	0 58 29	12 43 23	1 02	0 08	0 41	38
16	0 58 30	12 30 05	2 14	0 14	0 40	38
17	0 58 32	12 19 25	3 13	0 21	0 39	38
18	0 58 34	12 10 52	3 59	0 28	0 38	38
19	0 58 36	12 03 56	4 32	0 35	0 37	38
20	0 58 37	11 58 19	4 53	0 42	0 36	38
21	0 58 39	11 53 55	5 04	0 48	0 34	38
22	0 58 41	11 50 56	5 04	0 54	0 33	38
23	0 58 44	11 49 47	4 54	0 59	0 32	38
24	0 58 46	11 51 04	4 35	1 03	0 30	38
25	0 58 48	11 55 31	4 04	1 06	0 29	38
26	0 58 50	12 03 48	3 22	1 07	0 27	38
27	0 58 52	12 16 34	2 27	1 06	0 26	38
28	0 58 55	12 34 10	1 19	1 04	0 24	38
29	0 58 57	12 56 34	0 00	1 00	0 22	38
30	0 58 59	13 23 07	1 27	0 54	0 20	38

OCTOBER

D	☉	☽	☽Dec.	☿	♀	♂
	° ′ ″	° ′ ″	° ′	° ′	° ′	′
1	0 59 02	13 52 20	2 55	0 47	0 19	38
2	0 59 04	14 21 46	4 16	0 39	0 17	38
3	0 59 06	14 48 09	5 23	0 29	0 15	38
4	0 59 08	15 07 52	6 11	0 19	0 13	38
5	0 59 10	15 17 53	6 33	0 09	0 11	38
6	0 59 12	15 16 41	6 29	0 02	0 09	38
7	0 59 14	15 04 45	5 57	0 13	0 06	38
8	0 59 16	14 44 22	5 01	0 23	0 04	38
9	0 59 18	14 18 47	3 45	0 33	0 02	38
10	0 59 20	13 51 21	2 17	0 42	0 01	38
11	0 59 22	13 24 44	0 45	0 50	0 03	38
12	0 59 23	13 00 47	0 43	0 58	0 05	38
13	0 59 25	12 40 30	1 59	1 05	0 08	38
14	0 59 27	12 24 11	3 02	1 11	0 10	38
15	0 59 29	12 11 44	3 51	1 16	0 13	38
16	0 59 30	12 02 44	4 26	1 21	0 15	38
17	0 59 32	11 56 38	4 50	1 25	0 17	38
18	0 59 34	11 52 57	5 04	1 28	0 20	38
19	0 59 36	11 51 14	5 07	1 31	0 22	38
20	0 59 38	11 51 16	5 01	1 33	0 24	38
21	0 59 40	11 52 57	4 44	1 35	0 26	38
22	0 59 42	11 56 30	4 16	1 37	0 28	38
23	0 59 44	12 02 13	3 35	1 38	0 30	38
24	0 59 46	12 10 34	2 43	1 39	0 31	38
25	0 59 48	12 22 03	1 37	1 39	0 33	38
26	0 59 51	12 37 03	0 22	1 40	0 34	38
27	0 59 53	12 55 45	1 01	1 40	0 35	38
28	0 59 55	13 17 55	2 24	1 40	0 36	38
29	0 59 57	13 42 41	3 43	1 40	0 36	38
30	0 59 59	14 08 29	4 51	1 40	0 36	38
31	1 00 02	14 32 56	5 45	1 40	0 37	38

NOVEMBER

D	☉	☽	☽Dec.	☿	♀	♂
	° ′ ″	° ′ ″	° ′	° ′	° ′	′
1	1 00 04	14 53 12	6 20	1 40	0 36	38
2	1 00 06	15 06 23	6 32	1 39	0 36	38
3	1 00 08	15 10 21	6 17	1 39	0 35	38
4	1 00 10	15 04 22	5 36	1 39	0 34	38
5	1 00 11	14 49 19	4 29	1 39	0 33	38
6	1 00 13	14 27 21	3 01	1 38	0 32	38
7	1 00 15	14 01 19	1 24	1 38	0 30	38
8	1 00 16	13 34 06	0 12	1 38	0 28	38
9	1 00 18	13 08 01	1 38	1 37	0 27	38
10	1 00 19	12 44 48	2 49	1 37	0 25	38
11	1 00 20	12 25 28	3 42	1 36	0 22	38
12	1 00 22	12 10 27	4 21	1 36	0 20	38
13	1 00 23	11 59 48	4 47	1 36	0 18	38
14	1 00 25	11 53 17	5 02	1 36	0 16	38
15	1 00 26	11 50 28	5 08	1 35	0 13	38
16	1 00 27	11 50 51	5 05	1 35	0 11	38
17	1 00 29	11 53 54	4 51	1 35	0 08	38
18	1 00 30	11 59 11	4 27	1 34	0 06	38
19	1 00 32	12 06 17	3 50	1 34	0 03	38
20	1 00 34	12 14 59	3 00	1 34	0 01	38
21	1 00 35	12 25 11	1 56	1 34	0 02	38
22	1 00 37	12 36 52	0 41	1 34	0 04	38
23	1 00 38	12 50 09	0 41	1 34	0 06	39
24	1 00 40	13 05 04	2 03	1 33	0 09	39
25	1 00 42	13 21 33	3 20	1 33	0 11	39
26	1 00 43	13 39 15	4 27	1 33	0 13	39
27	1 00 45	13 57 29	5 20	1 33	0 15	39
28	1 00 46	14 15 04	5 58	1 33	0 17	39
29	1 00 48	14 30 27	6 17	1 33	0 19	39
30	1 00 49	14 41 49	6 15	1 33	0 21	39

DECEMBER

D	☉	☽	☽Dec.	☿	♀	♂
	° ′ ″	° ′ ″	° ′	° ′	° ′	′
1	1 00 51	14 47 30	5 50	1 33	0 23	39
2	1 00 52	14 46 16	4 59	1 33	0 25	39
3	1 00 53	14 37 45	3 44	1 32	0 27	39
4	1 00 54	14 22 35	2 11	1 32	0 29	39
5	1 00 55	14 02 12	0 30	1 32	0 30	39
6	1 00 56	13 38 41	1 06	1 32	0 32	39
7	1 00 57	13 14 13	2 27	1 32	0 33	39
8	1 00 58	12 50 47	3 30	1 32	0 35	39
9	1 00 58	12 30 01	4 15	1 31	0 36	39
10	1 00 59	12 13 02	4 44	1 31	0 37	39
11	1 01 00	12 00 33	5 01	1 30	0 39	39
12	1 01 00	11 52 49	5 08	1 30	0 40	39
13	1 01 01	11 49 51	5 07	1 29	0 41	39
14	1 01 01	11 51 20	4 56	1 29	0 42	39
15	1 01 02	11 56 51	4 36	1 28	0 43	39
16	1 01 02	12 05 43	4 03	1 27	0 44	39
17	1 01 03	12 17 14	3 18	1 25	0 45	39
18	1 01 03	12 30 33	2 17	1 24	0 46	39
19	1 01 04	12 44 49	1 03	1 22	0 47	39
20	1 01 05	12 59 16	0 20	1 20	0 48	39
21	1 01 05	13 13 14	1 45	1 18	0 49	39
22	1 01 06	13 26 16	3 05	1 15	0 50	39
23	1 01 06	13 38 04	4 14	1 11	0 51	39
24	1 01 07	13 48 35	5 08	1 07	0 52	39
25	1 01 08	13 57 50	5 45	1 03	0 52	39
26	1 01 08	14 05 47	6 05	0 58	0 53	39
27	1 01 09	14 12 16	6 07	0 52	0 54	39
28	1 01 09	14 16 52	5 48	0 45	0 54	39
29	1 01 10	14 18 55	5 09	0 37	0 55	39
30	1 01 10	14 17 40	4 07	0 28	0 56	39
31	1 01 11	14 12 24	2 45	0 19	0 56	39

Day	Time	Aspect	
JANUARY			
1 Tu	0 48	☉∥☿	
	1 20	☽⚼♂	b
	1 56	☿#♃	
	5 05	☉#♃	
	5 34	♀⊻♆	
	5 53	♀∠♅	
	5 53	☉☍♃	
	10 29	☽☍♆	B
	13 29	☽✱♄	G
	15 37	☽⊻♃	g
	22 58	☽∥♄	B
2 We	0 40	☽△♇	G
	10 07	☽#♆	D
	11 16	☽☍♅	B
	13 57	☽⚼♀	b
	15 17	♀⊽♄	
	16 04	☽∠♃	b
	18 58	☽⚼☉	b
	23 34	☽♍	
3 Th	5 37	☽#♅	B
	12 22	♀☍♃	
	13 36	☽#♇	D
	14 41	☽□♄	B
	16 34	☽✱♃	G
	17 01	☽△♀	G
	21 36	☽△☉	G
	21 38	☿♒	
4 Fr	0 40	☽⚼☿	b
	2 15	☽□♇	B
	7 30	☽☍♂	B
	12 57	☽⚼♆	b
	16 33	☿∠♇	
5 Sa	1 23	☽♎	
	2 24	☽#♂	B
	4 35	☽△☿	G
	13 48	☉±♄	
	14 14	☽△♆	G
	14 21	☽⚼♅	b
	16 39	☽△♄	G
	18 20	☽□♃	B
6 Su	0 11	☽□♀	B
	3 55	☽□☉	B
	4 54	☽✱♇	G
	14 44	☽∥♂	B
	16 05	☽△♅	G
	17 52	☉⊻♇	
	18 14	☽⚼♄	b
7 Mo	4 38	♀±♄	
	4 41	☽♏	
	6 07	☉⊥♅	
	6 52	☽∠♇	b
	13 52	☽□☿	B
	16 32	☽⚼♂	b
	18 08	☽□♆	B
	21 45	☽△♃	G
8 Tu	6 06	♀⊻♇	
	6 36	☿#♄	
	7 08	♀#♃	
	7 19	☽∥♇	D
	9 22	☽⊻♇	g
	9 41	☽✱♀	G
	12 29	☽✱☉	G
	15 22	☽∥♅	B
	16 24	♀⊥♅	
	20 41	☽△♂	G
	21 03	☽□♅	B
	23 51	♂∠♆	
9 We	0 12	☽⚼♃	b
	3 56	♂⊻♅	
	9 57	☽♐	
	11 56	☿☌♆	
	12 41	☽∥♆	D
	15 28	☽∠♀	b
	17 45	☽∠☉	b
	19 44	☽∥☿	G
10 Th	0 05	☽✱♆	G
	1 05	☽#♄	B
	1 17	☽✱☿	G
	1 59	☽☍♄	B
	5 24	☿∠♂	
	8 37	☿△♄	
	15 54	☽☌♇	D
	17 18	☽∥☉	G
	20 19	☿⊽♃	
	21 57	☽⊻♀	g
	23 40	☽⊻☉	g
11 Fr	2 21	☽∥♀	G
	3 51	☽∠♆	b
	4 07	☽✱♅	G
	6 49	☽□♂	B
	7 42	☽∠☿	b
	7 49	☽#♃	G
	17 18	☽♑	
12 Sa	0 49	☿∥♆	
	8 07	☽⊻♆	g
	8 26	☽∠♅	b
	10 34	☽☍♃	B
	14 29	☽⊻☿	g
	19 57	☉⊥♇	
13 Su	0 31	☽⊻♇	g
	3 40	♀⊥♇	
	10 47	☉⊻♅	
	13 00	☽☌♀	G
	13 16	☽⊻♅	g
	13 29	☽☌☉	D
	14 20	☽⚼♄	b
	15 41	♀⊻♅	
	19 24	☽✱♂	G
	23 11	☽#♃	G
	23 30	☉⚼♄	
14 Mo	1 43	♀⚼♄	
	2 41	☽♒	
	5 35	☽∠♇	b
	6 58	♂Q♄	
	11 32	☉☌♀	
	12 18	☽∥♀	G
	18 13	☽☌♆	D
	19 27	☽△♄	G
	21 51	☽∥☉	G
15 Tu	2 35	☽∠♂	b
	4 43	☽☌☿	G
	8 28	☽#♄	B
	11 09	☽✱♇	G
	22 18	☽∥♆	D
16 We	0 25	☽☌♅	B
	1 22	☽⚼♃	b
	5 50	☽⊻☉	g
	6 46	☽⊻♀	g
	10 19	☽⊻♂	g
	11 25	☽∥☿	G
	14 00	☽♓	
	22 30	☽∥♅	B
17 Th	6 09	☽⊻♆	g
	6 42	☽∥♇	D
	7 02	☽□♄	B
	7 09	☽△♃	G
	14 47	☽∠☉	b
	16 29	☽∠♀	b
	18 57	☽⊻☿	g
	23 27	☽□♇	B
18 Fr	0 15	♂⊥♅	
	0 33	♃⊻♄	
	2 48	☿±♃	
	4 29	☿∠♂	
	12 34	☽∠♆	b
	13 06	☽⊻♅	g
	18 25	♃⚼♅	
	20 50	☿Stat	
	22 53	♂♈	
19 Sa	0 00	☽✱☉	G
	1 32	☽∠☿	b
	2 27	☽✱♀	G
	2 35	☽♈	
	2 49	☽☌♂	B
	3 42	♀♒	
	10 20	♀✱♂	
	19 01	☽✱♆	G
	19 14	☽□♃	B
	19 31	☽✱♄	G
	19 35	☽∠♅	b
20 Su	2 08	☽#♂	B
	2 16	☽∥♂	B
	6 02	☉♒	
	7 26	☽✱☿	G
	10 57	♃⊽♆	
	11 49	♀∠♇	
	12 15	☽△♇	G
	20 08	☿±♃	
21 Mo	0 11	☉#♄	
	1 33	☽∠♄	b
	1 50	☽✱♅	G
	14 47	☽♉	
	17 46	☽□☉	B
	18 11	☽⚼♇	b
	18 51	☽⊻♂	g
	21 35	☽□♀	B
	22 44	☉∠♇	
22 Tu	6 23	☽✱♃	G
	6 56	☽□♆	B
	7 04	☽⊻♄	g
	16 22	☽□☿	B
	20 03	☽#♇	D
23 We	1 49	☽∠♂	b
	3 09	☽#♅	B
	5 08	☽#☿	G
	8 16	♄△♆	
	10 58	☽∠♃	b
	12 25	☉✱♂	
	12 29	☽□♅	B
	13 45	♀#♄	
24 Th	0 28	☽♊	
	1 54	☽#♆	D
	7 42	☽✱♂	G
	8 10	☽△☉	G
	9 25	☽#☉	G
	12 57	☽△♀	G
	12 59	☽#♀	G
	14 38	☽⊻♃	g
	15 04	☽∥♄	B
	15 37	☽●♄	B
	15 47	☽△♆	G
	20 52	☽△☿	G
25 Fr	5 15	♀⊽♃	
	7 08	☽☍♇	B
	13 30	☽⚼☉	b
	16 17	♀△♄	
	18 39	☽⚼♀	b
	18 42	☽⚼♆	b
	19 17	♀☌♆	
	19 23	☽△♅	G
	21 32	☽⚼☿	b
	22 48	☽∥♃	G
26 Sa	6 17	☽♋	
	12 17	☿☌♀	
	15 55	☽□♂	B
	19 03	☽●♃	G
	20 16	☽⊻♄	g
	21 20	☽⚼♅	b
27 Su	4 38	☿☌♆	
	9 26	☿△♄	
	12 17	☉⊽♃	
	18 55	☉☌☿	
	21 18	☽∠♄	b
28 Mo	1 18	☿⊽♃	
	3 56	☽∥♃	G
	6 12	☉△♄	
	8 31	☽♌	
	9 52	☿✱♂	
	11 37	☽⚼♇	b
	13 45	☉☌♆	
	18 54	☽☍☿	B
	20 10	☽△♂	G
	20 16	☽⊻♃	g
	21 41	☽✱♄	G
	21 58	♂□♃	
	22 15	☽☍♆	B
	22 47	☉∥♆	
	22 50	☽☍☉	B
29 Tu	4 55	☽☍♀	B
	8 58	☽∥♄	B
	11 50	☽△♇	G
	15 20	♀±♃	
	18 15	♀∥♆	
	20 10	☽∠♃	b
	20 45	☽#♆	D
	20 58	☽#♀	G
	21 26	☽⚼♂	b
	22 10	☽#☉	G
	23 04	☽☍♅	B
30 We	2 35	♂✱♄	
	8 40	☽♍	
	9 19	☽#☿	G
	16 25	☽#♅	B
	17 00	♂✱♆	
	19 55	☽✱♃	G
	21 33	☽□♄	B
	21 41	☽#♇	D
31 Th	9 58	♂∠♅	
	11 46	☽□♇	B
	13 34	☽⚼☿	b
	22 22	☽⚼♆	b
FEBRUARY			
1 Fr	4 03	☽⚼☉	b
	8 44	☽♎	
	11 34	☽⚼♀	b
	12 13	☽△☿	G
	12 27	☽∥♂	B
	13 07	☉∥♀	
	15 11	☿∠♇	
	16 53	♀✱♇	
	19 57	☽□♃	B
	21 54	☽△♄	G
	22 03	☉±♃	
	22 49	☽△♆	G
	23 40	☽⚼♅	b
2 Sa	1 29	☽☍♂	B
	6 24	☽△☉	G
	12 44	☽✱♇	G
	14 36	☽△♀	G
	20 36	☽#♂	B
	20 40	☿∥♀	
	22 49	☽⚼♄	b
3 Su	0 45	☽△♅	G
	1 17	☉∥☿	
	10 35	☽♏	
	11 23	☽□☿	B
	14 07	☽∠♇	b
	22 06	☽△♃	G
4 Mo	1 34	☽□♆	B
	4 19	☿♑	
	8 21	☿Q♂	
	12 10	☽∥♇	D
	13 33	☽□☉	B
	16 16	☽⊻♇	g
	17 29	☽∥♅	B
	23 25	☽□♀	B
5 Tu	0 17	☽⚼♃	b
	2 13	☽∥♀	G
	3 47	☽∥☉	G
	5 08	☽□♅	B
	8 17	♀⚼♃	
	10 57	☽∥☿	G
	11 12	☽⚼♂	b
	14 02	☽✱☿	G
	15 21	☽♐	
	15 31	☽∥♆	D
6 We	2 43	☉✱♇	
	5 26	☽#♄	B
	6 01	☽☍♄	B
	7 25	☽✱♆	G
	16 16	☽△♂	G
	16 51	☽∠☿	b
	22 54	☽☌♇	D
7 Th	0 35	☽✱☉	G
	11 28	☽∠♆	b
	12 21	☽✱♀	G
	12 38	☽✱♅	G
	15 23	♀☌♅	
	15 25	☽#♃	G
	20 38	☽⊻☿	g
	23 08	☽♑	
8 Fr	1 33	♄Stat	
	7 27	☽∠☉	b
	11 18	☽☍♃	B
	16 08	☽⊻♆	g
	17 23	☽∠♅	b
	17 29	☿Stat	
	18 33	☿∥♆	
	20 10	☽∠♀	b
9 Sa	4 43	☽□♂	B
	8 01	♀∥♅	
	8 13	☽⊻♇	g
	15 00	☽⊻☉	g
	19 35	☽⚼♄	b
	22 39	☽⊻♅	g
10 Su	2 42	☽#♃	G
	4 20	☉⚼♃	
	4 40	☽⊻♀	g
	6 50	☽☌☿	G
	9 15	☽♒	
	13 37	☽∠♇	b
11	1 06	☽△♄	G

Mo	2 57	☽☌♆	D		11 09	♀⊻♆		28	3 17	☽☍♀	B	Fr	1 59	☽∠♅	b		4 27	♀✱♆	
	6 12	☿⊻♀			15 03	☽∠♃	b	Th	5 13	☽⧺☉	G		8 27	☉□♇			11 57	♀⊻♂	
	10 46	♀Q♇			19 22	☽⊻♂	g		8 57	☉⊻♆			12 38	♂⧺♅			12 07	☽∠☿	b
	14 37	♀∥♇			23 34	☽□♅	B		10 17	☽⚼♆	b		14 34	☽⊻♇	g		16 30	☽∠♄	b
	14 46	☽⧺♄	B	20	0 41	♂∠♄			17 30	☽⧺♀	G		15 06	☽✱☉	G		20 06	☽⊻☉	g
	15 06	☉∥♅		We	2 07	♀⧺♂			17 43	☽⚼☿	b	9	2 45	☽⚼♄	b		21 07	☽✱♅	G
	18 32	♂△♇			7 08	☽⧺♆	D		18 47	☽♎		Sa	7 02	☽⊻☿	g	17	4 01	☽♉	
	19 23	☽✱♇	G		8 50	☽♊			MARCH				7 21	☽⊻♅	g	Su	8 56	☉⊻♅	
	19 26	☽✱♂	G		12 02	☽□☉	B						9 39	☽⧺♃	G		9 16	☽⚼♇	b
12	1 18	♀♓			13 03	☽⧺☿	G	1	3 38	☽□♃	B		9 52	☿☌♅			9 28	♀∠♅	
Tu	2 47	☽∥☿	G		19 06	☽△☿	G	Fr	8 07	☽△♄	G		14 56	☽♒			16 05	☽✱♃	G
	3 07	☽⚼♃	b		19 46	☽⊻♃	g		9 59	☽△♆	G		17 46	♂✱♃			16 44	☽⧺☿	G
	6 40	☽∥♆	D		20 18	♂Q♃			11 44	☽⚼♅	b		19 12	☽✱♀	G		21 29	☿□♄	
	7 41	☽☌☉	D		23 03	☽∥♄	B		15 05	♂♉			19 52	♀⊥♅			22 40	☽⊻♄	g
	10 21	☽☌♅	B	21	0 22	☽●♄	B		15 14	♃Stat			20 05	☽∠♇	b		22 51	☽✱☿	G
	20 02	☽⊻☿	g	Th	1 43	☽∠♂	b		19 39	☽△☿	G		23 16	☽∠☉	b	18	0 15	☽□♆	B
	20 53	☽♓			2 31	☽△♆	G		22 36	☽✱♇	G	10	2 50	☽□♂	B	Mo	3 12	☽☌♂	B
	23 10	☽☌♀	G		3 34	☿▽♃		2	4 37	☽∥♀	G	Su	8 34	☽△♄	G		3 21	♂±♇	
13	3 22	☽∠♂	b		6 39	☽□♀	B	Sa	8 14	☽⚼♄	b		10 38	☽☌♆	D		3 26	☉Q♄	
We	7 56	☽∥♅	B		17 32	☽☍♇	B		11 57	☽△♅	G		15 50	☿⧺♂			4 46	☽∠☉	b
	9 03	☽△♃	G	22	1 15	☽⚼☿	b		13 36	☽⚼☉	b		19 22	☽⧺♄	B		5 09	☽⊻♀	g
	11 18	☽∥☉	G	Fr	6 11	☽⚼♆	b		16 25	☽∥☉	G	11	2 01	☽✱♇	G		6 49	☽⧺♇	D
	13 05	☽□♄	B		6 55	☽✱♂	G		18 51	☽♏		Mo	4 35	☽∠♀	b		8 54	☽⧺♅	B
	13 07	☽∥♇	D		7 53	☽△♅	G		20 16	☽☍♂	B		7 57	☽⊻☉	g		9 20	☿⊻♆	
	15 06	☽⊻♆	g		7 56	☽∥♃	G		23 02	☽∠♇	b		8 23	☽⚼♃	b		21 57	☽∠♃	b
	17 06	☉☌♅			16 16	☽♋		3	4 10	☽△♃	G		14 43	☽∥♆	D	19	0 08	☽∥♂	B
	17 20	☿♒			16 31	☿⊥♀		Su	5 39	☿✱♇			17 19	☿Q♇		Tu	8 53	☽□♅	B
	18 28	☽∥♀	G		23 39	☽△☉	G		10 09	☽⚼♀	b		19 28	☽☌♅	B		10 26	☽⧺♆	D
14	3 32	☽∠☿	b	23	1 03	☉⧺♂			10 57	☽□♆	B		21 47	☿∥♅			12 53	☽✱☉	G
Th	7 43	☽□♇	B	Sa	2 19	☽●♃	G		14 42	☽⧺♂	B		23 34	☿♓			13 58	☽∠♀	b
	9 56	☉∥♇			2 28	♂✱♅			16 23	☽△☉	G	12	2 56	☽♓			15 20	☽♊	
	11 33	☽⊻♂	g		6 47	☽⊻♄	g		18 09	☽∥♇	D	Tu	3 26	☽☌☿	G	20	2 12	☿✱♂	
	18 03	☽⧺♂	B		10 28	☽⚼♅	b		19 40	♀∠♆			11 04	☽⧺♂	B	We	3 17	☽⊻♃	g
	21 30	☽∠♆	b		13 52	☿△♄			20 58	☽∥♅	B		14 18	☽⊻♀	g		6 08	☽∥♄	B
	23 05	☽⊻♅	g		17 47	☽△♀	G	4	0 16	☽⊻♇	g		14 41	☽△♃	G		9 40	☽●♄	B
15	1 43	☽⊻☉	g	24	3 30	☽⚼☉	b	Mo	2 13	☽□☿	B		17 04	☽∥♅	B		11 00	☽△♆	G
Fr	9 26	☽♈		Su	8 26	☽∠♄	b		5 34	☽⚼♃	b		18 05	♀□♃			14 58	♇Stat	
	11 31	☽✱☿	G		9 43	♀⊥♆			11 34	☽∥☿	G		18 50	☽✱♂	G		17 08	☽⊻♂	g
	18 54	☽⊻♀	g		11 16	☉△♃			14 19	☽△♀	G		19 31	☽∥☿	G		18 29	☽□☿	B
	21 27	☽□♃	B		13 39	☽□♂	B		14 43	☽□♅	B		19 40	☽∥♇	D		19 16	☉♈	
16	1 49	☽✱♄	G		14 28	☽∥♃	G		18 52	♀⊻♅			20 50	☿∥♇			21 56	☽✱♀	G
Sa	3 58	☽✱♆	G		15 59	☿☌♆			19 04	☽∥♆	D		21 09	☽□♄	B	21	1 05	☽☍♇	B
	5 36	☽∠♅	b		19 36	☽♌			21 55	☽♐			23 07	☽⊻♆	g	Th	11 56	☽∥♃	G
	10 55	☽∠☉	b		21 21	☽⚼♀	b	5	5 55	♂⚼♇		13	12 21	♂Q♅			15 19	☽⚼♆	b
	15 17	♀∠♂			23 40	☽⚼♇	b	Tu	8 10	♂⊥♄		We	14 31	☽□♇	B		18 14	☽△♅	G
	18 18	♀△♃		25	4 53	☽⊻♃	g		8 43	♀Q♄		14	2 02	☽☌☉	D		22 48	☽∠♂	b
	20 31	☽△♇	G	Mo	9 12	☽✱♄	G		9 24	♀⊥♂		Th	3 04	☽∠♂	b	22	0 06	☽♋	
17	4 08	☽☌♂	B		11 06	☽☍♆	B		11 23	☽⧺♄	B		5 31	☽∠♆	b	Fr	0 06	☿⊥♆	
Su	4 47	☽∠♀	b		12 39	☽☍☿	B		12 49	☿⚼♃			8 21	☽⊻♅	g		2 28	☽□☉	B
	6 40	♂Q♆			19 28	☽∥♄	B		13 19	☽☍♄	B		13 40	♂⊻♄			6 20	♀△♇	
	7 43	☿∠♇			23 57	☽△♇	G		15 21	☽✱♆	G		15 34	☽♈			11 37	☽●♃	G
	8 09	☽∠♄	b	26	0 44	♀□♇			16 56	☿Q♂			21 24	☉⧺♀			17 40	☽⊻♄	g
	12 01	☽✱♅	G	Tu	4 59	☽∠♃	b	6	1 24	☽□☉	B	15	1 11	☽⊻☿	g		19 10	☿□♇	
	19 55	☽✱☉	G		8 20	☽⧺☿	G	We	5 36	☽☌♇	D	Fr	1 53	☽⧺♀	G		21 35	☽⚼♅	b
	21 58	☽♉			9 27	☽⧺♆	D		6 56	☽⚼♂	b		2 47	☽∥☉	G	23	3 21	☽✱♂	G
18	2 42	☽⚼♇	b		12 47	☽☍♅	B		11 27	♂⧺♇			3 32	☽□♃	B	Sa	7 06	☿⧺♀	
Mo	3 02	☽∥♂	B		13 05	☿±♃			13 30	☉⊥♆			10 02	☽☌♀	G		9 38	☽△☿	G
	4 01	☽□☿	B		16 30	☽△♂	G		14 00	☽✱☿	G		10 07	☽✱♄	G		10 19	☽□♀	B
	5 11	☉Q♇			19 47	☽♍			18 52	☽⧺♃	G		10 54	♀✱♄			17 39	☉⊥♅	
	9 36	☽✱♃	G	27	3 54	☉□♄			19 01	☽∠♆	b		11 17	☽⊻♂	g		20 13	☽∠♄	b
	9 57	☽⧺♀	G	We	4 38	☽✱♃	G		19 59	☿⊥♀			11 55	☽✱♆	G	24	1 52	☿⊻♀	
	13 14	♀□♄			5 39	☽⧺♅	B		21 19	☽✱♅	G		14 48	☽∠♅	b	Su	2 35	☽∥♃	G
	14 11	☽⊻♄	g		8 36	☽⧺♇	D	7	2 31	☽□♀	B		16 27	☉∠♂			5 13	☽♌	
	14 17	☽✱♀	G		8 56	☽□♄	B	Th	4 48	☽♑			19 13	☿△♃			9 40	☽⚼♇	b
	16 23	☽□♆	B		9 17	☽☍☉	B		12 43	☽△♂	G		20 35	☉∠♆			11 24	☽△☉	G
	18 14	☽⧺☉	G		9 46	☿∥♆			15 36	☽☍♃	B		22 24	♂□♆			15 07	☽⚼☿	b
	20 13	☉♓			16 15	☽∥♂	B		21 57	☽∠☿	b		23 03	☽⧺☉	G		16 10	☽⊻♃	g
19	2 23	☽⧺♇	D		17 10	☽⚼♂	b		23 34	☽⊻♆	g	16	3 09	☽△♇	G		21 48	☽✱♄	G
Tu	6 49	☽⧺♅	B		23 12	☽□♇	B	8	1 42	♀♈		Sa	4 20	☽∥♀	G		22 37	☽☍♆	B

25	4 35	☽∥♄	B
Mo	9 06	☽□♂	B
	10 40	☽△♇	G
	14 09	☽⚼☉	b
	17 05	☽∠♃	b
	17 41	☽△♀	G
	22 00	☽#♆	D
	22 38	☽∥♂	B
26	1 57	☽☍♅	B
Tu	2 03	♀Q♆	
	6 44	☽♍	
	12 07	♂#♆	
	17 18	☽✱♃	G
	17 47	♂⚻♇	
	19 15	☽#♅	B
	19 55	☽⚼♀	b
	20 27	☽#♇	D
	22 39	☽□♄	B
27	3 15	☿∠♆	
We	10 39	☽□♇	B
	11 28	☽△♂	G
	13 24	☉□♃	
	13 49	☽∥♀	G
	22 52	☽⚼♆	b
28	0 14	♀Q♃	
Th	1 31	☽☍☿	B
	1 51	☿⚺♅	
	4 37	☉#☿	
	6 04	☽♎	
	7 37	♀∠♄	
	11 50	☽∥☉	G
	12 04	☽⚼♂	b
	13 23	☽#☿	G
	14 58	☿Q♄	
	16 41	☽□♃	B
	18 25	☽☍☉	B
	21 58	☽△♄	G
	22 23	☽△♆	G
29	1 07	☽⚼♅	b
Fr	6 51	☽∥☿	G
	9 40	☽✱♇	G
	12 10	☽#☉	G
	14 44	☿♈	
	21 46	☽⚼♄	b
30	0 24	♀✱♅	
Sa	0 54	☽△♅	G
	0 57	☽☍♀	B
	5 21	☽♏	
	9 32	☽∠♇	b
	15 01	☽#♀	G
	16 34	☽△♃	G
	22 16	☽□♆	B
31	2 38	☽∥♇	D
Su	3 38	☽∥♅	B
	6 22	☉✱♄	
	7 52	☿⊥♅	
	9 19	☉✱♆	
	9 58	☽⚺♇	g
	11 35	☽⚼☿	b
	15 39	☽☍♂	B
	17 23	☽⚼♃	b
APRIL			
1	0 10	☽⚼☉	b
Mo	1 38	☽∥♆	D
	2 13	☽□♅	B
	6 39	♀♉	
	6 48	☽♐	
	8 27	☽#♂	B
	17 02	☽△☿	G
	20 42	☽#♄	B
2	0 58	☽☍♄	B
Tu	0 58	☽✱♆	G
	2 40	♄△♆	
	3 59	☽△☉	G
	7 02	☉∠♅	
	7 52	☿∠♂	
	8 18	☿□♃	
	9 15	♂∠♃	
	11 30	☽⚼♀	b
	13 27	☽☌♇	D
	22 14	☽#♃	G
3	3 48	☽∠♆	b
We	7 13	☽✱♅	G
	8 49	♀⚼♇	
	11 58	☽♑	
	17 34	☽△♀	G
4	0 45	☿✱♆	
Th	1 41	☽☍♃	B
	2 22	☿✱♄	
	3 39	☽⚼♂	b
	7 41	☽⚺♆	g
	8 58	☽□☿	B
	11 16	☽∠♅	b
	15 29	☽□☉	B
	21 00	☽⚺♇	g
	23 36	☿∠♅	
5	4 03	♀⊥♄	
Fr	8 20	♀#♇	
	9 59	☽△♂	G
	12 58	☽⚼♄	b
	16 14	☽⚺♅	g
	16 55	♀#♅	
	20 00	☽#♃	G
	21 07	☽♒	
6	2 07	☽∠♇	b
Sa	9 32	☽□♀	B
	18 04	☽☌♆	D
	18 43	☽△♄	G
	23 43	☽#♄	B
7	6 47	☽#♂	B
Su	7 15	☽✱☿	G
	7 25	☽✱☉	G
	7 54	☽✱♇	G
	8 55	☉☌☿	
	10 59	☿△♇	
	13 14	☉△♇	
	13 38	♀✱♃	
	18 23	☽⚼♃	b
	23 00	☽∥♆	D
8	1 06	☽□♂	B
Mo	4 09	☽☌♅	B
	8 57	☽♓	
	16 20	☽∠☉	b
	18 19	☽#♀	G
	19 50	☽∠☿	b
	21 20	☉∥☿	
9	0 21	☿⊥♂	
Tu	0 57	☽△♃	G
	2 15	☽∥♅	B
	2 53	♀Q♅	
	2 58	☽∥♇	D
	4 40	☽✱♀	G
	6 32	☽⚺♆	g
	7 35	☽□♄	B
	20 24	☽□♇	B
	22 15	☿Q♆	
	22 51	♀□♆	
10	1 27	☽⚺☉	g
We	2 00	☽#☿	G
	5 09	☽#☉	G
	8 42	☽⚺☿	g
	9 04	♂□♅	
	10 56	♀⚺♄	
	12 57	☽∠♆	b
	14 33	☽∠♀	b
	15 06	♀±♇	
	17 04	☽⚺♅	g
	17 31	☽✱♂	G
	21 40	☽♈	
11	14 14	☽□♃	B
Th	14 44	☿Q♃	
	17 08	☿∠♄	
	19 17	☽✱♆	G
	20 44	☽✱♄	G
	23 26	☽∠♅	b
12	0 18	☽⚺♀	g
Fr	1 37	☽∠♂	b
	8 46	☿✱♅	
	8 54	☽△♇	G
	19 21	☽☌☉	D
	19 57	☉Q♆	
13	3 04	☽∠♄	b
Sa	5 34	☽✱♅	G
	6 34	☿⚺♂	
	9 07	♂∥♄	
	9 28	☽⚺♂	g
	9 52	☽☌☿	G
	9 55	☽♉	
	10 10	☿♉	
	14 50	☽⚼♇	b
	16 19	☽∥☉	G
	17 36	♂♊	
14	2 49	☽✱♃	G
Su	7 14	☽□♆	B
	9 05	☽⚺♄	g
	9 20	☽∥☿	G
	11 17	☽#♇	D
	11 43	☽#♅	B
	14 30	☿⚼♇	
	18 46	☽☌♀	G
	19 09	☿#♇	
	21 15	☿#♅	
15	1 04	☉⊥♂	
Mo	8 37	☽∠♃	b
	11 20	♀⚻♇	
	11 52	☽⚺☉	g
	11 55	☽∥♀	G
	14 00	☽#♆	D
	16 53	☽□♅	B
	20 56	☽♊	
	23 56	☽☌♂	B
16	6 18	☿⊥♄	
Tu	8 40	♀#♆	
	8 42	☽⚺☿	g
	13 33	☽∥♄	B
	13 59	☽⚺♃	g
	17 10	☽∥♂	B
	17 44	☽△♆	G
	19 19	☽∠☉	b
	19 56	☽☌♄	B
17	2 09	☉Q♃	
We	4 02	☉∠♄	
	6 23	☽☍♇	B
	11 02	☽⚺♀	g
	13 18	☽∥♃	G
	18 42	☽∠☿	b
	19 12	☿✱♃	
	22 11	☽⚼♆	b
18	2 03	☽✱☉	G
Th	2 17	☽△♅	G
	4 49	♂⊥♃	
	5 15	☉✱♅	
	6 01	☽♋	
	7 23	☿Q♅	
	12 03	☽⚺♂	g
	17 13	☿□♆	
	17 58	☽∠♀	b
	22 54	☽☌♃	G
19	0 20	☿±♇	
Fr	3 29	☽✱☿	G
	4 27	☽⚺♄	g
	6 00	☽⚼♅	b
	10 23	☿⚺♄	
	16 54	☽∠♂	b
	23 55	☽✱♀	G
20	6 20	☉♉	
Sa	7 36	☽∠♄	b
	11 37	☿#♆	
	12 21	☽♌	
	12 48	☽□☉	B
	14 00	☽∥♃	G
	16 30	☽⚼♇	b
	20 51	☽✱♂	G
21	3 26	☽∥♂	B
Su	4 49	☽⚺♃	g
	4 53	♀∠♃	
	7 13	☽☍♆	B
	9 56	☽✱♄	G
	10 50	☽∥♄	B
	16 54	☽□☿	B
	18 20	☽△♇	G
	20 43	☽∥♀	G
22	1 59	☽∥☿	G
Mo	3 56	☿⚻♇	
	6 35	☽∠♃	b
	8 15	☽#♆	D
	8 42	☽□♀	B
	12 30	☽☍♅	B
	15 35	☽♍	
	15 52	☉⚼♇	
	19 43	☽△☉	G
23	2 05	☽□♂	B
Tu	6 51	☽#♅	B
	6 55	☽#♇	D
	7 39	☽✱♃	G
	8 04	☽∥☉	G
	12 23	☽□♄	B
	19 57	☽□♇	B
	21 58	☽⚼☉	b
24	1 23	☽△☿	G
We	2 25	☉#♇	
	3 08	☉#♅	
	6 32	♀□♅	
	9 46	☽⚼♆	b
	14 06	☽△♀	G
	16 22	☽♎	
25	4 26	☽⚼☿	b
Th	4 49	☽△♂	G
	8 26	☽□♃	B
	9 45	☽△♆	G
	12 17	☿∥♀	
	12 56	☽△♄	G
	13 30	☽⚼♅	b
	16 09	☽⚼♀	b
	17 57	♀♊	
	18 04	♅∥♇	
	19 56	☽✱♇	G
26	5 51	☽⚼♂	b
Fr	6 48	☿∥♄	
	13 02	☽⚼♄	b
	13 29	☽△♅	G
	16 15	☽♏	
	19 53	☽∠♇	b
	20 44	♀∥♄	
	22 13	☿∠♃	
27	3 00	☽☍☉	B
Sa	8 56	☽△♃	G
	9 50	☽□♆	B
	12 35	☽∥♅	B
	12 38	☽∥♇	D
	13 29	☉⊥♄	
	17 59	☽#☉	G
	20 08	☽⚺♇	g
28	9 45	☽⚼♃	b
Su	10 55	☽∥♆	D
	13 19	☽☍☿	B
	14 25	☽□♅	B
	17 12	☽♐	
	23 50	☽☍♀	B
29	1 03	☿□♅	
Mo	8 56	☽#♄	B
	11 15	☽☍♂	B
	11 41	☽✱♆	G
	11 53	♂⚺♃	
	14 21	☽#♀	G
	14 51	♀⊥♃	
	15 50	☽☍♄	B
	20 24	☽#☿	G
	20 27	♂△♆	
	22 30	☽☌♇	D
30	0 16	☽#♂	B
Tu	3 21	☽#♃	G
	7 15	☿♊	
	12 05	☽⚼☉	b
	13 48	☽∠♆	b
	18 10	☽✱♅	G
	21 02	☽♑	
	22 37	☉Q♅	
MAY			
1	1 45	♃⚻♆	
We	12 11	☉□♆	
	14 09	☉✱♃	
	16 54	☽⚺♆	g
	17 05	☽☍♃	B
	17 16	☽△☉	G
	17 50	☉±♇	
	18 36	☿∥♂	
	21 28	☽∠♅	b
2	4 25	☽⚺♇	g
Th	4 27	☿∥♃	
	4 36	☽⚼☿	b
	16 11	☽⚼♀	b
	19 53	♂∥♃	
3	1 02	☽⚼♂	b
Fr	1 45	☽⚺♅	g
	2 20	☽⚼♄	b
	4 43	☽♒	
	5 54	☽#☿	G
	8 22	☽#♂	B
	8 50	☽∠♇	b
	9 00	☽#♃	G
	11 46	☽△☿	G
	13 42	☽#♀	G

Day	Time	Aspect	
4 Sa	0 10	☽△♀	G
	1 58	☽☌♆	D
	4 44	☽#♄	B
	5 58	♂☌♄	
	7 16	☽□☉	B
	7 44	☽△♄	G
	7 49	☽△♂	G
	14 00	☉⊻♄	
	14 05	☽⚹♇	G
	18 29	♀△♆	
5 Su	4 52	☉⊻♂	
	7 34	☽∥♆	D
	7 47	♀⊻♃	
	9 02	☽⚼♃	b
	10 13	♀∥♃	
	12 46	☽☌♅	B
	14 23	☽#☉	G
	15 45	☿⊥♃	
	15 46	☽♓	
6 Mo	4 03	☽□☿	B
	11 06	☽∥♇	D
	11 23	☽∥♅	B
	13 52	☽⊻♆	g
	15 39	☽△♃	G
	18 46	☽□♀	B
	20 23	☽□♄	B
	23 27	☽□♂	B
7 Tu	0 37	☽⚹☉	G
	2 10	☽□♇	B
	12 11	♀☌♄	
	16 45	♀∥♂	
	19 15	☉▽♇	
	20 13	☽∠♆	b
8 We	1 28	☽⊻♅	g
	4 22	☽♈	
	9 40	☽∠☉	b
	20 29	☽⚹☿	G
	22 12	♂☍♇	
9 Th	2 31	☽⚹♆	G
	5 10	☽□♃	B
	7 46	☽∠♅	b
	9 36	☽⚹♄	G
	12 59	☉#♆	
	14 12	☽⚹♀	G
	14 37	☽△♇	G
	15 37	☽⚹♂	G
	18 15	♀☍♇	
	18 31	☽⊻☉	g
10 Fr	3 43	☿∥♀	
	3 57	☽∠☿	b
	13 47	☽⚹♅	G
	15 51	☽∠♄	b
	16 32	☽♉	
	19 56	♀☌♂	
	20 26	☽⚼♇	b
	23 14	☽∠♂	b
	23 23	☽∠♀	b
11 Sa	10 42	☽⊻☿	g
	14 11	☽□♆	B
	16 48	☽#♅	B
	17 10	☽#♇	D
	17 37	☽⚹♃	G
	21 40	☽⊻♄	g
	22 43	☿∥♂	
12 Su	6 19	☽⊻♂	g
	7 58	☽⊻♀	g
	10 45	☽☌☉	D
	19 37	☽#♆	D
	23 08	☽∠♃	b
13 Mo	0 29	☽□♅	B
	1 16	☽∥☉	G
	3 04	☽♊	
	12 14	♆Stat	
	21 50	☽☌☿	G
	22 28	☽∥♄	B
	23 59	☽△♆	G
14 Tu	4 07	☽⊻♃	g
	7 47	☽●♄	B
	11 08	☽☍♇	B
	14 15	☽∥♃	G
	18 41	☽●♂	B
	19 26	☽∥☿	G
	23 04	☽●♀	G
15 We	0 28	☽⊻☉	g
	3 06	☽∥♂	B
	4 07	☽⚼♆	b
	9 08	☽△♅	G
	11 33	☽♋	
	14 14	☽∥♀	G
	18 50	☿Stat	
16 Th	5 52	☽⊻☿	g
	6 18	☽∠☉	b
	12 26	☽☌♃	G
	12 39	☽⚼♅	b
	15 43	☽⊻♄	g
	22 22	☽∥♀	G
17 Fr	3 17	☿∥♃	
	4 33	☽⊻♂	g
	5 03	♀⚼♆	
	5 10	♃⚼♅	
	8 46	☽∠☿	b
	10 24	☽∥♂	B
	11 16	☽⊻♀	g
	11 27	☽⚹☉	G
	17 52	☽♌	
	18 50	☽∠♄	b
	20 30	☉⊻♀	
	21 04	☽⚼♇	b
18 Sa	0 48	☽∥♃	G
	3 08	☽∥☿	G
	8 30	☽∠♂	b
	10 58	☽⚹☿	G
	13 11	☽☍♆	B
	14 25	☽∥♄	B
	16 16	☽∠♀	b
	18 29	☽⊻♃	g
	21 23	☽⚹♄	G
	23 17	☽△♇	G
19 Su	1 50	☽∥☉	G
	11 51	☽⚹♂	G
	12 26	♀△♅	
	15 22	☽#♆	D
	19 42	☽□☉	B
	19 53	☽☍♅	B
	20 34	☽⚹♀	G
	20 40	☽∠♃	b
	22 01	☽♍	
	22 13	♅Q♇	
	22 25	☉□♅	
20 Mo	13 02	☉∠♃	
	13 27	♀♋	
	13 29	☽□☿	B
	14 45	☽#♇	D
	15 07	☽#♅	B
	22 22	☽⚹♃	G
21 Tu	0 56	☽□♄	B
	2 14	☽□♇	B
	5 29	☉♊	
	16 53	☽□♂	B
	17 37	☽⚼♆	b
	22 14	☿⊥♃	
22 We	0 19	☽♎	
	1 39	☽△☉	G
	3 27	☽□♀	B
	5 31	☿∥♄	
	8 51	♂⚼♆	
	14 02	☽△☿	G
	18 23	☽△♆	G
	23 01	☽⚼♅	b
23 Th	0 43	☽□♃	B
	3 01	☽△♄	G
	3 46	☽⚹♇	G
	4 05	☽⚼☉	b
	13 54	☽⚼☿	b
	20 37	☽△♂	G
	23 39	☽△♅	G
24 Fr	1 38	☽♏	
	3 00	☉∥☿	
	3 51	☽⚼♄	b
	4 20	☽∠♇	b
	9 09	☽△♀	G
	16 38	♀±♆	
	19 39	☽□♆	B
	21 46	☽∥♅	B
	22 08	☽∥♇	D
	22 28	☽⚼♂	b
25 Sa	2 42	☽△♃	G
	5 01	☽⊻♇	g
	12 09	☽⚼♀	b
	20 56	☽∥♆	D
26 Su	0 44	☿⊻♀	
	1 20	☽□♅	B
	2 33	♄☍♇	
	3 20	☽♐	
	4 02	☽⚼♃	b
	10 52	☽#☿	G
	11 51	☽☍☉	B
	13 51	☽☍☿	B
	16 30	♂△♅	
	19 58	☽#☉	G
	21 50	☽⚹♆	G
	21 57	☽#♄	B
27 Mo	7 09	☉☌☿	
	7 29	☽☌♇	D
	7 48	☽☍♄	B
	8 32	☽#♃	G
	23 44	☽∠♆	b
28 Tu	4 17	☽#♂	B
	4 49	☽⚹♅	G
	6 39	☽☍♂	B
	6 54	☽♑	
	11 43	♂♋	
	13 52	☽#♀	G
	15 16	☉∥♄	
29 We	0 59	☽☍♀	B
	2 24	☽⊻♆	g
	7 40	☽∠♅	b
	10 49	☿⊥♀	
	11 46	☽☍♃	B
	12 33	☽⊻♇	g
	16 38	♀▽♆	
	17 58	☽⚼☿	b
	18 08	☽#♀	G
30 Th	1 24	☽⚼☉	b
	1 41	☽#♂	B
	11 23	☽⊻♅	g
	13 35	☽♒	
	16 22	☽∠♇	b
	17 43	☽⚼♄	b
	20 53	☽△☿	G
	23 58	☽#♃	G
31 Fr	7 18	☽#☉	G
	8 00	☽△☉	G
	9 57	♃▽♇	
	10 18	☽☌♆	D
	10 27	☽#♄	B
	21 01	☽⚹♇	G
	22 38	☽⚼♂	b
	22 46	☽△♄	G
JUNE			
1 Sa	3 37	♀⚼♅	
	7 24	☉⊥♃	
	13 38	☉△♆	
	14 01	☽#☿	G
	15 56	☽∥♆	D
	21 19	☽☌♅	B
	21 40	☿⊻♂	
	23 14	☽⚼♀	b
	23 37	☽♓	
2 Su	3 12	☽⚼♃	b
	5 07	☽□☿	B
	5 50	☽△♂	G
	12 34	♀∥♂	
	16 12	☿#♆	
	19 35	☽∥♇	D
	19 59	☽∥♅	B
	21 18	☽⊻♆	g
3 Mo	0 05	☽□☉	B
	0 11	♅Stat	
	7 06	♀▽♇	
	8 22	☽□♇	B
	8 30	☽△♀	G
	9 44	☽△♃	G
	10 58	☽□♄	B
	20 57	☿∠♃	
	22 25	☿∠♀	
	23 12	♀☌♃	
4 Tu	3 29	☽∠♆	b
	9 30	☽⊻♅	g
	11 51	☽♈	
	12 04	♀⊻♄	
	15 44	☽⚹☿	G
	20 48	♂±♆	
	21 42	☽□♂	B
5 We	9 45	☽⚹♆	G
	10 28	☉∥♃	
	15 46	☽∠♅	b
	17 54	☽⚹☉	G
	20 45	☽△♇	G
	21 23	☽∠☿	b
	23 19	☽□♃	B
6 Th	0 09	☽⚹♄	G
	3 41	☽□♀	B
	21 47	☽⚹♅	G
7 Fr	0 07	☽♉	
	2 28	☽∠☉	b
	2 39	☽⚼♇	b
	2 58	☽⊻☿	g
	4 43	☉☍♇	
	6 23	☽∠♄	b
	13 10	☽⚹♂	G
	21 26	☽□♆	B
8 Sa	0 16	☽#♅	B
	0 36	☽#♇	D
	6 07	♀±♇	
	10 23	☽⊻☉	g
	11 38	☽⚹♃	G
	12 04	☽⊻♄	g
	15 11	☿Stat	
	16 37	☿⊥♂	
	17 50	♀±♅	
	20 02	☽∠♂	b
	21 03	☽⚹♀	G
	21 30	☽∥☿	G
9 Su	3 31	☽#♆	D
	6 43	☉⊻♃	
	8 14	☽□♅	B
	10 29	☽♊	
	11 24	☉☌♄	
	13 07	☽☌☿	G
	16 51	☽∠♃	b
10 Mo	2 07	☽⊻♂	g
	4 28	☽∠♀	b
	5 01	♀⊥♄	
	6 49	☽△♆	G
	8 52	☽∥♄	B
	15 25	☽∥♃	G
	16 53	☽☍♇	B
	17 40	☉∥♀	
	21 14	☽∥♀	G
	21 22	☽⊻♃	g
	21 26	☽☌♄	B
	21 41	☽∥☉	G
	23 46	☽●●	D
11 Tu	7 37	♃⊻♄	
	10 32	☽⚼♆	b
	11 00	☽⊻♀	g
	11 18	☽∥♂	B
	16 05	☽△♅	G
	18 15	☽♋	
	21 26	☽⊻☿	g
12 We	12 00	☽●♂	B
	19 04	☽⚼♅	b
	23 08	☉⊥♀	
13 Th	0 54	☽∠☿	b
	4 12	☽⊻♄	g
	4 28	☽☌♃	G
	10 00	☽⊻☉	g
	18 11	☽∥♂	B
	19 29	♀▽♅	
	20 30	♂▽♆	
	21 44	☽☌♀	G
	22 03	♀∥♃	
	23 39	☽♌	
14 Fr	1 34	☽⚼♇	b
	3 40	☽∥☉	G
	4 02	☽⚹☿	G
	6 46	☽∠♄	b
	12 34	☽∥♃	G
	13 46	☽∥♀	G
	14 11	☽∠☉	b
	17 21	☽∥♄	B
	18 17	☽☍♆	B
	19 23	☽⊻♂	g
	20 16	♀♌	
15 Sa	3 31	☽△♇	G
	8 57	☽⚹♄	G
	9 31	☽⊻♃	g
	17 43	♀⚼♇	
	17 55	☽⚹☉	G
	20 27	☽#♆	D
	22 25	☽∠♂	b
	23 39	☽∥☿	G
16	1 17	☽☍♅	B

Day	Time	Aspect	
Su	3 23	☽♍	
	5 44	♀∥♄	
	6 13	☽⊻♀	g
	9 32	☽□☿	B
	11 32	☽∠♃	b
	20 27	☽#♇	D
	20 35	☽#♅	B
17 Mo	0 38	☉⚼♆	
	1 09	☽✱♂	G
	6 34	☽□♇	B
	9 57	☽∠♀	b
	12 28	☽□♄	B
	13 20	☽✱♃	G
	22 52	☽⚼♆	b
18 Tu	0 29	☽□☉	B
	6 11	☽♎	
	11 33	♂⚼♅	
	13 30	☽✱♀	G
	14 42	☽△☿	G
	20 05	♀∠♄	
	22 51	☿∠♃	
	23 27	☿#♆	
19 We	0 06	☽△♆	G
	5 18	☽⚼♅	b
	6 09	☽□♂	B
	9 02	☽✱♇	G
	15 28	☽△♄	G
	16 39	☽□♃	B
	17 24	☽⚼☿	b
20 Th	5 08	☉△♅	
	6 32	☽△♅	G
	6 38	☽△☉	G
	8 42	☽♏	
	8 52	☿✱♀	
	10 16	☽∠♇	b
	17 00	☽⚼♄	b
	20 34	☽□♀	B
21 Fr	2 38	☽□♆	B
	5 39	☽∥♅	B
	5 41	☽∥♇	D
	9 51	☽⚼☉	b
	11 15	☽△♂	G
	11 37	☽⊻♇	g
	13 24	☉♋	
	18 56	♂⚻♇	
	20 12	☽△♃	G
22 Sa	5 45	☽∥♆	D
	9 27	☽□♅	B
	10 54	☽#☿	G
	11 42	☽♐	
	14 07	☽⚼♂	b
	16 33	♅∥♇	
	19 15	☽#♀	G
	22 20	☽⚼♃	b
23 Su	3 20	☽☍☿	B
	4 29	☽△♀	G
	5 55	☽✱♆	G
	9 20	☽#♄	B
	9 36	☉∥♂	
	11 04	☽#♃	G
	15 06	☽☌♇	D
	21 21	♀☍♆	
	22 57	☽☍♄	B
	23 41	☽#♂	B
24 Mo	0 06	☽#☉	G
	8 07	☽∠♆	b
	9 08	☽⚼♀	b
	12 00	☿△♆	
	13 38	☽✱♅	G
	16 01	☽♑	
	19 06	☿∥♀	
	21 42	☽☍☉	B
25 Tu	10 51	☽⊻♆	g
	16 30	☽∠♅	b
	17 53	♃±♇	
	20 24	☽⊻♇	g
26 We	1 40	☽☍♂	B
	6 39	☉±♆	
	7 37	☽☍♃	B
	13 42	☿⊥♂	
	19 25	☽⚼☿	b
	20 01	☽⊻♅	g
	22 36	☽♒	
27 Th	0 01	☽∠♇	b
	1 45	☽#☉	G
	4 17	☽#♂	B
	9 25	☽⚼♄	b
	16 06	☽#♃	G
	16 24	☽#♄	B
	18 18	☽☌♆	D
28 Fr	2 57	☽△☿	G
	3 52	☽☍♀	B
	4 20	☽✱♇	G
	4 58	☽#☿	G
	8 49	♀△♇	
	11 05	♃∥♄	
	14 20	☽△♄	G
	15 37	☿☍♇	
	15 59	☽⚼☉	b
	22 34	☽#♀	G
	23 28	☽∥♆	D
29 Sa	5 12	☽☌♅	B
	6 07	☿⊥♃	
	6 56	♃±♅	
	7 45	♀#♆	
	8 00	☽♓	
	19 01	♂⊻♄	
	20 01	☽⚼♂	b
	22 15	☿✱♀	
	23 12	☽⚼♃	b
	23 52	☽△☉	G
30 Su	3 22	☽∥♅	B
	3 36	☽∥♇	D
	4 34	☽⊻♆	g
	15 02	☽□♇	B
	17 04	♂±♇	
	21 37	☽□☿	B
JULY			
1 Mo	2 11	☽□♄	B
	3 37	☽△♂	G
	5 43	☽△♃	G
	10 32	☽∠♆	b
	16 49	☽⊻♅	g
	19 49	☽♈	
2 Tu	0 18	♂±♅	
	6 19	☽⚼♀	b
	10 21	☉⚻♆	
	11 34	☿☌♄	
	14 42	☿∥♃	
	16 45	☽✱♆	G
	17 19	☽□☉	B
	23 04	☽∠♅	b
3 We	3 21	☽△♇	G
	5 45	☿∥♄	
	10 14	♀✱♄	
	13 24	♂☌♃	
	15 20	☽✱♄	G
	15 49	☽△♀	G
	19 06	☿⊻♃	
	19 22	☽□♃	B
	19 24	☽✱☿	G
	19 35	☽□♂	B
	21 27	☿⊻♂	
4 Th	5 11	☽✱♅	G
	8 16	☽♉	
	9 25	☽⚼♇	b
	18 45	☿∥♂	
	19 54	☿⚼♆	
	21 38	☽∠♄	b
5 Fr	4 44	☽□♆	B
	6 14	☽∠☿	b
	8 48	☽#♇	D
	9 13	☽#♅	B
	10 31	☽✱☉	G
	13 01	♀⊻♃	
	15 15	☉⚼♅	
	21 23	☽∥♀	G
6 Sa	3 22	☽⊻♄	g
	5 28	☉∥☿	
	7 43	☽✱♃	G
	9 14	☽□♀	B
	10 06	☽✱♂	G
	12 43	☽#♆	D
	13 42	☿△♅	
	15 57	☽□♅	B
	16 20	☽⊻☿	g
	18 02	☽∠☉	b
	19 01	☽♊	
7 Su	5 55	♀⊻♂	
	10 35	☿♋	
	12 46	☽∠♃	b
	14 23	☽△♆	G
	16 05	☽∠♂	b
	16 07	☽∥♃	G
	19 33	☉⚻♇	
	19 35	☽∥♄	B
	19 59	☽∥♂	B
8 Mo	0 09	☽☍♇	B
	0 31	☽⊻☉	g
	0 46	☽∥☉	G
	4 33	♂∥♄	
	6 58	☽∥☿	G
	12 24	☽☌♄	B
	16 56	☽⊻♃	g
	17 58	☽⚼♆	b
	21 05	☽⊻♂	g
	22 40	☽✱♀	G
	23 37	☽△♅	G
9 Tu	2 36	☽♋	
	9 14	☽☌☿	G
	9 38	♀☍♅	
	15 20	☿±♆	
10 We	2 14	☽⚼♅	b
	3 46	☽∠♀	b
	10 26	☽☌☉	D
	18 07	☽⊻♄	g
	21 09	♀♍	
	22 48	☽☌♃	G
	23 23	♂⚻♅	
11 Th	0 27	♀#♅	
	4 25	☽☌♂	B
	6 55	♀#♇	
	7 08	☽☊	
	7 28	♂⊥♄	
	7 51	☽⚼♇	b
	7 53	☽∥☿	G
	8 00	☽⊻♀	g
	20 00	☽∠♄	b
	21 32	☽∥☉	G
	22 02	☽⊻☿	g
	22 05	☽∥♄	B
12 Fr	0 22	☽☍♆	B
	2 03	☽∥♂	B
	2 45	☽∥♃	G
	3 10	♀⊥♃	
	8 54	☉∥♄	
	9 14	☽△♇	G
	14 00	☿⚻♆	
	17 16	☽⊻☉	g
	21 28	☽✱♄	G
13 Sa	1 40	☽#♆	D
	2 17	♂∥♃	
	2 22	☽⊻♃	g
	3 29	☽∠☿	b
	6 42	☽☍♅	B
	9 25	☽⊻♂	g
	9 41	☽♍	
	14 49	☽☌♀	G
	15 23	♂☊	
	20 05	☽∠☉	b
	23 12	☉±♇	
14 Su	1 14	☽#♅	B
	1 26	☿⚼♅	
	1 52	☽#♇	D
	3 46	☽∠♃	b
	5 03	♂⚼♇	
	7 55	☽∥♀	G
	8 43	☽✱☿	G
	11 15	☽□♇	B
	11 33	☽∠♂	b
	19 26	☉±♅	
	22 49	☽✱☉	G
	23 53	☽□♄	B
15 Mo	1 55	☿⚻♇	
	3 24	☽⚼♆	b
	5 08	☽✱♃	G
	7 32	♀Q♄	
	11 39	☽♎	
	13 43	☽✱♂	G
	16 55	☉⊻♄	
	21 02	☽⊻♀	g
16 Tu	4 27	☽△♆	G
	9 39	☽⚼♅	b
	13 21	☽✱♇	G
	19 38	☽□☿	B
17 We	0 26	☽∠♀	b
	2 39	☽△♄	G
	4 47	☽□☉	B
	8 23	☽□♃	B
	10 58	☽△♅	G
	14 13	☽♏	
	14 43	☽∠♇	b
	18 45	☽□♂	B
	19 35	☉∥♃	
	20 49	☿±♇	
	21 47	☽#♀	G
18 Th	4 11	☽✱♀	G
	4 26	☽⚼♄	b
	5 30	☿±♅	
	7 17	☽□♆	B
	11 18	☽∥♇	D
	12 07	☽∥♅	B
	16 25	☽⊻♇	g
	20 23	☿⊻♄	
19	8 22	☽△☿	G
Fr	8 32	☿∠♀	
	12 11	☽△☉	G
	12 31	☽∥♆	D
	12 54	☽△♃	G
	14 35	☽□♅	B
	18 02	☽♐	
	18 07	♀⊥♂	
	18 26	♀⚻♆	
20 Sa	1 16	☽△♂	G
	1 19	☉☌♃	
	4 34	☽#♂	B
	7 09	☽#☉	G
	9 35	☽#♃	G
	11 30	☽✱♆	G
	13 03	☽□♀	B
	15 38	☽⚼☿	b
	15 45	☽⚼♃	b
	16 24	☿☌♃	
	16 35	☽⚼☉	b
	17 25	☽#♄	B
	18 44	☽#☿	G
	20 57	☽☌♇	D
	21 34	☉⚻♅	
	23 51	☿⚻♅	
21 Su	1 47	☉☌☿	
	5 05	☿∥♄	
	5 12	☽⚼♂	b
	12 05	☽☍♄	B
	14 13	☽∠♆	b
	19 44	☽✱♅	G
	19 46	☿⊥♄	
	22 41	☿☊	
	23 26	☽♑	
22 Mo	1 10	☿⚼♇	
	5 43	♀∠♃	
	17 22	☽⊻♆	g
	20 44	☉⊥♄	
	22 58	☽∠♅	b
23 Tu	0 03	☽△♀	G
	0 15	☉☊	
	3 10	☽⊻♇	g
	5 15	☉⚼♇	
	7 18	♃⚻♅	
24 We	0 14	☿∥♃	
	2 41	☽⊻♅	g
	3 05	☽☍♃	B
	6 28	☽⚼♀	b
	6 40	☽♒	
	7 00	☽∠♇	b
	9 07	☽☍☉	B
	12 40	♀□♇	
	17 39	☽☍☿	B
	20 12	☽☍♂	B
	22 22	☽#♄	B
	23 50	☽⚼♄	b
25 Th	1 10	☽☌♆	D
	2 19	♀±♆	
	8 41	☽#♃	G
	11 23	☽✱♇	G
	14 01	☽#☿	G
	15 20	☿☌♂	
	17 41	☽#☉	G
	18 48	☽#♂	B
26 Fr	4 52	☽△♄	G
	5 53	☽∥♆	D
	9 45	☿∠♄	
	11 46	☽☌♅	B
	15 40	☿☍♆	
	16 04	☽♓	

Day	Time	Aspect	
27 Sa	2 53	☉∥☿	
	7 34	☿∥♂	
	9 17	☽∥♅	B
	10 37	☽∥♇	D
	11 12	☽⊻♆	g
	19 27	☽⚼♃	b
	21 52	☽□♇	B
28 Su	6 03	☽☍♀	B
	7 44	☽⚼☉	b
	9 25	☉∥♂	
	10 19	♂∠♄	
	13 13	☿⊥♀	
	16 37	☽□♄	B
	16 54	☽⚼♂	b
	17 00	☽∠♆	b
	18 32	♂☍♆	
	23 02	☽⊻♅	g
29 Mo	2 01	☽△♃	G
	3 00	☽⚼☿	b
	3 38	☽♈	
	5 15	☽#♀	G
	8 11	☿△♇	
	16 30	☽△☉	G
	17 14	☿#♆	
	23 09	☽✱♆	G
30 Tu	0 51	☽△♂	G
	2 41	♄⚼♆	
	5 13	☽∠♅	b
	10 08	☽△♇	G
	15 14	☽△☿	G
	18 12	☽∥♀	G
31 We	5 45	☽✱♄	G
	11 28	☽✱♅	G
	15 48	☽□♃	B
	16 17	☽♉	
	16 26	☽⚼♇	b
AUGUST			
1 Th	9 45	☽⚼♀	b
	10 22	☽□☉	B
	11 34	☽□♆	B
	12 12	☽∠♄	b
	16 46	☽#♇	D
	16 46	☽□♂	B
	17 20	♃♌	
	18 21	☽#♅	B
	23 23	♃⚼♇	
2 Fr	0 57	☉☍♆	
	5 43	♀⚼♆	
	7 13	☉#♆	
	7 44	☽∥☿	G
	11 58	☉∠♄	
	14 30	☽□☿	B
	16 10	♀□♄	
	18 08	☽⊻♄	g
	18 18	☽△♀	G
	20 47	☽∥☉	G
	21 43	☽#♆	D
	22 58	☽□♅	B
	23 04	☽∥♂	B
3 Sa	3 46	☽♊	
	4 24	☽✱♃	G
	15 17	☽∥♃	G
	16 11	☿✱♄	
	22 04	☽△♆	G
4 Su	1 52	☽✱☉	G
	2 00	♂#♆	
	3 11	☉∠♀	
	4 56	☽∥♄	B
	6 13	☽✱♂	G
	8 26	☽☍♇	B
	9 30	☽∠♃	b
	22 45	♀▽♅	
	22 59	☿☍♅	
	23 20	☿⊻♀	
5 Mo	2 01	☽⚼♆	b
	3 28	☽☌♄	B
	7 22	☽△♅	G
	7 55	☽∠☉	b
	8 09	☽□♀	B
	8 42	☽✱☿	G
	11 21	☽∠♂	b
	12 02	☽♋	
	13 34	☽⊻♃	g
	18 53	☿#♅	
6 Tu	1 56	♂△♇	
	6 04	☿#♇	
	9 51	☿♍	
	10 07	☽⚼♅	b
	12 44	☽⊻☉	g
	15 19	☽⊻♂	g
	15 23	☽∠☿	b
7 We	2 20	☿⊻♃	
	8 51	☽⊻♄	g
	9 09	♀♎	
	16 26	☽⚼♇	b
	16 27	☽♌	
	16 28	☉△♇	
	17 02	☽✱♀	G
	18 43	☽☌♃	G
	20 39	☽⊻☿	g
8 Th	6 01	☽∥♄	B
	8 14	☽☍♆	B
	10 16	☽∠♄	b
	17 28	☽△♇	G
	19 15	☽☌☉	D
	19 37	☽∥♃	G
	19 59	☽∠♀	b
	20 26	☽☌♂	B
	21 41	♀✱♃	
9 Fr	8 51	☽#♆	D
	11 06	☽✱♄	G
	11 21	♀∠♂	
	13 36	☽☍♅	B
	14 25	☽∥♂	B
	15 27	♃⊥♄	
	18 03	☽♍	
	19 27	☽∥☉	G
	20 58	☽⊻♃	g
	22 21	☽⊻♀	g
10 Sa	4 23	☽☌☿	G
	5 49	♀Q♇	
	7 16	☽#♅	B
	8 52	☽#♇	D
	11 59	♀±♅	
	18 17	☽□♇	B
	21 37	☽∠♃	b
	22 17	☉☌♂	
	22 59	☽∥☿	G
	23 25	☽⊻♂	g
	23 26	☽⊻☉	g
11 Su	2 50	☿Q♄	
	5 56	☿⊥♃	
	9 26	☽⚼♆	b
	12 01	☽□♄	B
	18 38	☽♎	
	22 17	☽✱♃	G
12 Mo	0 11	☿▽♆	
	0 49	☽∠♂	b
	1 26	☽∠☉	b
	1 54	☽#♀	G
	2 34	☽☌♀	G
	9 47	☽△♆	G
	10 58	☽⊻☿	g
	14 27	☽⚼♅	b
	19 02	☽✱♇	G
	23 57	☽∥♀	G
13 Tu	2 32	☽✱♂	G
	3 46	☽✱☉	G
	13 31	☽△♄	G
	14 43	☽∠☿	b
	15 11	☽△♅	G
	17 31	☽#☿	G
	19 55	☽∠♇	b
	20 00	☽♏	
14 We	0 32	☽□♃	B
	8 03	☽⊻♀	g
	11 36	☽□♆	B
	14 57	☽⚼♄	b
	16 32	☽∥♇	D
	18 22	☽∥♅	B
	19 06	☽✱☿	G
	21 18	☽⊻♇	g
	22 55	☽#☉	G
15 Th	6 00	☽#♂	B
	7 34	☽□♂	B
	10 12	☽□☉	B
	11 45	☽∠♀	b
	15 29	☿□♇	
	17 58	☽∥♆	D
	18 13	☽□♅	B
	20 02	☿±♆	
	23 25	☽♐	
16 Fr	5 00	☽△♃	G
	5 26	☽#♃	G
	9 01	♀△♆	
	15 40	☽✱♆	G
	16 12	☽✱♀	G
	22 18	☽#♄	B
17 Sa	1 54	☽☌♇	D
	2 55	☿#♀	
	6 12	☽□☿	B
	8 11	☽⚼♃	b
	15 22	☽△♂	G
	18 36	☽∠♆	b
	19 37	☽△☉	G
	21 05	☉#♅	
	22 53	☽☍♄	B
	23 39	☽✱♅	G
18 Su	3 30	☿∠♃	
	5 15	☽♑	
	12 13	♅Q♇	
	20 16	☽⚼♂	b
	22 06	☽⊻♆	g
19 Mo	1 24	☽⚼☉	b
	2 15	♀⚼♅	
	3 13	☽∠♅	b
	3 18	☽□♀	B
	3 50	☉#♇	
	8 51	☽⊻♇	g
	20 13	☽△☿	G
	20 35	☉✱♄	
20 Tu	0 54	☉☍♅	
	7 17	☽⊻♅	g
	13 06	☽∠♇	b
	13 16	☽♒	
	21 13	☽☍♃	B
21 We	4 09	☽⚼☿	b
	4 36	☽#♄	B
	6 36	☽☌♆	D
	7 17	♄△♅	
	11 52	☽⚼♄	b
	16 55	☽△♀	G
	17 49	☽✱♇	G
22 Th	1 00	☽#♃	G
	2 45	☿⚼♆	
	4 33	♀✱♇	
	11 28	☽∥♆	D
	14 28	☽☍♂	B
	16 49	☽☌♅	B
	17 09	☽△♄	G
	22 29	☽☍☉	B
	23 11	☽♓	
23 Fr	0 34	☽⚼♀	b
	7 17	☉♍	
	10 59	☽#♂	B
	14 03	☽∥♅	B
	16 31	☽∥♇	D
	16 55	☽⊻♆	g
	21 48	☿⊻♂	
24 Sa	1 13	☽#☉	G
	3 52	☿▽♅	
	4 36	☽□♇	B
	6 32	♀Q♃	
	9 29	♂☍♅	
	10 58	☿□♄	
	14 16	☽∥♀	G
	14 41	☽⚼♃	b
	22 43	☽∠♆	b
25 Su	1 40	♂✱♄	
	4 04	☽⊻♅	g
	5 00	☽□♄	B
	6 57	☽☍☿	B
	10 47	☽♈	
	21 20	☽△♃	G
	21 29	♂#♅	
26 Mo	3 34	☽∥☿	G
	4 51	☽✱♆	G
	10 12	☽∠♅	b
	11 00	♇Stat	
	13 09	☽⚼♂	b
	13 25	☽#☿	G
	16 53	☽△♇	G
	21 10	☿♎	
27 Tu	0 21	☽⚼☉	b
	2 18	☽☍♀	B
	13 35	☉#♀	
	16 32	☽✱♅	G
	18 05	☽✱♄	G
	21 18	☽△♂	G
	23 19	☽⚼♇	b
	23 31	☽♉	
	23 52	♂#♇	
28 We	7 18	☽∥☉	G
	9 29	☽△☉	G
	10 40	☽#♀	G
	11 13	☽□♃	B
	17 31	☽□♆	B
	22 42	☽∥♂	B
	23 53	☽#♇	D
29 Th	0 38	☽∠♄	b
	2 03	☿±♅	
	2 36	☽#♅	B
	11 01	☿Q♇	
	11 44	☽⚼☿	b
	12 11	☉⊻♃	
	14 38	♂♍	
30 Fr	4 44	☽□♅	B
	5 18	☽#♆	D
	6 49	☽⊻♄	g
	11 45	☽♊	
	12 37	☽∥♃	G
	12 55	☽□♂	B
	20 20	☽△☿	G
31 Sa	0 07	☽✱♃	G
	2 31	☽□☉	B
	3 53	☽⚼♀	b
	5 03	☽△♆	G
	11 48	☽∥♄	B
	16 47	☽☍♇	B
SEPTEMBER			
1 Su	1 04	♀#♂	
	5 25	☽∠♃	b
	9 41	☽⚼♆	b
	10 08	☉▽♆	
	10 44	☽△♀	G
	14 28	☽△♅	G
	16 55	☽☌♄	B
	21 14	☽♋	
2 Mo	1 17	☽✱♂	G
	7 53	☿✱♃	
	8 48	☉Q♄	
	9 41	☽⊻♃	g
	9 47	☽□☿	B
	15 29	☽✱☉	G
	17 52	☽⚼♅	b
3 Tu	5 40	☽∠♂	b
	6 33	♀∥♇	
	15 40	♀△♅	
	19 58	☽∠☉	b
	20 31	☽□♀	B
	22 52	☽⊻♄	g
4 We	2 28	☽⚼♇	b
	2 36	☽♌	
	8 51	☽⊻♂	g
	13 44	♀∥♅	
	14 52	☽☌♃	G
	14 54	☿△♆	
	16 41	☽∥♄	B
	17 23	☽☍♆	B
	17 32	☽✱☿	G
	23 14	☽⊻☉	g
5 Th	0 19	☽∠♄	b
	3 41	☽△♇	G
	14 07	☽∥♃	G
	14 26	♀△♄	
	18 18	☽#♆	D
	19 37	☽∠☿	b
	21 51	☉#☿	
	22 07	☽☍♅	B
6 Fr	0 58	☽✱♄	G
	1 33	☽✱♀	G
	3 21	☉∠♀	
	4 16	☽♍	
	8 23	☉⊥♃	
	12 13	☽#♀	G
	12 21	☽☌♂	B
	15 37	☽#♅	B
	16 31	☽⊻♃	g
	17 59	☽#♇	D
	20 53	☽⊻☿	g
7 Sa	2 56	☽∠♀	b
	3 10	☽☌☉	D
	3 59	☽∥♂	D

Day	Time	Aspect	
	4 07	☽□♇	B
	11 26	☉±♆	
	16 38	☽∠♃	b
	16 51	☽#☿	G
	17 56	☽⚼♆	b
	18 04	☉□♇	
	22 23	☽∥☉	G
8 Su	0 54	☽□♄	B
	1 01	☿⚼♅	
	1 23	♀∠♇	
	3 05	♀♏	
	3 57	☽♎	
	4 00	☽⊻♀	g
	13 59	☽⊻♂	g
	16 40	☽⚹♃	G
	17 38	☽△♆	G
	21 30	☽⚼♅	b
	22 20	☽☌☿	G
9 Mo	3 39	☽⚹♇	G
	5 56	☽⊻☉	g
	14 55	☽∠♂	b
	15 53	☽#☉	G
	21 25	☽△♅	G
10 Tu	0 52	☽△♄	G
	3 03	☽∥☿	G
	3 44	☽∠♇	b
	3 48	☽♏	
	6 34	☽☌♀	G
	7 46	☽∠☉	b
	9 58	☽#♂	B
	16 20	☽⚹♂	G
	17 35	☽□♃	B
	17 51	☽□♆	B
	23 32	☽∥♇	D
11 We	0 20	☽⊻☿	g
	1 30	☽⚼♄	b
	2 04	☽∥♅	B
	4 22	☽⊻♇	g
	10 17	☽⚹☉	G
	12 07	♃☍♆	
	14 55	☽∥♀	G
	22 52	☽□♅	B
12 Th	0 01	☽∥♆	D
	2 06	☽∠☿	b
	2 19	♂▽♆	
	2 22	☽#♃	G
	5 44	☽♐	
	9 07	♂⊻♃	
	11 33	☽⊻♀	g
	20 33	☽⚹♆	G
	21 04	☽△♃	G
	21 28	☽□♂	B
13 Fr	2 16	☽#♄	B
	4 31	☽⚹☿	G
	7 50	☽☌♇	D
	15 22	☽∠♀	b
	18 08	☽□☉	B
	23 06	☽∠♆	b
14 Sa	0 03	☽⚼♃	b
	3 20	☽⚹♅	G
	7 54	☽☍♄	B
	9 35	☿#♂	
	10 47	☽♑	
	19 37	☿Stat	
	20 07	☽⚹♀	G
15 Su	0 39	♂Q♄	
	2 27	☽⊻♆	g
	6 17	☽△♂	G
	6 47	☽∠♅	b
	11 11	☽□☿	B
	14 32	☽⊻♇	g
16 Mo	5 58	☽△☉	G
	10 55	☽⊻♅	g
	12 00	☽⚼♂	b
	13 12	☉⚼♆	
	13 13	♀∥♆	
	18 54	☽♒	
	18 57	☽∠♇	b
17 Tu	0 56	♀#♃	
	7 59	☽□♀	B
	11 14	☽☌♆	D
	11 28	☽#♄	B
	13 08	☽⚼☉	b
	13 40	☽☍♃	B
	19 30	☽△☿	G
	21 06	☽⚼♄	b
	21 18	☉∠♃	
	23 57	☽⚹♇	G
18 We	8 21	☿⊻♂	
	12 48	☽∥♀	G
	16 30	☽#♃	G
	16 59	☽∥♆	D
	20 14	☉▽♅	
	20 54	☽☌♅	B
	23 56	☽⚼☿	b
19 Th	2 35	☽△♄	G
	5 18	☽♓	
	18 35	☽∥♅	B
	21 19	♀□♆	
	21 47	☽∥♇	D
	22 02	☽⊻♆	g
	22 04	☽△♀	G
20 Fr	4 22	♃#♆	
	8 47	☽☍♂	B
	11 14	☽□♇	B
	22 19	♀⊥♇	
	23 41	☽∥☿	G
21 Sa	3 32	☽#♂	B
	3 58	☽∠♆	b
	5 38	☽⚼♀	b
	6 47	♂±♆	
	8 00	☽⚼♃	b
	8 27	☽⊻♅	g
	13 59	☽☍☉	B
	14 36	☽□♄	B
	14 43	☿⚼♅	
	17 11	☽♈	
	18 44	☿⚹♃	
	21 47	☉□♄	
22 Su	8 09	♂□♇	
	10 09	☽⚹♆	G
	11 00	☿⊻♀	
	12 34	☽#☉	G
	13 08	☽☍☿	B
	14 37	☽∠♅	b
	14 43	☽△♃	G
	14 54	☽∥☉	G
	23 42	☽△♇	G
23 Mo	4 55	☉♎	
	20 55	☽∥♂	B
	20 56	☽⚹♅	G
	21 34	☽#☿	G
24 Tu	3 29	☽⚹♄	G
	3 45	☿△♆	
	5 54	☽♉	
	6 10	☽⚼♇	b
	7 53	♀□♃	
	8 18	☿#♂	
	8 43	☽⚼♂	b
	18 58	☉±♅	
	22 53	☽□♆	B
25 We	4 28	☽□♃	B
	5 04	☽☍♀	B
	6 22	☽#♇	D
	9 41	☽#♅	B
	9 58	☽∠♄	b
	15 49	♂⊥♃	
	16 48	☽△♂	G
	17 16	☽⚼☉	b
26 Th	1 10	☽⚼☿	b
	9 20	☽∥♃	G
	9 27	☽□♅	B
	9 36	☿⊥♀	
	10 24	☉Q♇	
	11 18	☽#♆	D
	16 12	☽⊻♄	g
	18 26	☽♊	
27 Fr	2 00	☽△☉	G
	4 38	☽△☿	G
	9 17	☽#♀	G
	11 00	☽△♆	G
	16 31	☽∥♄	B
	17 22	☽⚹♃	G
	18 31	☉☌☿	
28 Sa	0 28	☽☍♇	B
	7 42	☽□♂	B
	16 15	☽⚼♆	b
	20 19	☽△♅	G
	22 23	☿Q♇	
	22 53	☽∠♃	b
29 Su	1 31	☽⚼♀	b
	3 01	☽☌♄	B
	5 01	☽♋	
	10 07	☽□☿	B
	17 03	☽□☉	B
	22 39	☉∥☿	
30 Mo	0 33	☽⚼♅	b
	3 28	☽⊻♃	g
	6 28	☽△♀	G
	17 43	☿±♅	
	18 59	☽⚹♂	G
OCTOBER			
1 Tu	8 19	☉⊥♀	
	8 38	♀⚼♄	
	10 11	☽⊻♄	g
	10 30	♀#♄	
	11 58	☽♌	
	12 25	☽⚼♇	b
	13 09	☽⚹☿	G
	15 50	☉△♆	
	22 50	☽∠♂	b
2 We	2 25	☽☍♆	B
	2 59	☽#♀	G
	3 14	☽⚹☉	G
	3 58	☽∥♄	B
	9 23	☽☌♃	G
	9 26	☿♍	
	12 12	☽∠♄	b
	12 48	☽□♀	B
	13 40	☽∠☿	b
	14 21	☽△♇	G
3 Th	1 31	☽⊻♂	g
	2 26	☿∠♀	
	4 47	☽#♆	D
	6 26	☽∠☉	b
	7 10	☽☍♅	B
	8 08	☽∥♃	G
	13 16	☽⚹♄	G
	13 37	☽⊻☿	g
	14 52	☽♍	
	15 59	☉#♂	
	17 00	☉⚼♅	
	23 08	☿□♄	
4 Fr	1 31	☽#♅	B
	4 11	☽#♇	D
	8 38	☽⊻☉	g
	11 25	☽⊻♃	g
	14 57	☽⚹♀	G
	15 37	☽□♇	B
5 Sa	3 53	♂⚼♆	
	4 14	☽⚼♆	b
	4 15	☽☌♂	B
	11 29	☽∠♃	b
	12 27	☽☌☿	G
	13 21	☽#☉	G
	13 22	☽□♄	B
	14 51	☽♎	
	15 01	☽∠♀	b
	18 00	☽∥♂	B
6 Su	3 48	☽△♆	G
	4 08	☽∥☿	G
	6 56	☽⚼♅	b
	9 58	☽#☿	G
	10 38	☉⚹♃	
	11 15	☽⚹♃	G
	11 18	☽☌☉	D
	14 49	☽⊻♀	g
	14 56	☽⚹♇	G
	18 50	☽#♂	B
	19 27	☿Stat	
7 Mo	2 39	☽∥☉	G
	5 24	☽⊻♂	g
	5 54	♀⊻♇	
	6 26	☽△♅	G
	11 22	☽⊻☿	g
	12 29	☽△♄	G
	13 57	☽♏	
	14 33	☽∠♇	b
8 Tu	3 02	☽□♆	B
	5 10	♂▽♅	
	6 13	☽∠♂	b
	9 25	☽∥♇	D
	11 10	☽□♃	B
	11 34	☽∠☿	b
	12 02	☽∥♅	B
	12 23	☽⚼♄	b
	14 03	☽⊻☉	g
	14 31	☽⊻♇	g
	14 42	☽☌♀	G
	21 03	☉⚹♇	
9 We	0 31	☉⊻♀	
	3 44	☽#♃	G
	6 25	☽□♅	B
	7 36	☽⚹♂	G
	8 18	☽∥♆	D
	12 38	☽⚹☿	G
	14 21	☽♐	
	16 20	☽∠☉	b
	18 28	☿□♄	
10 Th	4 05	☽⚹♆	G
	8 20	☽#♄	B
	13 16	☽△♃	G
	16 22	☽☌♇	D
	16 39	☽⊻♀	g
	17 30	☽∥♀	G
	18 34	♀Stat	
	19 35	☽⚹☉	G
11 Fr	5 49	☽∠♆	b
	5 56	☿♎	
	9 11	☽⚹♅	G
	13 01	☽□♂	B
	13 03	♄Stat	
	15 37	☽⚼♃	b
	16 08	☽☍♄	B
	17 45	☽♑	
	18 28	☽□☿	B
	18 48	☽∠♀	b
	23 44	☿∠♀	
12 Sa	8 28	☽⊻♆	g
	11 56	☽∠♅	b
	14 31	☿±♅	
	21 46	☽⊻♇	g
	21 48	☽⚹♀	G
13 Su	1 18	♀⊻♇	
	5 33	☽□☉	B
	14 24	♃∠♄	
	15 37	☽⊻♅	g
	22 42	☽△♂	G
14 Mo	0 51	☽♒	
	1 52	☽∠♇	b
	6 10	☽△☿	G
	6 56	♂□♄	
	8 29	☽∥♀	G
	11 51	♂∠♃	
	16 31	☽☌♆	D
	19 12	☽#♄	B
	22 10	☿Q♇	
15 Tu	3 52	☽⚼♄	b
	4 19	☽☍♃	B
	5 01	☽⚼♂	b
	6 04	☽□♀	B
	6 45	☽⚹♇	G
	14 09	☽⚼☿	b
	17 38	♂♎	
	19 54	☽△☉	G
	20 59	♀∠♂	
	23 19	☽∥♆	D
16 We	1 21	☽☌♅	B
	6 34	☽#♃	G
	9 15	☽△♄	G
	11 07	☽♓	
	23 58	☽∥♅	B
17 Th	0 23	☿#♂	
	3 06	☽∥♇	D
	3 25	☽⊻♆	g
	4 16	☽⚼☉	b
	8 49	♂±♅	
	16 20	☽△♀	G
	16 34	♀□♃	
	18 17	☽□♇	B
	22 50	☽∥☉	G
18 Fr	9 30	☽∠♆	b
	10 46	☿△♆	
	13 11	☽⊻♅	g
	13 57	☿⊥♀	
	14 08	☉△♅	
	21 17	☽□♄	B
	21 47	☽⚼♀	b
	22 51	☽⚼♃	b
	23 13	☽♈	
19 Sa	3 38	☽☍♂	B
	10 47	☽∥☿	G
	15 48	☽⚹♆	G
	16 09	♀⚼♄	

Day	Time	Aspect	
	16 21	☿⚼♅	
	19 28	☽∠♅	b
	19 41	☽∥♂	B
	19 55	☽☍☿	B
	20 17	☽#♂	B
20 Su	5 33	☽△♃	G
	6 59	☽△♇	G
	7 33	☽#☿	G
	13 46	♆Stat	
	14 45	☉Q♃	
21 Mo	1 48	☽⚹♅	G
	7 20	☽☍☉	B
	9 55	☽⚹♄	G
	11 57	☽♉	
	13 25	☽⚼♇	b
	14 02	♂Q♇	
	18 10	☿⊻♀	
22 Tu	0 24	☽#☉	G
	4 30	☽□♆	B
	13 02	☽#♇	D
	13 32	☉△♄	
	13 53	☽☍♀	B
	16 03	☽#♅	B
	16 09	☽∠♄	b
	18 51	☽□♃	B
23 We	2 20	☿⚹♃	
	3 44	☽⚼♂	b
	7 52	☽∥♃	G
	8 46	♀#♄	
	8 49	☿⚹♇	
	14 14	☽□♅	B
	14 18	☉♏	
	16 37	☽#♆	D
	22 11	☽⊻♄	g
24 Th	0 17	☽♊	
	4 30	☽⚼☿	b
	9 53	☉∠♇	
	11 23	☽△♂	G
	16 35	☽△♆	G
	17 53	☽#♀	G
	18 47	♀⊥♂	
	20 44	☽∥♄	B
25 Fr	7 11	☽⚹♃	G
	7 38	☽☍♇	B
	9 30	☽⚼☉	b
	14 43	☽△☿	G
	22 01	☽⚼♆	b
26 Sa	1 24	☽△♅	G
	3 32	☽⚼♀	b
	9 01	☽☌♄	B
	11 10	☽♋	
	12 37	☽∠♃	b
	17 08	☽△☉	G
27 Su	0 58	☽□♂	B
	6 07	☽⚼♅	b
	7 00	☽△♀	G
	17 19	☽⊻♃	g
	23 41	♃△♇	
28 Mo	2 52	♀⊥♇	
	8 22	☽□☿	B
	14 28	♂△♆	
	17 11	☽⊻♄	g
	19 20	☽♌	
	21 03	☽⚼♇	b
	21 43	☿△♅	
29 Tu	5 28	☽□☉	B
	6 06	☉∥♇	
	10 07	☽☍♆	B
	11 05	☽⚹♂	G
	11 42	☽□♀	B
	13 28	☽∥♄	B
	18 09	♀⊻♂	
	19 58	☽∠♄	b
	23 50	☽△♇	G
30 We	0 06	☽☌♃	G
	3 33	☽#♀	G
	14 19	☽#♆	D
	14 35	☽∠♂	b
	15 19	☽☍♅	B
	20 18	☉∥♅	
	20 57	☽⚹☿	G
	21 15	☿Q♃	
	21 51	☽⚹♄	G
	22 53	♀□♆	
	22 59	☽∥♃	G
	23 59	☽♍	
31 Th	4 28	☿△♄	
	6 21	♂⚼♅	
	10 14	☽#☉	G
	11 06	☽#♅	B
	12 06	☉☌♀	
	13 13	☽⚹♀	G
	13 21	☽⚹☉	G
	13 22	☽#♇	D
	17 07	☽⊻♂	g
	20 16	☉□♆	
	22 43	☿♏	

NOVEMBER

Day	Time	Aspect	
1 Fr	1 22	☽∠☿	b
	2 29	☽#☿	G
	2 47	☽□♇	B
	3 18	☽⊻♃	g
	12 57	☽∠♀	b
	14 03	☿∠♇	
	14 32	☽⚼♆	b
	15 51	☽∠☉	b
	23 19	☽□♄	B
2 Sa	1 28	☽♎	
	3 49	☽∠♃	b
	4 50	☽⊻☿	g
	5 11	☽#♂	B
	12 10	☽⊻♀	g
	14 41	☽△♆	G
	17 04	☉⊥♇	
	17 20	☽⚼♅	b
	17 41	☽⊻☉	g
	19 57	☽☌♂	B
3 Su	3 12	☽⚹♇	G
	3 54	☽⚹♃	G
	7 50	☽∥♂	B
	17 07	☽△♅	G
	21 58	♀∥♆	
	22 56	☽△♄	G
4 Mo	1 10	☽♏	
	2 59	☽∠♇	b
	6 26	♅Stat	
	7 43	☿☌♀	
	9 57	☽☌♀	G
	10 19	☽☌☿	G
	14 14	☽□♆	B
	18 25	☽∥☿	G
	20 34	☽☌☉	D
	21 18	☽∥♇	D
	21 34	☽⊻♂	g
	22 38	☽⚼♄	b
	23 18	☽∥♅	B
5 Tu	2 50	☽⊻♇	g
	3 43	☽□♃	B
	6 48	☽∥☉	G
	10 01	☽#♃	G
	15 11	☽∥♀	G
	16 48	☽□♅	B
	18 41	☽∥♆	D
	20 49	☿∥♇	
	22 37	☿□♆	
	22 40	☽∠♂	b
6 We	1 01	☽♐	
	2 20	☉⚼♄	
	8 16	☽⊻♀	g
	12 27	☉⊻♂	
	14 31	☽⚹♆	G
	14 33	☿∥♅	
	16 31	☽⊻☿	g
	17 36	☽#♄	B
7 Th	0 21	☽⚹♂	G
	0 41	☽⊻☉	g
	3 32	☿⊥♇	
	3 42	☽☌♇	D
	4 50	☽△♃	G
	8 11	☽∠♀	b
	11 29	☉#♃	
	15 32	☽∠♆	b
	18 17	☽⚹♅	G
	20 52	☽∠☿	b
8 Fr	0 14	☽☍♄	B
	0 27	☉∥♀	
	2 59	☽♑	
	3 57	☽∠☉	b
	6 26	☽⚼♃	b
	8 52	☽⚹♀	G
	11 04	♀#♃	
	17 23	☽⊻♆	g
	20 13	☽∠♅	b
	21 34	☉⊻♇	
9 Sa	1 16	☿⚼♄	
	2 26	☽⚹☿	G
	6 26	☽□♂	B
	7 35	☽⊻♇	g
	8 22	☽⚹☉	G
	16 26	☿∥♀	
	17 06	☉□♃	
	23 07	☽⊻♅	g
10 Su	7 52	♂⚹♇	
	8 27	☽♒	
	10 58	☽∠♇	b
	10 59	☿#♃	
	12 55	☽□♀	B
	22 04	☿⊻♇	
	23 59	☽☌♆	D
11 Mo	3 50	☽#♄	B
	6 55	☿⊻♂	
	9 16	☽⚼♄	b
	11 09	☿□♃	
	15 19	☽⚹♇	G
	16 55	☽△♂	G
	16 59	☽☍♃	B
	17 49	☽□☿	B
	18 22	♂⚹♃	
	20 52	☽□☉	B
12 Tu	7 06	☽∥♆	D
	7 48	☽☌♅	B
	9 44	☽∥☉	G
	11 37	☽∥☿	G
	14 06	☽△♄	G
	17 42	☽♓	
	18 28	☽#♃	G
	20 40	☽△♀	G
	23 43	☽⚼♂	b
13 We	1 23	♀∠♇	
	3 58	☽∥♀	G
	7 01	☽∥♅	B
	9 07	☽∥♇	D
	10 12	☽⊻♆	g
	17 31	☉∥☿	
	20 58	☿∥♆	
14 Th	0 24	☉∥♆	
	1 42	☽⚼♀	b
	2 25	☽□♇	B
	4 40	☉☌☿	
	11 08	☿±♄	
	13 29	☽△☉	G
	13 59	☽△☿	G
	14 43	☉±♄	
	16 15	☽∠♆	b
	19 26	☽⊻♅	g
	19 30	☽∥♂	B
	20 14	♀∥♅	
15 Fr	1 38	☽□♄	B
	5 38	☽♈	
	10 43	☽⚼♃	b
	22 37	☽⚼☉	b
	22 37	☽⚹♆	G
16 Sa	0 12	♀∥♇	
	1 01	☽⚼☿	b
	1 49	☽∠♅	b
	7 03	☿□♅	
	15 13	☽△♇	G
	17 16	☽△♃	G
	23 24	☽☍♂	B
17 Su	4 52	☿Q♆	
	8 15	☽⚹♅	G
	12 34	☉□♅	
	13 09	☽#♂	B
	13 46	☿⊥♂	
	14 06	☽⚹♄	G
	18 23	☽♉	
	19 01	☽☍♀	B
	21 40	☽⚼♇	b
18 Mo	2 36	☿⊽♄	
	11 23	☽□♆	B
	16 26	☽#♀	G
	20 09	☽∠♄	b
	20 32	☽#♇	D
	22 19	☽#♅	B
	23 12	☉Q♆	
19 Tu	6 01	☽□♃	B
	10 30	☽∥♃	G
	11 29	☿♐	
	13 16	☿⊻♀	
	20 32	☽□♅	B
	22 20	☽#♆	D
20 We	1 34	☽☍☉	B
	1 54	☽⊻♄	g
	5 22	☉⊽♄	
	6 25	☽♊	
	8 27	☽#☉	G
	9 14	☽☍☿	B
	20 59	☽#☿	G
	22 28	☽⚼♂	b
	23 06	☽△♆	G
21 Th	2 09	☽∥♄	B
	7 13	♀Stat	
	11 57	☽⚼♀	b
	15 16	☽☍♇	B
	17 22	☽⚹♃	G
22 Fr	4 18	☽⚼♆	b
	5 14	☽△♂	G
	7 18	☽△♅	G
	11 54	☉♐	
	12 04	☿#♄	
	12 07	☽☌♄	B
	13 58	☉⊻♀	
	16 48	☽♋	
	16 58	☽△♀	G
	21 50	☉⊥♂	
	22 18	☽∠♃	b
23 Sa	9 37	☿⊥♀	
	11 55	☽⚼♅	b
	22 20	♂△♅	
24 Su	0 02	☽⚼☉	b
	2 40	☽⊻♃	g
	11 48	☽⚼☿	b
	16 51	☽□♂	B
	20 12	☽⊻♄	g
	22 38	☿⚹♆	
25 Mo	1 00	☽♌	
	1 37	☽□♀	B
	4 27	☽⚼♇	b
	6 06	☽△☉	G
	11 28	☽#☿	G
	16 35	☽☍♆	B
	18 56	☽△☿	G
	20 12	☽∥♄	B
	23 21	☽∠♄	b
26 Tu	4 37	☽#☉	G
	7 37	☽△♇	G
	9 31	☽☌♃	G
	21 41	☽#♆	D
	22 09	☽☍♅	B
27 We	1 35	☽⚹♂	G
	1 51	☽⚹♄	G
	6 34	♂△♄	
	6 42	☽♍	
	7 57	☿∠♂	
	8 02	☽⚹♀	G
	8 19	☽∥♃	G
	15 46	☽□☉	B
	18 55	☽#♅	B
	19 57	☽#♇	D
	21 43	☿Q♅	
28 Th	4 51	☽∠♂	b
	6 23	☽□☿	B
	6 46	☽#♀	G
	10 22	☽∠♀	b
	12 01	☽□♇	B
	12 08	☽#♂	B
	13 46	☽⊻♃	g
	23 13	☽⚼♆	b
29 Fr	5 01	☽□♄	B
	7 27	☽⊻♂	g
	9 54	☽♎	
	12 10	☽⊻♀	g
	15 01	☽∠♃	b
	21 21	☉⊥♀	
	22 25	☽⚹☉	G
30 Sa	0 17	☽△♆	G
	2 27	☿∠♀	
	2 50	☽⚼♅	b
	10 50	☿☌♇	
	14 11	☽⚹♇	G
	14 34	☽⚹☿	G
	15 48	☽⚹♃	G

DECEMBER

Day	Time	Aspect	
1	0 54	☽∠☉	b
Su	1 38	☉⚹♆	
	2 19	☿△♃	
	3 28	☽△♅	G
	6 15	☽△♄	G
	11 07	☽☌♂	B
	11 15	☽♏	
	14 26	♂♏	
	14 38	☽☌♀	G
	14 43	☽∠♇	b
	17 52	♂Q♃	
	17 54	☽∠☿	b
	18 21	♀∠♇	
	20 31	☽∥♂	B
	21 50	☽∥♀	G
2	1 22	☽□♆	B
Mo	3 05	☽⊻☉	g
	6 29	☽⚼♄	b
	8 43	☽∥♇	D
	9 26	☽∥♅	B
	15 07	☽⊻♇	g
	16 37	☽□♃	B
	19 23	☽#♃	G
	21 03	☽⊻☿	g
3	4 15	☽□♅	B
Tu	4 49	☉#♄	
	5 01	☽∥♆	D
	6 02	♀∥♂	
	11 58	☽♐	
	14 03	☽⊻♂	g
	16 45	☽⊻♀	g
4	2 16	☽⚹♆	G
We	4 20	☽#♄	B
	5 20	☽∥☉	G
	7 34	☽●●	D
	12 20	♃Stat	
	15 50	☽∠♂	b
	16 18	☽☌♇	D
	17 43	☽△♃	G
	18 14	☽∠♀	b
	18 39	☿∠♆	
5	3 03	♂∠♇	
Th	3 10	☽∠♆	b
	4 10	☽●☿	G
	5 45	☽⚹♅	G
	7 55	☽☍♄	B
	13 39	☽♑	
	14 18	☽∥☿	G
	15 40	☉Q♅	
	18 10	☽⚹♂	G
	18 54	☽⚼♃	b

Day	Time	Aspect	
	19 09	☿⚹♅	
	20 20	☽⚹♀	G
6	4 38	☽⊻♆	g
Fr	7 18	☽∠♅	b
	13 36	☿☍♄	
	14 06	☽⊻☉	g
	19 26	☽⊻♇	g
	21 22	☽∥☿	G
7	9 37	☽⊻♅	g
Sa	14 29	☽⊻☿	g
	17 54	☽♒	
	18 47	☽∠☉	b
	22 11	☽∠♇	b
8	1 24	☽□♂	B
Su	3 13	☽□♀	B
	8 00	☽∥☉	G
	9 59	☽☌♆	D
	13 13	☽#♄	B
	14 35	☽⚼♄	b
	20 21	☿♑	
	21 30	☽∠☿	b
9	0 38	☽⚹☉	G
Mo	1 52	☽⚹♇	G
	3 06	☽☍♃	B
	16 21	☽∥♆	D
	16 55	☉☌♇	
	17 02	☽☌♅	B
	18 35	☽△♄	G
10	1 46	☽♓	
Tu	3 19	☽#♃	G
	5 52	☽⚹☿	G
	7 16	☉△♃	
	12 53	☽△♂	G
	14 32	☽△♀	G
	15 58	☽∥♅	B
	16 11	☽∥♇	D
	18 18	☿⊥♆	
	19 04	☽⊻♆	g
	20 17	☿⚼♃	
	21 06	☽∥♂	B
11	3 18	☽∥♀	G
We	12 00	☽□♇	B
	15 49	☽□☉	B
	20 06	☽⚼♂	b
	21 45	☽⚼♀	b
12	0 49	☽∠♆	b
Th	3 57	☽⊻♅	g
	5 02	☽□♄	B
	12 58	☽♈	
	19 00	☽⚼♃	b
13	1 54	☽□☿	B
Fr	7 06	☽⚹♆	G
	7 47	♅∥♇	

Day	Time	Aspect	
	10 17	☽∠♅	b
14	0 35	☽△♇	G
Sa	1 18	☽△♃	G
	5 25	☿⚹♂	
	7 18	♀□♆	
	9 58	☽△☉	G
	16 48	☽⚹♅	G
	17 18	☽⚹♄	G
	20 05	☿⊻♆	
15	1 43	☽♉	
Su	6 41	♂∥♅	
	7 05	☽⚼♇	b
	7 09	☿⚹♀	
	10 17	♂∥♇	
	16 08	♂□♆	
	19 09	☽⚼☉	b
	20 00	☽□♆	B
	20 13	☽☍♂	B
	20 24	☽#♀	G
	22 13	☽☍♀	B
	22 20	☿∠♅	
	23 18	☽△☿	G
	23 24	☽∠♄	b
16	4 28	☽#♅	B
Mo	4 43	☽#♇	D
	5 16	☉∠♆	
	5 36	☽#♂	B
	13 40	☽□♃	B
	15 47	♀⚼♄	
	18 13	☽∥♃	G
	18 28	☿±♃	
	21 36	♄△♅	
17	2 53	☉∠♂	
Tu	4 42	☽#♆	D
	5 07	☽⊻♄	g
	5 11	☽□♅	B
	9 17	☽⚼☿	b
	13 43	☽♊	
	17 28	☉☍♄	
	19 50	☉⚹♅	
18	0 58	♂⚼♄	
We	2 19	♀⊥♇	
	7 34	☽△♆	G
	9 09	☽∥♄	B
	13 40	♃△♇	
	21 10	☽#☉	G
19	0 14	☽⚹♃	G
Th	0 18	☽☍♇	B
	11 24	☽#☿	G
	12 27	☽⚼♆	b
	14 53	☽☌♄	B
	15 30	☽△♅	G
	17 10	☽⚼♂	b

Day	Time	Aspect	
	19 10	☽☍☉	B
	19 55	☽⚼♀	b
	23 30	☽♋	
	23 57	♂⊥♇	
20	4 34	☽∠♃	b
Fr	19 42	☽⚼♅	b
	21 58	☿⚻♃	
	22 43	☽△♂	G
21	1 46	☿⊻♇	
Sa	1 46	☽△♀	G
	8 18	☽⊻♃	g
	9 31	☽☍☿	B
	11 48	☉∠♀	
	22 12	☽⊻♄	g
22	1 14	☉♑	
Su	6 48	☽♌	
	9 33	☽#☿	G
	12 05	☽⚼♇	b
	14 06	☽#☉	G
	14 41	☿⊥♅	
	23 27	☽☍♆	B
23	1 03	☽∠♄	b
Mo	1 42	☽∥♄	B
	7 51	☽□♂	B
	11 34	☽□♀	B
	12 18	☽⚼☉	b
	14 07	☽☌♃	G
	14 56	☽△♇	G
	23 17	♀∥♅	
24	0 13	☉∥☿	
Tu	3 27	☽⚹♄	G
	3 50	☽#♆	D
	4 58	☽☍♅	B
	11 06	☉⚼♃	
	12 05	☽♍	
	12 05	☽∥♃	G
	15 45	☽#♂	B
	16 48	☽△☉	G
	20 40	♀∥♇	
25	0 25	☽#♀	G
We	0 34	☽#♇	D
	1 26	♀□♃	
	1 28	☽#♅	B
	1 43	☽⚼☿	b
	8 02	☉⊥♆	
	14 56	☽⚹♂	G
	18 13	☽⊻♃	g
	19 02	♀⊻♇	
	19 24	☽□♇	B
	19 25	☽⚹♀	G
26	5 29	☿⊥♇	
Th	5 45	☽△☿	G
	6 16	☽⚼♆	b

Day	Time	Aspect	
	7 10	☽□♄	B
	15 53	☽♎	
	17 18	♀±♄	
	17 54	☽∠♂	b
	19 48	☽∠♃	b
	22 49	☽∠♀	b
27	0 07	☿⚻♄	
Fr	0 31	☽□☉	B
	7 54	☽△♆	G
	10 43	☽⚼♅	b
	20 36	☽⊻♂	g
	21 08	☽⚹♃	G
	22 41	☽⚹♇	G
28	1 58	☽⊻♀	g
Sa	3 35	☿#♄	
	7 22	♂□♃	
	9 49	☽△♄	G
	10 19	☿⊻♅	
	12 09	☽△♅	G
	12 15	☽□☿	B
	18 41	☽♏	
29	0 01	☽∠♇	b
Su	2 01	♂#♃	
	7 05	☽⚹☉	G
	10 36	☽□♆	B
	10 53	☽⚼♄	b
	16 00	☽∥♅	B
	17 13	☽∥♇	D
	21 08	♂⊻♇	
	21 56	☽∥♀	G
	23 19	☽□♃	B
30	1 15	☽⊻♇	g
Mo	1 26	☽●♂	B
	5 47	☽#♃	G
	6 43	☽∥♂	B
	7 48	☽☌♀	G
	10 10	☽∠☉	b
	10 43	♂±♄	
	12 38	☽∥♆	D
	14 39	☽□♅	B
	17 04	☽⚹☿	G
	21 01	☽♐	
	22 28	♄⚼♆	
31	6 20	☽∥☿	G
Tu	10 03	☉⊻♆	
	13 04	☽⚹♆	G
	13 17	☽⊻☉	g
	13 30	☽#♄	B
	19 04	☽∠☿	b
	21 13	☽∥☉	G

DISTANCES APART OF ALL ☌s AND ☍s IN 2002

Note: The Distances Apart are in Declination

JANUARY

1	05	53	☉☍♃	0 00
1	10	29	☽☍♆	3 24
2	11	16	☽☍♅	3 26
3	12	22	♀☍♃	0 29
4	07	30	☽☍♂	4 12
9	11	56	☿☌♆	1 12
10	01	59	☽☍♄	0 07
10	15	54	☽☌♇	8 45
12	10	34	☽☍♃	1 04
13	13	00	☽☌♀	1 25
13	13	29	☽☌☉	2 16
14	11	32	☉☌♀	0 52
14	18	13	☽☌♆	3 24
15	04	43	☽☌☿	3 42
16	00	25	☽☌♅	3 26
19	02	49	☽☌♂	4 26
24	15	37	☽•♄	0 04
25	07	08	☽☍♇	8 53
25	19	17	♀☌♆	1 15
26	12	17	☿☌♀	4 16
26	19	03	☽•♃	0 55
27	04	38	☿☌♆	3 07
27	18	55	☉☌☿	3 18
28	13	45	☉☌♆	0 06
28	18	54	☽☍☿	6 37
28	22	15	☽☍♆	3 25
28	22	50	☽☍☉	3 21
29	04	55	☽☍♀	2 21
29	23	04	☽☍♅	3 26

FEBRUARY

2	01	29	☽☍♂	4 28
6	06	01	☽☍♄	0 05
6	22	54	☽☌♇	9 00
7	15	23	♀☌♅	0 40
8	11	18	☽☍♃	0 50
10	06	50	☽☌☿	4 55
11	02	57	☽☌♆	3 27
12	07	41	☽☌☉	4 03
12	10	21	☽☌♅	3 26
12	23	10	☽☌♀	2 57
13	17	06	☉☌♅	0 39
17	04	08	☽☌♂	4 17
21	00	22	☽•♄	0 10
21	17	32	☽☍♇	9 13
23	02	19	☽•♃	0 52
24	15	59	☿☌♆	0 29
25	11	06	☽☍♆	3 32
25	12	39	☽☍☿	2 59
26	12	47	☽☍♅	3 30
27	09	17	☽☍☉	4 29
28	03	17	☽☍♀	3 19

MARCH

2	20	16	☽☍♂	4 00
5	13	19	☽☍♄	0 16
6	05	36	☽☌♇	9 23
7	15	36	☽☍♃	0 56
9	09	52	☿☌♅	1 06
10	10	38	☽☌♆	3 36
11	19	28	☽☌♅	3 32
12	03	26	☽☌☿	2 24
14	02	02	☽☌☉	4 34
15	10	02	☽☌♀	3 22
18	03	12	☽☌♂	3 30
20	09	40	☽•♄	0 26
21	01	05	☽☍♇	9 37
22	11	37	☽•♃	1 08
24	22	37	☽☍♆	3 45
26	01	57	☽☍♅	3 38
28	01	31	☽☍☿	2 43
28	18	25	☽☍☉	4 25
30	00	57	☽☍♀	3 11
31	15	39	☽☍♂	2 57

APRIL

2	00	58	☽☍♄	0 34
2	13	27	☽☌♇	9 46
4	01	41	☽☍♃	1 19
6	18	04	☽☌♆	3 50
7	08	55	☉☌☿	0 50
8	04	09	☽☌♅	3 43
12	19	21	☽☌☉	3 56
13	09	52	☽☌☿	3 42
14	18	46	☽☌♀	2 40
15	23	56	☽☌♂	2 12
16	19	56	☽•♄	0 46
17	06	23	☽☍♇	9 55
18	22	54	☽☌♃	1 35
21	07	13	☽☍♆	3 58
22	12	30	☽☍♅	3 50
27	03	00	☽☍☉	3 15
28	13	19	☽☍☿	4 09
28	23	50	☽☍♀	1 56
29	11	15	☽☍♂	1 29
29	15	50	☽☍♄	0 54
29	22	30	☽☌♇	9 59

MAY

1	17	05	☽☍♃	1 47
4	01	58	☽☌♆	4 03
4	05	58	♂☌♄	2 11
5	12	46	☽☌♅	3 54
7	12	11	♀☌♄	2 22
8	22	12	♂☍♇	10 58
9	18	15	♀☍♇	11 14
10	19	56	♀☌♂	0 18
12	10	45	☽☌☉	2 15
13	21	50	☽☌☿	2 25
14	07	47	☽•♄	1 04
14	11	08	☽☍♇	10 01
14	18	41	☽•♂	0 38
14	23	04	☽•♀	0 51
16	12	26	☽☌♃	2 02
18	13	11	☽☍♆	4 07
19	19	53	☽☍♅	3 57
26	02	33	♄☍♇	8 48
26	11	51	☽☍☉	1 09
26	13	51	☽☍☿	0 31
27	07	09	☉☌☿	1 46
27	07	29	☽☌♇	9 59
27	07	48	☽☍♄	1 12
28	06	39	☽☍♂	0 08
29	00	59	☽☍♀	0 14
29	11	46	☽☍♃	2 14
31	10	18	☽☌♆	4 08

JUNE

1	21	19	☽☌♅	3 59
3	23	12	♀☌♃	1 37
7	04	43	☉☍♇	10 05
9	11	24	☉☌♄	1 17
9	13	07	☽☌☿	2 33
10	16	53	☽☍♇	9 55
10	21	26	☽☌♄	1 21
10	23	46	☽•●	0 11
12	12	00	☽•♂	0 57
13	04	28	☽☌♃	2 27
13	21	44	☽☌♀	1 27
14	18	17	☽☍♆	4 07
16	01	17	☽☍♅	3 58
23	03	20	☽☍☿	2 23
23	15	06	☽☌♇	9 51
23	21	21	♀☍♆	1 56
23	22	57	☽☍♄	1 30
24	21	42	☽☍☉	1 24
26	01	40	☽☍♂	1 36
26	07	37	☽☍♃	2 38
27	18	18	☽☌♆	4 06
28	03	52	☽☍♀	2 27
28	15	37	☿☍♇	7 47
29	05	12	☽☌♅	3 56

JULY

2	11	34	☿☌♄	0 13
3	13	24	♂☌♃	0 48
8	00	09	☽☍♇	9 47
8	12	24	☽☌♄	1 40
9	09	14	☽☌☿	1 31
9	09	38	♀☍♅	0 43
10	10	26	☽☌☉	2 37
10	22	48	☽☌♃	2 49
11	04	25	☽☌♂	2 14
12	00	22	☽☍♆	4 03
13	06	42	☽☍♅	3 52
13	14	49	☽☌♀	3 25
20	01	19	☉☌♃	0 18
20	16	24	☿☌♃	1 13
20	20	57	☽☌♇	9 44
21	01	47	☉☌☿	1 33
21	12	05	☽☍♄	1 50
24	03	05	☽☍♃	2 59
24	09	07	☽☍☉	3 29
24	17	39	☽☍☿	2 02
24	20	12	☽☍♂	2 43
25	01	10	☽☌♆	4 00
25	15	20	☿☌♂	0 37
26	11	46	☽☌♅	3 49
26	15	40	☿☍♆	1 48
28	06	03	☽☍♀	4 15
28	18	32	♂☍♆	1 10

AUGUST

2	00	57	☉☍♆	0 04
4	08	26	☽☍♇	9 43
4	22	59	☿☍♅	0 35
5	03	28	☽☌♄	2 03
7	18	43	☽☌♃	3 10
8	08	14	☽☍♆	3 59
8	19	15	☽☌☉	4 11
8	20	26	☽☌♂	3 07
9	13	36	☽☍♅	3 46
10	04	23	☽☌☿	3 48
10	22	17	☉☌♂	1 05
12	02	34	☽☌♀	5 05
17	01	54	☽☌♇	9 42
17	22	53	☽☍♄	2 15
20	00	54	☉☍♅	0 44
20	21	13	☽☍♃	3 20
21	06	36	☽☌♆	3 59
22	14	28	☽☍♂	3 22
22	16	49	☽☌♅	3 44
22	22	29	☽☍☉	4 31
24	09	29	♂☍♅	0 21
25	06	57	☽☍☿	5 36
27	02	18	☽☍♀	5 56
31	16	47	☽☍♇	9 45

SEPTEMBER

1	16	55	☽☌♄	2 29
4	14	52	☽☌♃	3 31
4	17	23	☽☍♆	4 02
5	22	07	☽☍♅	3 46
6	12	21	☽☌♂	3 32
7	03	10	☽☌☉	4 37
8	22	20	☽☌☿	7 11
10	06	34	☽☌♀	6 50
11	12	07	♃☍♆	0 27
13	07	50	☽☌♇	9 46
14	07	54	☽☍♄	2 40
17	11	14	☽☌♆	4 05
17	13	40	☽☍♃	3 40
18	20	54	☽☌♅	3 48
20	08	47	☽☍♂	3 35
21	13	59	☽☍☉	4 24
22	13	08	☽☍☿	7 30
25	05	04	☽☍♀	7 50
27	18	31	☉☌☿	2 23
28	00	28	☽☍♇	9 51
29	03	01	☽☌♄	2 53

OCTOBER

2	02	25	☽☍♆	4 11
2	09	23	☽☌♃	3 50
3	07	10	☽☍♅	3 53
5	04	15	☽☌♂	3 32
5	12	27	☽☌☿	4 30
6	11	18	☽☌☉	3 57
8	14	42	☽☌♀	8 40
10	16	22	☽☌♇	9 53
11	16	08	☽☍♄	3 00
14	16	31	☽☌♆	4 16
15	04	19	☽☍♃	3 57
16	01	21	☽☌♅	3 57
19	03	38	☽☍♂	3 22
19	19	55	☽☍☿	2 12
21	07	20	☽☍☉	3 12
22	13	53	☽☍♀	8 47
25	07	38	☽☍♇	9 56
26	09	01	☽☌♄	3 06
29	10	07	☽☍♆	4 22
30	00	06	☽☌♃	4 04
30	15	19	☽☍♅	4 03
31	12	06	☉☌♀	5 23

NOVEMBER

2	19	57	☽☌♂	3 07
4	07	43	☿☌♀	5 31
4	09	57	☽☌♀	7 17
4	10	19	☽☌☿	1 47
4	20	34	☽☌☉	2 14
7	03	42	☽☌♇	9 56

Note: The Distances Apart are in Declination

8	00 14	☽☍♄	3 06	25	16 35	☽☍♆	4 28	5	07 55	☽☍♄	2 58	19	19 10	☽☍☉	1 43
10	23 59	☽☌♆	4 25	26	09 31	☽☌♃	4 06	6	13 36	☿☍♄	3 26	21	09 31	☽☍☿	1 20
11	16 59	☽☍♃	4 06	26	22 09	☽☍♅	4 09	8	09 59	☽☌♆	4 28	22	23 27	☽☍♆	4 27
12	07 48	☽☌♅	4 06	30	10 50	☿☌♇	10 54	9	03 06	☽☍♃	4 03	23	14 07	☽☌♃	3 57
14	04 40	☉☌☿	0 07		DECEMBER			9	16 55	☉☌♇	9 10	24	04 58	☽☍♅	4 07
16	23 24	☽☍♂	2 45					9	17 02	☽☌♅	4 09	30	01 26	☽•♂	1 04
17	19 01	☽☍♀	4 30	1	11 07	☽☌♂	2 17	15	20 13	☽☍♂	1 43	30	07 48	☽☌♀	1 59
20	01 34	☽☍☉	1 00	1	14 38	☽☌♀	1 48	15	22 13	☽☍♀	0 20				
20	09 14	☽☍☿	1 26	4	07 34	☽•●	0 18	17	17 28	☉☍♄	1 19				
21	15 16	☽☍♇	9 57	4	16 18	☽☌♇	9 58	19	00 18	☽☍♇	10 00				
22	12 07	☽☌♄	3 03	5	04 10	☽•☿	0 36	19	14 53	☽☌♄	2 50				

PHENOMENA IN 2002

d	h	JANUARY
2	07	☽ in Perigee
2	15	⊕ in perihelion
5	21	☽ Zero Dec.
12	00	☿ Gt.Elong. 19 ° E.
12	15	☽ Max. Dec.24°S14′
14	20	☿ ☊
18	09	☽ in Apogee
19	12	☿ in perihelion
20	02	☽ Zero Dec.
25	12	♀ in aphelion
27	02	☽ Max. Dec.24°N16′
30	09	☽ in Perigee
		FEBRUARY
2	04	☽ Zero Dec.
8	21	☽ Max. Dec.24°S18′
10	13	♂ ☊
14	22	☽ in Apogee
16	08	☽ Zero Dec.
21	16	☿ Gt.Elong. 27 ° W.
22	04	☿ ☋
23	12	☽ Max. Dec.24°N25′
27	20	☽ in Perigee
		MARCH
1	12	☽ Zero Dec.
4	12	☿ in aphelion
8	02	☽ Max. Dec.24°S31′
14	01	☽ in Apogee
15	14	☽ Zero Dec.
20	19	☉ enters ♈,Equinox
22	20	☽ Max. Dec.24°N40′
28	08	☽ in Perigee
28	23	☽ Zero Dec.
		APRIL
4	08	☽ Max. Dec.24°S46′
10	06	☽ in Apogee
11	20	☽ Zero Dec.
12	20	☿ ☊
13	23	♀ ☊
17	12	☿ in perihelion
19	02	☽ Max. Dec.24°N55′
25	10	☽ Zero Dec.
25	16	☽ in Perigee

d	h	MAY
1	17	☽ Max. Dec.24°S59′
4	04	☿ Gt.Elong. 21 ° E.
7	19	☽ in Apogee
9	03	☽ Zero Dec.
16	08	☽ Max. Dec.25°N02′
17	19	♀ in perihelion
21	03	☿ ☋
22	19	☽ Zero Dec.
23	16	☽ in Perigee
29	03	☽ Max. Dec.25°S03′
31	11	☿ in aphelion
		JUNE
4	13	☽ in Apogee
5	11	☽ Zero Dec.
11	00	☽ Annular eclipse
12	14	☽ Max. Dec.25°N03′
19	01	☽ Zero Dec.
19	07	☽ in Perigee
21	13	☉ enters ♋,Solstice
21	14	☿ Gt.Elong. 23 ° W.
25	12	☽ Max. Dec.25°S03′
		JULY
2	08	☽ in Apogee
2	18	☽ Zero Dec.
6	04	⊕ in aphelion
9	19	☿ ☊
9	22	☽ Max. Dec.25°N03′
14	11	☿ in perihelion
14	13	☽ in Perigee
16	06	☽ Zero Dec.
22	19	☽ Max. Dec.25°S03′
30	02	☽ in Apogee
30	02	☽ Zero Dec.
		AUGUST
3	13	♀ ☋
6	07	☽ Max. Dec.25°N06′
11	00	☽ in Perigee
12	12	☽ Zero Dec.
17	02	☿ ☋
19	01	☽ Max. Dec.25°S10′
22	13	♀ Gt.Elong. 46 ° E.
26	08	☽ Zero Dec.
26	18	☽ in Apogee
27	10	☿ in aphelion

d	h	SEPTEMBER
1	10	☿ Gt.Elong. 27 ° E.
2	16	☽ Max. Dec.25°N17′
7	04	♀ in aphelion
8	03	☽ in Perigee
8	20	☽ Zero Dec.
15	06	☽ Max. Dec.25°S23′
21	01	♂ in aphelion
22	14	☽ Zero Dec.
23	03	☽ in Apogee
23	05	☉ enters ♎,Equinox
30	00	☽ Max. Dec.25°N32′
		OCTOBER
5	18	☿ ☊
6	07	☽ Zero Dec.
6	13	☽ in Perigee
10	10	☿ in perihelion
12	12	☽ Max. Dec.25°S37′
13	07	☿ Gt.Elong. 18 ° W.
19	20	☽ Zero Dec.
20	05	☽ in Apogee
27	07	☽ Max. Dec.25°N44′
		NOVEMBER
2	18	☽ Zero Dec.
4	01	☽ in Perigee
8	21	☽ Max. Dec.25°S47′
13	01	☿ ☋
16	03	☽ Zero Dec.
16	11	☽ in Apogee
23	10	☿ in aphelion
23	12	☽ Max. Dec.25°N49′
24	16	♀ ☊
30	03	☽ Zero Dec.
		DECEMBER
2	09	☽ in Perigee
4	08	☽ Total eclipse
6	07	☽ Max. Dec.25°S49′
13	10	☽ Zero Dec.
14	04	☽ in Apogee
20	18	☽ Max. Dec.25°N47′
22	01	☉ enters ♑,Solstice
26	05	☿ Gt.Elong. 20 ° E.
27	09	☽ Zero Dec.
28	12	♀ in perihelion
30	01	☽ in Perigee

LOCAL MEAN TIME OF SUNRISE FOR LATITUDES
60° North to 50° South
FOR ALL SUNDAYS IN 2002 (ALL TIMES ARE A.M.)

Date	Northern Latitudes								Southern Latitudes					
	LONDON	60°	55°	50°	40°	30°	20°	10°	0°	10°	20°	30°	40°	50°
2001	H M	H M	H M	H M	H M	H M	H M	H M	H M	H M	H M	H M	H M	H M
Dec. 30	8 5	9 4	8 25	7 59	7 22	6 55	6 34	6 16	5 59	5 41	5 22	5 1	4 33	3 53
2002														
Jan. 6	8 5	9 0	8 24	7 58	7 22	6 57	6 36	6 19	6 2	5 45	5 27	5 6	4 39	4 0
,, 13	8 1	8 51	8 18	7 54	7 21	6 57	6 38	6 21	6 5	5 49	5 32	5 12	4 46	4 10
,, 20	7 54	8 40	8 10	7 49	7 18	6 56	6 38	6 22	6 8	5 52	5 37	5 18	4 54	4 21
,, 27	7 45	8 26	8 0	7 41	7 13	6 53	6 37	6 23	6 9	5 55	5 41	5 24	5 2	4 32
Feb. 3	7 35	8 10	7 48	7 31	7 7	6 49	6 35	6 22	6 10	5 58	5 45	5 30	5 11	4 44
,, 10	7 23	7 52	7 34	7 20	6 59	6 44	6 32	6 21	6 11	6 1	5 49	5 36	5 20	4 57
,, 17	7 11	7 33	7 19	7 7	6 50	6 38	6 28	6 19	6 11	6 2	5 53	5 42	5 28	5 9
,, 24	6 57	7 13	7 3	6 54	6 41	6 32	6 24	6 17	6 10	6 3	5 56	5 47	5 36	5 21
Mar. 3	6 41	6 53	6 46	6 40	6 31	6 24	6 19	6 14	6 9	6 4	5 58	5 52	5 44	5 33
,, 10	6 26	6 33	6 28	6 25	6 20	6 16	6 13	6 10	6 7	6 4	6 1	5 57	5 52	5 45
,, 17	6 10	6 12	6 11	6 10	6 9	6 8	6 7	6 6	6 5	6 4	6 3	6 1	5 59	5 56
,, 24	5 54	5 50	5 53	5 55	5 58	5 59	6 1	6 2	6 3	6 4	6 5	6 5	6 6	6 7
,, 31	5 38	5 29	5 35	5 40	5 46	5 51	5 55	5 58	6 1	6 4	6 7	6 9	6 13	6 18
Apr. 7	5 22	5 8	5 17	5 25	5 35	5 43	5 49	5 54	5 59	6 3	6 8	6 14	6 20	6 30
,, 14	5 7	4 47	5 0	5 10	5 24	5 35	5 43	5 50	5 57	6 3	6 10	6 18	6 27	6 40
,, 21	4 53	4 27	4 43	4 56	5 14	5 27	5 38	5 47	5 55	6 3	6 12	6 22	6 34	6 50
,, 28	4 39	4 7	4 27	4 42	5 4	5 20	5 33	5 44	5 54	6 4	6 15	6 27	6 42	7 1
May 5	4 26	3 48	4 12	4 30	4 56	5 14	5 29	5 42	5 53	6 5	6 17	6 31	6 49	7 11
,, 12	4 14	3 30	3 58	4 19	4 48	5 9	5 25	5 40	5 53	6 6	6 20	6 35	6 56	7 22
,, 19	4 3	3 14	3 46	4 9	4 42	5 4	5 23	5 38	5 53	6 7	6 22	6 40	7 2	7 31
,, 26	3 55	3 0	3 36	4 1	4 36	5 1	5 21	5 38	5 53	6 9	6 25	6 44	7 8	7 40
June 2	3 48	2 48	3 28	3 55	4 33	4 59	5 20	5 38	5 54	6 11	6 28	6 48	7 13	7 48
,, 9	3 43	2 40	3 23	3 51	4 31	4 58	5 20	5 38	5 55	6 12	6 30	6 51	7 17	7 53
,, 16	3 42	2 36	3 20	3 50	4 31	4 58	5 20	5 39	5 57	6 14	6 32	6 53	7 20	7 57
,, 23	3 43	2 36	3 21	3 51	4 31	5 0	5 22	5 41	5 58	6 16	6 34	6 55	7 22	8 0
,, 30	3 46	2 41	3 24	3 54	4 34	5 2	5 24	5 43	6 0	6 17	6 35	6 56	7 23	8 0
July 7	3 52	2 49	3 31	3 59	4 38	5 5	5 26	5 44	6 1	6 18	6 35	6 56	7 21	7 57
,, 14	3 59	3 1	3 39	4 6	4 43	5 8	5 29	5 46	6 2	6 18	6 35	6 54	7 18	7 53
,, 21	4 8	3 15	3 50	4 14	4 48	5 12	5 31	5 48	6 3	6 18	6 34	6 52	7 14	7 46
,, 28	4 18	3 31	4 2	4 23	4 54	5 16	5 34	5 49	6 3	6 17	6 31	6 48	7 9	7 37
Aug. 4	4 29	3 47	4 14	4 33	5 1	5 20	5 36	5 50	6 3	6 15	6 28	6 43	7 2	7 27
,, 11	4 39	4 4	4 26	4 43	5 7	5 25	5 39	5 51	6 2	6 13	6 24	6 38	6 54	7 16
,, 18	4 50	4 21	4 39	4 54	5 14	5 29	5 41	5 51	6 1	6 10	6 20	6 31	6 45	7 4
,, 25	5 1	4 37	4 53	5 4	5 21	5 33	5 43	5 51	5 59	6 6	6 15	6 24	6 35	6 50
Sept. 1	5 12	4 54	5 6	5 14	5 27	5 37	5 44	5 51	5 57	6 2	6 9	6 15	6 24	6 35
,, 8	5 24	5 11	5 19	5 25	5 34	5 41	5 46	5 50	5 54	5 58	6 2	6 7	6 12	6 20
,, 15	5 35	5 27	5 32	5 35	5 41	5 44	5 47	5 50	5 52	5 54	5 56	5 59	6 1	6 6
,, 22	5 46	5 43	5 45	5 46	5 47	5 48	5 49	5 49	5 50	5 49	5 49	5 50	5 49	5 50
,, 29	5 57	6 0	5 58	5 56	5 54	5 52	5 50	5 49	5 47	5 45	5 43	5 42	5 38	5 34
Oct. 6	6 8	6 17	6 11	6 7	6 1	5 56	5 52	5 48	5 45	5 41	5 37	5 34	5 27	5 19
,, 13	6 19	6 34	6 25	6 18	6 8	6 0	5 54	5 48	5 43	5 37	5 31	5 25	5 16	5 4
,, 20	6 32	6 51	6 39	6 30	6 15	6 5	5 56	5 49	5 42	5 34	5 26	5 17	5 6	4 50
,, 27	6 44	7 9	6 53	6 41	6 23	6 10	5 59	5 50	5 41	5 32	5 22	5 10	4 56	4 36
Nov. 3	6 56	7 27	7 7	6 53	6 31	6 15	6 2	5 51	5 40	5 30	5 18	5 4	4 47	4 23
,, 10	7 8	7 45	7 22	7 4	6 39	6 21	6 6	5 53	5 40	5 29	5 15	4 59	4 40	4 13
,, 17	7 20	8 3	7 36	7 16	6 47	6 27	6 10	5 55	5 41	5 28	5 13	4 55	4 34	4 3
,, 24	7 32	8 19	7 49	7 27	6 55	6 32	6 14	5 58	5 43	5 28	5 11	4 53	4 29	3 55
Dec. 1	7 43	8 35	8 1	7 37	7 2	6 38	6 19	6 1	5 45	5 29	5 12	4 52	4 26	3 50
,, 8	7 52	8 47	8 11	7 45	7 9	6 43	6 23	6 5	5 48	5 31	5 13	4 51	4 24	3 46
,, 15	7 59	8 57	8 19	7 52	7 15	6 48	6 27	6 9	5 51	5 34	5 15	4 53	4 25	3 45
,, 22	8 3	9 2	8 23	7 56	7 18	6 52	6 30	6 12	5 54	5 37	5 18	4 56	4 28	3 47
,, 29	8 5	9 4	8 25	7 59	7 21	6 55	6 34	6 16	5 58	5 41	5 22	5 1	4 33	3 52
2003														
Jan. 5	8 5	9 1	8 24	7 58	7 22	6 57	6 36	6 19	6 2	5 45	5 27	5 6	4 39	3 59

Example:—To find the time of Sunrise in Jamaica (Latitude 18° N.) on Wednesday June 19th, 2002. On June 16th, L.M.T. = 5h. 20m + $\frac{2}{10}$ × 19m. = 5h. 24m., on June 23rd, L.M.T. = 5h. 22m. + $\frac{2}{10}$ × 19m. = 5h. 26m., therefore L.M.T. on June 19th = 5h. 24m. + $\frac{3}{7}$ × 2m. = 5h. 25m. A.M.

LOCAL MEAN TIME OF SUNSET FOR LATITUDES
60° North to 50° South
FOR ALL SUNDAYS IN 2002 (ALL TIMES ARE P.M.)

Date	Northern Latitudes									Southern Latitudes				
	LON-DON	60°	55°	50°	40°	30°	20°	10°	0°	10°	20°	30°	40°	50°
	H M	H M	H M	H M	H M	H M	H M	H M	H M	H M	H M	H M	H M	H M
2001 Dec. 30	4 0	3 2	3 40	4 6	4 43	5 10	5 31	5 49	6 6	6 23	6 42	7 4	7 32	8 12
2002 Jan. 6	4 7	3 12	3 48	4 14	4 49	5 15	5 35	5 53	6 10	6 26	6 44	7 5	7 32	8 11
„ 13	4 17	3 27	4 0	4 24	4 57	5 21	5 40	5 57	6 13	6 29	6 46	7 6	7 31	8 7
„ 20	4 28	3 43	4 13	4 34	5 5	5 27	5 45	6 0	6 15	6 30	6 46	7 4	7 27	8 0
„ 27	4 40	4 1	4 27	4 46	5 13	5 33	5 49	6 3	6 16	6 29	6 44	7 1	7 22	7 52
Feb. 3	4 53	4 19	4 41	4 57	5 21	5 39	5 53	6 6	6 17	6 29	6 42	6 57	7 16	7 42
„ 10	5 6	4 38	4 56	5 9	5 30	5 45	5 57	6 8	6 18	6 28	6 39	6 52	7 8	7 31
„ 17	5 19	4 56	5 10	5 22	5 38	5 50	6 0	6 9	6 18	6 26	6 35	6 46	7 0	7 18
„ 24	5 31	5 14	5 25	5 33	5 46	5 55	6 3	6 10	6 17	6 23	6 30	6 39	6 50	7 4
Mar. 3	5 44	5 32	5 39	5 45	5 54	6 0	6 6	6 11	6 15	6 20	6 25	6 31	6 39	6 49
„ 10	5 56	5 49	5 53	5 57	6 1	6 5	6 8	6 11	6 14	6 17	6 20	6 24	6 28	6 35
„ 17	6 8	6 7	6 7	6 8	6 9	6 10	6 10	6 11	6 12	6 13	6 14	6 16	6 17	6 20
„ 24	6 19	6 24	6 21	6 19	6 16	6 14	6 12	6 11	6 10	6 9	6 8	6 7	6 6	6 5
„ 31	6 31	6 41	6 35	6 30	6 23	6 18	6 14	6 11	6 8	6 4	6 2	5 58	5 54	5 49
Apr. 7	6 43	6 58	6 48	6 41	6 30	6 22	6 16	6 11	6 6	6 1	5 56	5 50	5 43	5 34
„ 14	6 55	7 15	7 2	6 52	6 37	6 26	6 18	6 11	6 4	5 57	5 50	5 42	5 33	5 20
„ 21	7 6	7 32	7 16	7 3	6 44	6 31	6 20	6 11	6 2	5 53	5 45	5 34	5 23	5 6
„ 28	7 17	7 50	7 29	7 14	6 51	6 35	6 22	6 11	6 1	5 51	5 40	5 28	5 13	4 53
May 5	7 29	8 7	7 43	7 24	6 58	6 40	6 25	6 12	6 0	5 48	5 36	5 22	5 4	4 42
„ 12	7 40	8 24	7 56	7 35	7 5	6 44	6 28	6 13	6 0	5 47	5 33	5 17	4 57	4 31
„ 19	7 51	8 41	8 8	7 45	7 12	6 49	6 30	6 15	6 0	5 46	5 31	5 13	4 51	4 21
„ 26	8 0	8 56	8 19	7 53	7 18	6 53	6 33	6 16	6 1	5 45	5 29	5 10	4 46	4 13
June 2	8 8	9 9	8 29	8 1	7 23	6 57	6 36	6 18	6 2	5 45	5 28	5 8	4 43	4 8
„ 9	8 15	9 19	8 36	8 7	7 28	7 0	6 39	6 20	6 3	5 46	5 27	5 7	4 41	4 4
„ 16	8 19	9 26	8 41	8 11	7 31	7 3	6 41	6 22	6 4	5 47	5 28	5 7	4 40	4 3
„ 23	8 21	9 28	8 43	8 13	7 33	7 4	6 42	6 23	6 6	5 48	5 30	5 9	4 42	4 4
„ 30	8 21	9 26	8 42	8 13	7 33	7 5	6 43	6 25	6 7	5 50	5 32	5 11	4 45	4 8
July 7	8 17	9 19	8 38	8 10	7 31	7 5	6 44	6 25	6 8	5 51	5 34	5 14	4 49	4 12
„ 14	8 12	9 9	8 31	8 5	7 29	7 3	6 43	6 26	6 9	5 53	5 36	5 17	4 53	4 18
„ 21	8 4	8 56	8 22	7 58	7 24	7 0	6 41	6 25	6 10	5 55	5 39	5 21	4 58	4 27
„ 28	7 55	8 41	8 11	7 49	7 18	6 56	6 39	6 24	6 10	5 56	5 42	5 25	5 4	4 36
Aug. 4	7 43	8 24	7 57	7 38	7 11	6 51	6 36	6 22	6 10	5 57	5 44	5 29	5 10	4 45
„ 11	7 30	8 5	7 43	7 26	7 2	6 45	6 32	6 20	6 9	5 57	5 46	5 33	5 17	4 55
„ 18	7 17	7 45	7 27	7 13	6 53	6 38	6 27	6 17	6 7	5 58	5 48	5 37	5 23	5 5
„ 25	7 2	7 25	7 10	6 59	6 43	6 31	6 21	6 13	6 5	5 58	5 50	5 41	5 29	5 15
Sept. 1	6 47	7 4	6 53	6 45	6 32	6 23	6 15	6 9	6 3	5 57	5 51	5 45	5 36	5 25
„ 8	6 31	6 43	6 36	6 30	6 21	6 14	6 9	6 5	6 1	5 57	5 53	5 48	5 43	5 36
„ 15	6 15	6 22	6 18	6 14	6 9	6 6	6 3	6 1	5 58	5 57	5 55	5 52	5 50	5 46
„ 22	5 59	6 1	6 0	5 59	5 58	5 57	5 57	5 56	5 56	5 56	5 56	5 56	5 57	5 57
„ 29	5 43	5 39	5 42	5 43	5 46	5 48	5 50	5 52	5 54	5 56	5 58	6 0	6 4	6 8
Oct. 6	5 28	5 18	5 24	5 28	5 35	5 40	5 44	5 48	5 52	5 56	6 0	6 4	6 10	6 19
„ 13	5 12	4 58	5 7	5 14	5 24	5 32	5 38	5 44	5 50	5 56	6 2	6 8	6 17	6 30
„ 20	4 57	4 38	4 50	4 59	5 14	5 24	5 33	5 41	5 48	5 56	6 4	6 13	6 24	6 41
„ 27	4 43	4 18	4 34	4 46	5 4	5 18	5 29	5 38	5 47	5 57	6 7	6 19	6 32	6 53
Nov. 3	4 30	4 0	4 19	4 34	4 56	5 12	5 25	5 36	5 47	5 58	6 10	6 24	6 40	7 5
„ 10	4 19	3 42	4 6	4 23	4 48	5 7	5 22	5 35	5 48	6 0	6 14	6 30	6 49	7 17
„ 17	4 8	3 27	3 54	4 14	4 42	5 3	5 20	5 35	5 49	6 3	6 18	6 36	6 57	7 28
„ 24	4 0	3 14	3 44	4 6	4 38	5 1	5 19	5 35	5 50	6 6	6 22	6 42	7 5	7 39
Dec. 1	3 55	3 3	3 37	4 1	4 35	5 0	5 19	5 37	5 53	6 9	6 27	6 47	7 13	7 50
„ 8	3 52	2 56	3 33	3 59	4 35	5 0	5 21	5 39	5 56	6 13	6 31	6 52	7 20	7 59
„ 15	3 52	2 53	3 32	3 58	4 36	5 2	5 23	5 42	5 59	6 16	6 35	6 57	7 25	8 5
„ 22	3 53	2 54	3 33	4 0	4 38	5 4	5 25	5 45	6 2	6 20	6 39	7 1	7 29	8 10
„ 29	3 59	3 1	3 39	4 6	4 43	5 9	5 30	5 49	6 6	6 24	6 42	7 4	7 32	8 12
2003 Jan. 5	4 7	3 10	3 48	4 13	4 49	5 14	5 35	5 52	6 9	6 26	6 45	7 6	7 32	8 12

EXAMPLE:—To find the time of Sunset in Canberra (Latitude 35°.3S.) on Thursday August 1st, 2002. On July 28th, L.M.T. = 5h. 25m. − $\frac{5.3}{10}$ × 21m. = 5h. 14m., on August 4th, L.M.T. = 5h. 29m. − $\frac{5.3}{10}$ × 19m. = 5h. 19m., therefore L.M.T. on August 1st = 5h. 14m. + $\frac{4}{7}$ × 5m. = 5h. 17m. P.M.

TABLES OF HOUSES FOR LONDON, Latitude 51º 32' *N.*

Sidereal Time.	10 ♈	11 ♉	12 ♊	Ascen ♋		2 ♌	3 ♍
H. M. S.	º	º	º	º	'	º	º
0 0 0	0	9	22	26	36	12	3
0 3 40	1	10	23	27	17	13	3
0 7 20	2	11	24	27	56	14	4
0 11 0	3	12	25	28	42	15	5
0 14 41	4	13	25	29	17	15	6
0 18 21	5	14	26	29	55	16	7
0 22 2	6	15	27	0♌	34	17	8
0 25 42	7	16	28	1	14	18	8
0 29 23	8	17	29	1	55	18	9
0 33 4	9	18	♋	2	33	19	10
0 36 45	10	19	1	3	14	20	11
0 40 26	11	20	1	3	54	20	12
0 44 8	12	21	2	4	33	21	13
0 47 50	13	22	3	5	12	22	14
0 51 32	14	23	4	5	52	23	15
0 55 14	15	24	5	6	30	23	15
0 58 57	16	25	6	7	9	24	16
1 2 40	17	26	6	7	50	25	17
1 6 23	18	27	7	8	30	26	18
1 10 7	19	28	8	9	9	26	19
1 13 51	20	29	9	9	48	27	19
1 17 35	21	♊	10	10	28	28	20
1 21 20	22	1	10	11	8	28	21
1 25 6	23	2	11	11	48	29	22
1 28 52	24	3	12	12	28	♍	23
1 32 38	25	4	13	13	8	1	24
1 36 25	26	5	14	13	48	1	25
1 40 12	27	6	14	14	28	2	25
1 44 0	28	7	15	15	8	3	26
1 47 48	29	8	16	15	48	4	27
1 51 37	30	9	17	16	28	4	28

Sidereal Time.	10 ♉	11 ♊	12 ♋	Ascen ♌		2 ♍	3 ♍
H. M. S.	º	º	º	º	'	º	º
1 51 37	0	9	17	16	28	4	28
1 55 27	1	10	18	17	8	5	29
1 59 17	2	11	19	17	48	6	♎
2 3 8	3	12	19	18	28	7	1
2 6 59	4	13	20	19	9	8	2
2 10 51	5	14	21	19	49	9	2
2 14 44	6	15	22	20	29	9	3
2 18 37	7	16	22	21	10	10	4
2 22 31	8	17	23	21	51	11	5
2 26 25	9	18	24	22	32	11	6
2 30 20	10	19	25	23	14	12	7
2 34 16	11	20	25	23	55	13	8
2 38 13	12	21	26	24	36	14	9
2 42 10	13	22	27	25	17	15	10
2 46 8	14	23	28	25	58	15	11
2 50 7	15	24	29	26	40	16	12
2 54 7	16	25	29	27	22	17	12
2 58 7	17	26	♌	28	4	18	13
3 2 8	18	27	1	28	46	18	14
3 6 9	19	27	2	29	28	19	15
3 10 12	20	28	3	0♍	12	20	16
3 14 15	21	29	3	0	54	21	17
3 18 19	22	♋	4	1	36	22	18
3 22 23	23	1	5	2	20	22	19
3 26 29	24	2	6	3	2	23	20
3 30 35	25	3	7	3	45	24	21
3 34 41	26	4	7	4	28	25	22
3 38 49	27	5	8	5	11	26	23
3 42 57	28	6	9	5	54	27	24
3 47 6	29	7	10	6	38	27	25
3 51 15	30	8	11	7	21	28	25

Sidereal Time.	10 ♊	11 ♋	12 ♌	Ascen ♍		2 ♍	3 ♎
H. M. S.	º	º	º	º	'	º	º
3 51 15	0	8	11	7	21	28	25
3 55 25	1	9	12	8	5	29	26
3 59 36	2	10	12	8	49	♎	27
4 3 48	3	10	13	9	33	1	28
4 8 0	4	11	14	10	17	2	29
4 12 13	5	12	15	11	2	2	♏
4 16 26	6	13	16	11	46	3	1
4 20 40	7	14	17	12	30	4	2
4 24 55	8	15	17	13	15	5	3
4 29 10	9	16	18	14	0	6	4
4 33 26	10	17	19	14	45	7	5
4 37 42	11	18	20	15	30	8	6
4 41 59	12	19	21	16	15	8	7
4 46 16	13	20	21	17	0	9	8
4 50 34	14	21	22	17	45	10	9
4 54 52	15	22	23	18	30	11	10
4 59 10	16	23	24	19	16	12	11
5 3 29	17	24	25	20	3	13	12
5 7 49	18	25	26	20	49	14	13
5 12 9	19	25	27	21	35	14	14
5 16 29	20	26	28	22	20	15	14
5 20 49	21	27	28	23	6	16	15
5 25 9	22	28	29	23	51	17	16
5 29 30	23	29	♏	24	37	18	17
5 33 51	24	♌	1	25	23	19	18
5 38 12	25	1	2	26	9	20	19
5 42 34	26	2	3	26	55	21	20
5 46 55	27	3	4	27	41	21	21
5 51 17	28	4	4	28	27	22	22
5 55 38	29	5	5	29	13	23	23
6 0 0	30	6	6	30	0	24	24

Sidereal Time.	10 ♋	11 ♌	12 ♍	Ascen ♎		2 ♎	3 ♏
H. M. S.	º	º	º	º	'	º	º
6 0 0	0	6	6	0	0	24	24
6 4 22	1	7	7	0	47	25	25
6 8 43	2	8	8	1	33	26	26
6 13 5	3	9	9	2	19	27	27
6 17 26	4	10	10	3	5	27	28
6 21 48	5	11	10	3	51	28	29
6 26 9	6	12	11	4	37	29	♐
6 30 30	7	13	12	5	23	♏	1
6 34 51	8	14	13	6	9	1	2
6 39 11	9	15	14	6	55	2	3
6 43 31	10	16	15	7	40	2	4
6 47 51	11	16	16	8	26	3	4
6 52 11	12	17	16	9	12	4	5
6 56 31	13	18	17	9	58	5	6
7 0 50	14	19	18	10	43	6	7
7 5 8	15	20	19	11	28	7	8
7 9 26	16	21	20	12	14	8	9
7 13 44	17	22	21	12	59	8	10
7 18 1	18	23	22	13	45	9	11
7 22 18	19	24	23	14	30	10	12
7 26 34	20	25	24	15	15	11	13
7 30 50	21	26	25	16	0	12	14
7 35 5	22	27	25	16	45	13	15
7 39 20	23	28	26	17	30	13	16
7 43 34	24	29	27	18	15	14	17
7 47 47	25	♍	28	18	59	15	18
7 52 0	26	1	29	19	43	16	19
7 56 12	27	2	29	20	27	17	20
8 0 24	28	3	♎	21	11	18	20
8 4 35	29	4	1	21	56	18	21
8 8 45	30	5	2	22	40	19	22

Sidereal Time.	10 ♌	11 ♍	12 ♎	Ascen ♎		2 ♏	3 ♐
H. M. S.	º	º	º	º	'	º	º
8 8 45	0	5	2	22	40	19	22
8 12 54	1	5	3	23	24	20	23
8 17 3	2	6	3	24	7	21	24
8 21 11	3	7	4	24	50	22	25
8 25 19	4	8	5	25	34	23	26
8 29 26	5	9	6	26	18	23	27
8 33 31	6	10	7	27	1	24	28
8 37 37	7	11	8	27	44	25	29
8 41 41	8	12	8	28	26	26	♑
8 45 45	9	13	9	29	8	27	1
8 49 48	10	14	10	29	50	27	2
8 53 51	11	15	11	0♏	32	28	3
8 57 52	12	16	12	1	15	29	4
9 1 53	13	17	12	1	58	♐	4
9 5 53	14	18	13	2	39	1	5
9 9 53	15	18	14	3	21	1	6
9 13 52	16	19	15	4	3	2	7
9 17 50	17	20	16	4	44	3	8
9 21 47	18	21	16	5	26	3	9
9 25 44	19	22	17	6	7	4	10
9 29 40	20	23	18	6	48	5	11
9 33 35	21	24	18	7	29	5	12
9 37 29	22	25	19	8	9	6	13
9 41 23	23	26	20	8	50	7	14
9 45 16	24	27	21	9	31	8	15
9 49 9	25	28	22	10	11	9	16
9 53 1	26	28	23	10	51	9	17
9 56 52	27	29	23	11	32	10	18
10 0 43	28	♎	24	12	12	11	19
10 4 33	29	1	25	12	53	12	20
10 8 23	30	2	26	13	33	13	20

Sidereal Time.	10 ♍	11 ♎	12 ♎	Ascen ♏		2 ♐	3 ♑
H. M. S.	º	º	º	º	'	º	º
10 8 23	0	2	26	13	33	13	20
10 12 12	1	3	26	14	13	14	21
10 16 0	2	4	27	14	53	15	22
10 19 48	3	5	28	15	33	15	23
10 23 35	4	5	29	16	13	16	24
10 27 22	5	6	29	16	52	17	25
10 31 8	6	7	♏	17	32	18	26
10 34 54	7	8	1	18	12	19	27
10 38 40	8	9	2	18	52	20	28
10 42 25	9	10	2	19	31	20	29
10 46 9	10	11	3	20	11	21	♒
10 49 53	11	11	4	20	50	22	1
10 53 37	12	12	4	21	30	23	2
10 57 20	13	13	5	22	9	24	3
11 1 3	14	14	6	22	49	24	4
11 4 46	15	15	7	23	28	25	5
11 8 28	16	16	7	24	8	26	6
11 12 10	17	17	8	24	47	27	8
11 15 52	18	17	9	25	27	28	9
11 19 34	19	18	10	26	6	29	10
11 23 15	20	19	10	26	45	♑	11
11 26 56	21	20	11	27	25	0	12
11 30 37	22	21	12	28	5	1	13
11 34 18	23	22	13	28	44	2	14
11 37 58	24	23	13	29	24	3	15
11 41 39	25	23	14	0♐	3	4	16
11 45 19	26	24	15	0	43	5	17
11 49 0	27	25	15	1	23	6	18
11 52 40	28	26	16	2	3	6	19
11 56 20	29	27	17	2	43	7	20
12 0 0	30	27	17	3	23	8	21

TABLES OF HOUSES FOR LONDON, *Latitude* 51º 32' *N.*

Sidereal Time.	10 ♎	11 ♎	12 ♏	Ascen ♐	2 ♑	3 ♒
H. M. S.	º	º	º	º '	º	º
12 0 0	0	27	17	3 23	8	21
12 3 40	1	28	18	4 4	9	23
12 7 20	2	29	19	4 45	10	24
12 11 0	3	♏	20	5 26	11	25
12 14 41	4	1	20	6 7	12	26
12 18 21	5	1	21	6 48	13	27
12 22 2	6	2	22	7 29	14	28
12 25 42	7	3	23	8 10	15	29
12 29 23	8	4	23	8 51	16	♓
12 33 4	9	5	24	9 33	17	2
12 36 45	10	6	25	10 15	18	3
12 40 26	11	6	25	10 57	19	4
12 44 8	12	7	26	11 40	20	5
12 47 50	13	8	27	12 22	21	6
12 51 32	14	9	28	13 4	22	7
12 55 14	15	10	28	13 47	23	9
12 58 57	16	11	29	14 30	24	10
13 2 40	17	11	♐	15 14	25	11
13 6 23	18	12	1	15 59	26	12
13 10 7	19	13	1	16 44	27	13
13 13 51	20	14	2	17 29	28	15
13 17 35	21	15	3	18 14	29	16
13 21 20	22	16	4	19 0	♒	17
13 25 6	23	16	4	19 45	1	18
13 28 52	24	17	5	20 31	2	20
13 32 38	25	18	6	21 18	4	21
13 36 25	26	19	7	22 6	5	22
13 40 12	27	20	7	22 54	6	23
13 44 0	28	21	8	23 42	7	25
13 47 48	29	21	9	24 31	8	26
13 51 37	30	22	10	25 20	10	27

Sidereal Time.	10 ♏	11 ♏	12 ♐	Ascen ♐	2 ♒	3 ♓
H. M. S.	º	º	º	º '	º	º
13 51 37	0	22	10	25 20	10	27
13 55 27	1	23	11	26 10	11	28
13 59 17	2	24	11	27 2	12	♈
14 3 8	3	25	12	27 53	14	1
14 6 59	4	26	13	28 45	15	2
14 10 51	5	26	14	29 36	16	4
14 14 44	6	27	15	0♑29	18	5
14 18 37	7	28	15	1 23	19	6
14 22 31	8	29	16	2 18	20	8
14 26 25	9	♐	17	3 14	22	9
14 30 20	10	1	18	4 11	23	10
14 34 16	11	2	19	5 9	25	11
14 38 13	12	2	20	6 7	26	13
14 42 10	13	3	20	7 6	28	14
14 46 8	14	4	21	8 6	29	15
14 50 7	15	5	22	9 8	♓	17
14 54 7	16	6	23	10 11	2	18
14 58 7	17	7	24	11 15	4	19
15 2 8	18	8	25	12 20	6	21
15 6 9	19	9	26	13 27	8	22
15 10 12	20	9	27	14 35	9	23
15 14 15	21	10	27	15 43	11	24
15 18 19	22	11	28	16 52	13	26
15 22 23	23	12	29	18 3	14	27
15 26 29	24	13	♑	19 16	16	28
15 30 35	25	14	1	20 32	17	29
15 34 41	26	15	2	21 48	19	♉
15 38 49	27	16	3	23 8	21	2
15 42 57	28	17	4	24 29	22	3
15 47 6	29	18	5	25 51	24	5
15 51 15	30	18	6	27 15	26	6

Sidereal Time.	10 ♐	11 ♐	12 ♑	Ascen ♑	2 ♓	3 ♉
H. M. S.	º	º	º	º '	º	º
15 51 15	0	18	6	27 15	26	6
15 55 25	1	19	7	28 42	28	7
15 59 36	2	20	8	0♒11	♈	9
16 3 48	3	21	9	1 42	2	10
16 8 0	4	22	10	3 16	3	11
16 12 13	5	23	11	4 53	5	12
16 16 26	6	24	12	6 32	7	14
16 20 40	7	25	13	8 13	9	15
16 24 55	8	26	14	9 57	11	16
16 29 10	9	27	16	11 44	12	17
16 33 26	10	28	17	13 34	14	18
16 37 42	11	29	18	15 26	16	20
16 41 59	12	♑	19	17 20	18	21
16 46 16	13	1	20	19 18	20	22
16 50 34	14	2	21	21 22	21	23
16 54 52	15	3	22	23 29	23	25
16 59 10	16	4	24	25 36	25	26
17 3 29	17	5	25	27 46	27	27
17 7 49	18	6	26	0♓0	28	28
17 12 9	19	7	27	2 19	♉	29
17 16 29	20	8	29	4 40	2	♊
17 20 49	21	9	♒	7 2	3	1
17 25 9	22	10	1	9 26	5	2
17 29 30	23	11	3	11 54	7	3
17 33 51	24	12	4	14 24	8	5
17 38 12	25	13	5	17 0	10	6
17 42 34	26	14	7	19 33	11	7
17 46 55	27	15	8	22 6	13	8
17 51 17	28	16	10	24 40	14	9
17 55 38	29	17	11	27 20	16	10
18 0 0	30	18	13	30 0	17	11

Sidereal Time.	10 ♑	11 ♑	12 ♒	Ascen ♈	2 ♉	3 ♊
H. M. S.	º	º	º	º '	º	º
18 0 0	0	18	13	0 0	17	11
18 4 22	1	20	14	2 39	19	13
18 8 43	2	21	16	5 19	20	14
18 13 5	3	22	17	7 55	22	15
18 17 26	4	23	19	10 29	23	16
18 21 48	5	24	20	13 2	25	17
18 26 9	6	25	22	15 36	26	18
18 30 30	7	26	23	18 6	28	19
18 34 51	8	27	25	20 34	29	20
18 39 11	9	29	27	22 59	♊	21
18 43 31	10	♒	28	25 22	1	22
18 47 51	11	1	♓	27 42	2	23
18 52 11	12	2	2	29 58	4	24
18 56 31	13	3	3	2♉13	5	25
19 0 50	14	4	5	4 24	6	26
19 5 8	15	6	7	6 30	8	27
19 9 26	16	7	9	8 36	9	28
19 13 44	17	8	10	10 40	10	29
19 18 1	18	9	12	12 39	11	♋
19 22 18	19	10	14	14 35	12	1
19 26 34	20	12	16	16 28	13	2
19 30 50	21	13	18	18 17	14	3
19 35 5	22	14	19	20 3	16	4
19 39 20	23	15	21	21 48	17	5
19 43 34	24	16	23	23 29	18	6
19 47 47	25	18	25	25 9	19	7
19 52 0	26	19	27	26 45	20	8
19 56 12	27	20	28	28 18	21	9
20 0 24	28	21	♈	29 49	22	10
20 4 35	29	23	2	1♊19	23	11
20 8 45	30	24	4	2 45	24	12

Sidereal Time.	10 ♒	11 ♒	12 ♈	Ascen ♊	2 ♊	3 ♋
H. M. S.	º	º	º	º '	º	º
20 8 45	0	24	4	2 45	24	12
20 12 54	1	25	6	4 9	25	12
20 17 3	2	27	7	5 32	26	13
20 21 11	3	28	9	6 53	27	14
20 25 19	4	29	11	8 12	28	15
20 29 26	5	♓	13	9 27	29	16
20 33 31	6	2	14	10 43	♋	17
20 37 37	7	3	16	11 58	1	18
20 41 41	8	4	18	13 9	2	19
20 45 45	9	6	19	14 18	3	20
20 49 48	10	7	21	15 25	3	21
20 53 51	11	8	23	16 32	4	21
20 57 52	12	9	24	17 39	5	22
21 1 53	13	11	26	18 44	6	23
21 5 53	14	12	28	19 48	7	24
21 9 53	15	13	29	20 51	8	25
21 13 52	16	15	♉	21 53	9	26
21 17 50	17	16	2	22 53	10	27
21 21 47	18	17	4	23 52	10	28
21 25 44	19	19	5	24 51	11	28
21 29 40	20	20	7	25 48	12	29
21 33 35	21	22	8	26 44	13	♌
21 37 29	22	23	10	27 40	14	1
21 41 23	23	24	11	28 34	15	2
21 45 16	24	25	13	29 29	15	3
21 49 9	25	26	14	0♋22	16	4
21 53 1	26	28	15	1 15	17	4
21 56 52	27	29	16	2 7	18	5
22 0 43	28	♈	18	2 57	19	6
22 4 33	29	2	19	3 48	19	7
22 8 23	30	3	20	4 38	20	8

Sidereal Time.	10 ♓	11 ♈	12 ♉	Ascen ♋	2 ♋	3 ♌
H. M. S.	º	º	º	º '	º	º
22 8 23	0	3	20	4 38	20	8
22 12 12	1	4	21	5 28	21	8
22 16 0	2	6	23	6 17	22	9
22 19 48	3	7	24	7 5	23	10
22 23 35	4	8	25	7 53	23	11
22 27 22	5	9	26	8 42	24	12
22 31 8	6	10	28	9 29	25	13
22 34 54	7	12	29	10 16	26	14
22 38 40	8	13	♊	11 2	26	14
22 42 25	9	14	1	11 47	27	15
22 46 9	10	15	2	12 31	28	16
22 49 53	11	17	3	13 16	29	17
22 53 37	12	18	4	14 1	29	18
22 57 20	13	19	5	14 45	♌	19
23 1 3	14	20	6	15 28	1	19
23 4 46	15	21	7	16 11	2	20
23 8 28	16	23	8	16 54	2	21
23 12 10	17	24	9	17 37	3	22
23 15 52	18	25	10	18 20	4	23
23 19 34	19	26	11	19 3	5	24
23 23 15	20	27	12	19 45	5	24
23 26 56	21	29	13	20 26	6	25
23 30 37	22	♉	14	21 8	7	26
23 34 18	23	1	15	21 50	7	27
23 37 58	24	2	16	22 31	8	28
23 41 39	25	3	17	23 12	9	28
23 45 19	26	4	18	23 53	9	29
23 49 0	27	5	19	24 32	10	♍
23 52 40	28	6	20	25 15	11	1
23 56 20	29	8	21	25 56	12	2
24 0 0	30	9	22	26 36	13	3

TABLES OF HOUSES FOR LIVERPOOL, Latitude 53° 25' *N.*

Sidereal Time.	10 ♈	11 ♉	12 ♊	Ascen ♋	2 ♌	3 ♍
H. M. S.	°	°	°	° '	°	°
0 0 0	0	9	24	28 12	14	3
0 3 40	1	10	25	28 51	14	4
0 7 20	2	12	25	29 30	15	4
0 11 0	3	13	26	0♌ 9	16	5
0 14 41	4	14	27	0 48	17	6
0 18 21	5	15	28	1 27	17	7
0 22 2	6	16	29	2 6	18	8
0 25 42	7	17	♋	2 44	19	9
0 29 23	8	18	1	3 22	19	10
0 33 4	9	19	1	4 1	20	10
0 36 45	10	20	2	4 39	21	11
0 40 26	11	21	3	5 18	22	12
0 44 8	12	22	4	5 56	22	13
0 47 50	13	23	5	6 34	23	14
0 51 32	14	24	6	7 13	24	14
0 55 14	15	25	6	7 51	24	15
0 58 57	16	26	7	8 30	25	16
1 2 40	17	27	8	9 8	26	17
1 6 23	18	28	9	9 47	26	18
1 10 7	19	29	10	10 25	27	19
1 13 51	20	♊	11	11 4	28	19
1 17 35	21	1	11	11 43	28	20
1 21 20	22	2	12	12 21	29	21
1 25 6	23	3	13	13 0	♍	22
1 28 52	24	4	14	13 39	1	23
1 32 38	25	5	15	14 17	1	24
1 36 25	26	6	15	14 56	2	25
1 40 12	27	7	16	15 35	3	25
1 44 0	28	8	17	16 14	3	26
1 47 48	29	9	18	16 53	4	27
1 51 37	30	10	18	17 32	5	28

Sidereal Time.	10 ♉	11 ♊	12 ♋	Ascen ♌	2 ♍	3 ♍
H. M. S.	°	°	°	° '	°	°
1 51 37	0	10	18	17 32	5	28
1 55 27	1	11	19	18 11	6	29
1 59 17	2	12	20	18 51	6	♎
2 3 8	3	13	21	19 30	7	1
2 6 59	4	14	22	20 9	8	2
2 10 51	5	15	22	20 49	9	2
2 14 44	6	16	23	21 28	9	3
2 18 37	7	17	24	22 8	10	4
2 22 31	8	18	25	22 48	11	5
2 26 25	9	19	25	23 28	12	6
2 30 20	10	20	26	24 8	12	7
2 34 16	11	21	27	24 48	13	8
2 38 13	12	22	28	25 28	14	9
2 42 10	13	23	29	26 8	15	10
2 46 8	14	24	29	26 49	15	10
2 50 7	15	25	♌	27 29	16	11
2 54 7	16	26	1	28 10	17	12
2 58 7	17	27	2	28 51	18	13
3 2 8	18	28	2	29 32	19	14
3 6 9	19	29	3	0♍13	19	15
3 10 12	20	29	4	0 54	20	16
3 14 15	21	♋	5	1 36	21	17
3 18 19	22	1	5	2 17	22	18
3 22 23	23	2	6	2 59	23	19
3 26 29	24	3	7	3 41	23	20
3 30 35	25	4	8	4 23	24	21
3 34 41	26	5	9	5 5	25	22
3 38 49	27	6	10	5 47	26	22
3 42 57	28	7	10	6 29	27	23
3 47 6	29	8	11	7 12	27	24
3 51 15	30	9	12	7 55	28	25

Sidereal Time.	10 ♊	11 ♋	12 ♌	Ascen ♍	2 ♍	3 ♎
H. M. S.	°	°	°	° '	°	°
3 51 15	0	9	12	7 55	28	25
3 55 25	1	10	13	8 37	29	26
3 59 36	2	11	13	9 20	♎	27
4 3 48	3	12	14	10 3	1	28
4 8 0	4	12	15	10 46	2	29
4 12 13	5	13	16	11 30	2	♏
4 16 26	6	14	17	12 13	3	1
4 20 40	7	15	18	12 56	4	2
4 24 55	8	16	18	13 40	5	3
4 29 10	9	17	19	14 24	6	4
4 33 26	10	18	20	15 8	7	5
4 37 42	11	19	21	15 52	7	6
4 41 59	12	20	21	16 36	8	6
4 46 16	13	21	22	17 20	9	7
4 50 34	14	22	23	18 4	10	8
4 54 52	15	23	24	18 48	11	9
4 59 10	16	24	25	19 32	12	10
5 3 29	17	24	26	20 17	12	11
5 7 49	18	25	26	21 1	13	12
5 12 9	19	26	27	21 46	14	13
5 16 29	20	27	28	22 31	15	14
5 20 49	21	28	29	23 16	16	15
5 25 9	22	29	♍	24 0	17	16
5 29 30	23	♌	1	24 45	18	17
5 33 51	24	1	1	25 30	18	18
5 38 12	25	2	2	26 15	19	19
5 42 34	26	3	3	27 0	20	20
5 46 55	27	4	4	27 45	21	21
5 51 17	28	5	5	28 30	22	21
5 55 38	29	6	6	29 15	23	22
6 0 0	30	7	7	30 0	23	23

Sidereal Time.	10 ♋	11 ♌	12 ♍	Ascen ♎	2 ♎	3 ♏
H. M. S.	°	°	°	° '	°	°
6 0 0	0	7	7	0 0	23	23
6 4 22	1	8	7	0 45	24	24
6 8 43	2	9	8	1 30	25	25
6 13 5	3	9	9	2 15	26	26
6 17 26	4	10	10	3 0	27	27
6 21 48	5	11	11	3 45	28	28
6 26 9	6	12	12	4 30	29	29
6 30 30	7	13	12	5 15	29	♐
6 34 51	8	14	13	6 0	♏	1
6 39 11	9	15	14	6 44	1	2
6 43 31	10	16	15	7 29	2	3
6 47 51	11	17	16	8 14	3	4
6 52 11	12	18	17	8 59	4	5
6 56 31	13	19	18	9 43	4	6
7 0 50	14	20	18	10 27	5	6
7 5 8	15	21	19	11 11	6	7
7 9 26	16	22	20	11 56	7	8
7 13 44	17	23	21	12 40	8	9
7 18 1	18	24	22	13 24	8	10
7 22 18	19	24	23	14 8	9	11
7 26 34	20	25	23	14 52	10	12
7 30 50	21	26	24	15 36	11	13
7 35 5	22	27	25	16 20	12	14
7 39 20	23	28	26	17 4	13	15
7 43 34	24	29	27	17 47	13	16
7 47 47	25	♍	28	18 30	14	17
7 52 0	26	1	28	19 13	15	18
7 56 12	27	2	29	19 57	16	18
8 0 24	28	3	♎	20 40	17	19
8 4 35	29	4	1	21 23	17	20
8 8 45	30	5	2	22 5	18	21

Sidereal Time.	10 ♌	11 ♍	12 ♎	Ascen ♎	2 ♏	3 ♐
H. M. S.	°	°	°	° '	°	°
8 8 45	0	5	2	22 5	18	21
8 12 54	1	6	2	22 48	19	22
8 17 3	2	7	3	23 30	20	23
8 21 11	3	8	4	24 13	20	24
8 25 19	4	8	5	24 55	21	25
8 29 26	5	9	6	25 37	22	26
8 33 31	6	10	7	26 19	23	27
8 37 37	7	11	7	27 1	24	28
8 41 41	8	12	8	27 43	25	29
8 45 45	9	13	9	28 24	25	♑
8 49 48	10	14	10	29 6	26	1
8 53 51	11	15	11	29 47	27	1
8 57 52	12	16	11	0♏28	28	2
9 1 53	13	17	12	1 9	28	3
9 5 53	14	18	13	1 50	29	4
9 9 53	15	19	14	2 31	♐	5
9 13 52	16	19	15	3 11	1	6
9 17 50	17	20	15	3 52	1	7
9 21 47	18	21	16	4 32	2	8
9 25 44	19	22	17	5 12	3	9
9 29 40	20	23	18	5 52	4	10
9 33 35	21	24	18	6 32	5	11
9 37 29	22	25	19	7 12	5	12
9 41 23	23	26	20	7 52	6	13
9 45 16	24	27	21	8 32	7	14
9 49 9	25	27	21	9 12	8	15
9 53 1	26	28	22	9 51	8	16
9 56 52	27	29	23	10 30	9	17
10 0 43	28	♎	24	11 9	10	17
10 4 33	29	1	24	11 49	11	18
10 8 23	30	2	25	12 28	11	19

Sidereal Time.	10 ♍	11 ♎	12 ♎	Ascen ♏	2 ♐	3 ♑
H. M. S.	°	°	°	° '	°	°
10 8 23	0	2	25	12 28	11	19
10 12 12	1	3	26	13 6	12	20
10 16 0	2	4	27	13 45	13	21
10 19 48	3	4	27	14 25	14	22
10 23 35	4	5	28	15 4	15	23
10 27 22	5	6	29	15 42	15	24
10 31 8	6	7	29	16 21	16	25
10 34 54	7	8	♏	17 0	17	26
10 38 40	8	9	1	17 39	18	27
10 42 25	9	10	2	18 17	18	28
10 46 9	10	10	2	18 55	19	29
10 49 53	11	11	3	19 34	20	♒
10 53 37	12	12	4	20 13	21	1
10 57 20	13	13	4	20 52	22	2
11 1 3	14	14	5	21 30	22	3
11 4 46	15	15	6	22 8	23	5
11 8 28	16	16	7	22 46	24	6
11 12 10	17	16	7	23 25	25	7
11 15 52	18	17	8	24 4	26	8
11 19 34	19	18	9	24 42	26	9
11 23 15	20	19	9	25 21	27	10
11 26 56	21	20	10	25 59	28	11
11 30 37	22	20	11	26 38	29	12
11 34 18	23	21	12	27 16	♑	13
11 37 58	24	22	12	27 54	1	14
11 41 39	25	23	13	28 33	1	15
11 45 19	26	24	14	29 11	2	16
11 49 0	27	25	14	29 50	3	17
11 52 40	28	26	15	0♐30	4	18
11 56 20	29	26	16	1 9	5	20
12 0 0	30	27	16	1 48	6	21

TABLES OF HOUSES FOR LIVERPOOL, Latitude 53º 25' *N.*

Sidereal Time.	10 ♎	11 ♎	12 ♏	Ascen ♐	2 ♑	3 ♒
H. M. S.	º	º	º	º '	º	º
12 0 0	0	27	16	1 48	6	21
12 3 40	1	28	17	2 27	7	22
12 7 20	2	29	18	3 6	8	23
12 11 0	3	♏	18	3 46	9	24
12 14 41	4	0	19	4 25	10	25
12 18 21	5	1	20	5 6	10	26
12 22 2	6	2	21	5 46	11	28
12 25 42	7	3	21	6 26	12	29
12 29 23	8	4	22	7 6	13	♓
12 33 4	9	4	23	7 46	14	1
12 36 45	10	5	24	8 27	15	2
12 40 26	11	6	24	9 8	16	3
12 44 8	12	7	25	9 49	17	5
12 47 50	13	8	26	10 30	18	6
12 51 32	14	9	26	11 12	19	7
12 55 14	15	9	27	11 54	20	8
12 58 57	16	10	28	12 36	21	10
13 2 40	17	11	28	13 19	22	11
13 6 23	18	12	29	14 2	23	12
13 10 7	19	13	♐	14 45	25	13
13 13 51	20	13	1	15 28	26	15
13 17 35	21	14	1	16 12	27	16
13 21 20	22	15	2	16 56	28	17
13 25 6	23	16	3	17 41	29	18
13 28 52	24	17	4	18 26	♒	19
13 32 38	25	17	4	19 11	1	21
13 36 25	26	18	5	19 57	3	22
13 40 12	27	19	6	20 44	4	23
13 44 0	28	20	7	21 31	5	24
13 47 48	29	21	7	22 18	7	26
13 51 37	30	21	8	23 6	8	27

Sidereal Time.	10 ♏	11 ♏	12 ♐	Ascen ♐	2 ♒	3 ♓
H. M. S.	º	º	º	º '	º	º
13 51 37	0	21	8	23 6	8	27
13 55 27	1	22	9	23 55	9	28
13 59 17	2	23	10	24 43	10	♈
14 3 8	3	24	10	25 33	12	1
14 6 59	4	25	11	26 23	13	2
14 10 51	5	26	12	27 14	15	4
14 14 44	6	26	13	28 6	16	5
14 18 37	7	27	13	28 59	18	6
14 22 31	8	28	14	29 52	19	8
14 26 25	9	29	15	0♑46	20	9
14 30 20	10	♐	16	1 41	22	10
14 34 16	11	1	17	2 36	23	11
14 38 13	12	2	18	3 33	25	13
14 42 10	13	2	18	4 30	26	14
14 46 8	14	3	19	5 29	28	16
14 50 7	15	4	20	6 29	♓	17
14 54 7	16	5	21	7 30	1	18
14 58 7	17	6	22	8 32	3	20
15 2 8	18	7	23	9 35	5	21
15 6 9	19	8	24	10 39	6	22
15 10 12	20	8	24	11 45	8	23
15 14 15	21	9	25	12 52	10	25
15 18 19	22	10	26	14 1	11	26
15 22 23	23	11	27	15 11	13	27
15 26 29	24	12	28	16 23	15	29
15 30 35	25	13	29	17 37	17	♉
15 34 41	26	14	♑	18 53	19	1
15 38 49	27	15	1	20 10	21	3
15 42 57	28	16	2	21 29	22	4
15 47 6	29	16	3	22 51	24	5
15 51 15	30	17	4	24 15	26	7

Sidereal Time.	10 ♐	11 ♐	12 ♑	Ascen ♑	2 ♓	3 ♉
H. M. S.	º	º	º	º '	º	º
15 51 15	0	17	4	24 15	26	7
15 55 25	1	18	5	25 41	28	8
15 59 36	2	19	6	27 10	♈	9
16 3 48	3	20	7	28 41	2	10
16 8 0	4	21	8	0♒14	4	12
16 12 13	5	22	9	1 50	5	13
16 16 26	6	23	10	3 30	7	14
16 20 40	7	24	11	5 13	9	15
16 24 55	8	25	12	6 58	11	17
16 29 10	9	26	13	8 46	13	18
16 33 26	10	27	14	10 38	15	19
16 37 42	11	28	15	12 32	17	20
16 41 59	12	29	16	14 31	19	22
16 46 16	13	♑	18	16 33	20	23
16 50 34	14	1	19	18 40	22	24
16 54 52	15	2	20	20 50	24	25
16 59 10	16	3	21	23 4	26	26
17 3 29	17	4	22	25 21	28	28
17 7 49	18	5	24	27 42	29	29
17 12 9	19	6	25	0♓8	♉	♊
17 16 29	20	7	26	2 37	3	1
17 20 49	21	8	28	5 10	5	3
17 25 9	22	9	29	7 46	6	4
17 29 30	23	10	♒	10 24	8	5
17 33 51	24	11	2	13 7	10	6
17 38 12	25	12	3	15 52	11	7
17 42 34	26	13	4	18 38	13	8
17 46 55	27	14	6	21 27	15	9
17 51 17	28	15	7	24 17	16	10
17 55 38	29	16	9	27 8	18	12
18 0 0	30	17	11	30 0	19	13

Sidereal Time.	10 ♑	11 ♑	12 ♒	Ascen ♈	2 ♉	3 ♊
H. M. S.	º	º	º	º '	º	º
18 0 0	0	17	11	0 0	19	13
18 4 22	1	18	12	2 52	21	14
18 8 43	2	20	14	5 43	23	15
18 13 5	3	21	15	8 33	24	16
18 17 26	4	22	17	11 22	25	17
18 21 48	5	23	19	14 8	27	18
18 26 9	6	24	20	16 53	28	19
18 30 30	7	25	22	19 36	♊	20
18 34 51	8	26	24	22 14	1	21
18 39 11	9	27	25	24 50	2	22
18 43 31	10	29	27	27 23	4	23
18 47 51	11	♒	28	29 52	5	24
18 52 11	12	1	♓	2♉18	6	25
18 56 31	13	2	2	4 39	8	26
19 0 50	14	4	4	6 56	9	27
19 5 8	15	5	6	9 10	10	28
19 9 26	16	6	8	11 20	11	29
19 13 44	17	7	10	13 27	12	♋
19 18 1	18	8	11	15 29	14	1
19 22 18	19	9	13	17 28	15	2
19 26 34	20	11	15	19 22	16	3
19 30 50	21	12	17	21 14	17	4
19 35 5	22	13	19	23 2	18	5
19 39 20	23	15	21	24 47	19	6
19 43 34	24	16	23	26 30	20	7
19 47 47	25	17	25	28 10	21	8
19 52 0	26	18	26	29 46	22	9
19 56 12	27	20	28	1♊19	23	10
20 0 24	28	21	♈	2 50	24	11
20 4 35	29	22	2	4 19	25	12
20 8 45	30	23	4	5 45	26	13

Sidereal Time.	10 ♒	11 ♒	12 ♈	Ascen ♊	2 ♊	3 ♋
H. M. S.	º	º	º	º '	º	º
20 8 45	0	23	4	5 45	26	13
20 12 54	1	25	6	7 9	27	14
20 17 3	2	26	8	8 31	28	14
20 21 11	3	27	9	9 50	29	15
20 25 19	4	29	11	11 7	♋	16
20 29 26	5	♓	13	12 23	1	17
20 33 31	6	1	15	13 37	2	18
20 37 37	7	3	17	14 49	3	19
20 41 41	8	4	19	15 59	4	20
20 45 45	9	5	20	17 8	5	21
20 49 48	10	7	22	18 15	6	22
20 53 51	11	8	24	19 21	7	22
20 57 52	12	10	25	20 25	7	23
21 1 53	13	11	27	21 28	8	24
21 5 53	14	12	29	22 30	9	25
21 9 53	15	13	♉	23 31	10	26
21 13 52	16	14	2	24 31	11	27
21 17 50	17	16	4	25 30	12	28
21 21 47	18	17	5	26 27	12	28
21 25 44	19	18	7	27 24	13	29
21 29 40	20	20	8	28 19	14	♌
21 33 35	21	21	10	29 14	15	1
21 37 29	22	22	11	0♋8	16	2
21 41 23	23	24	12	1 1	17	3
21 45 16	24	25	14	1 54	17	4
21 49 9	25	26	15	2 46	18	4
21 53 1	26	28	17	3 37	19	5
21 56 52	27	29	18	4 27	20	6
22 0 43	28	♈	20	5 17	20	7
22 4 33	29	2	21	6 5	21	8
22 8 23	30	3	22	6 54	22	8

Sidereal Time.	10 ♓	11 ♈	12 ♉	Ascen ♋	2 ♋	3 ♌
H. M. S.	º	º	º	º '	º	º
22 8 23	0	3	22	6 54	22	8
22 12 12	1	4	23	7 42	23	9
22 16 0	2	5	25	8 29	23	10
22 19 48	3	7	26	9 16	24	11
22 23 35	4	8	27	10 3	25	12
22 27 22	5	9	29	10 49	26	13
22 31 8	6	11	♊	11 34	26	13
22 34 54	7	12	1	12 19	27	14
22 38 40	8	13	2	13 3	28	15
22 42 25	9	14	3	13 48	29	16
22 46 9	10	16	4	14 32	29	17
22 49 53	11	17	5	15 15	♌	17
22 53 37	12	18	7	15 58	1	18
22 57 20	13	19	8	16 41	2	19
23 1 3	14	20	9	17 24	2	20
23 4 46	15	22	10	18 6	3	21
23 8 28	16	23	11	18 48	4	21
23 12 10	17	24	12	19 30	4	22
23 15 52	18	25	13	20 11	5	23
23 19 34	19	27	14	20 52	6	24
23 23 15	20	28	15	21 33	6	25
23 26 56	21	29	16	22 14	7	26
23 30 37	22	♉	17	22 54	8	26
23 34 18	23	1	18	23 34	9	27
23 37 58	24	2	19	24 14	9	28
23 41 39	25	4	20	24 54	10	29
23 45 19	26	5	21	25 35	11	♍
23 49 0	27	6	22	26 14	11	0
23 52 40	28	7	22	26 54	12	1
23 56 20	29	8	23	27 33	13	2
24 0 0	30	9	24	28 12	14	3

TABLES OF HOUSES FOR NEW YORK, Latitude 40º 43' *N.*

Sidereal Time.	10 ♈	11 ♉	12 ♊	Ascen ♋	2 ♌	3 ♍
H. M. S.	°	°	°	° '	°	°
0 0 0	0	6	15	18 53	8	1
0 3 40	1	7	16	19 38	9	2
0 7 20	2	8	17	20 23	10	3
0 11 0	3	9	18	21 12	11	4
0 14 41	4	11	19	21 55	12	5
0 18 21	5	12	20	22 40	12	5
0 22 2	6	13	21	23 24	13	6
0 25 42	7	14	22	24 8	14	7
0 29 23	8	15	23	24 54	15	8
0 33 4	9	16	23	25 37	15	9
0 36 45	10	17	24	26 22	16	10
0 40 26	11	18	25	27 5	17	11
0 44 8	12	19	26	27 50	18	12
0 47 50	13	20	27	28 33	19	13
0 51 32	14	21	28	29 18	19	13
0 55 14	15	22	28	0♌ 3	20	14
0 58 57	16	23	29	0 46	21	15
1 2 40	17	24	♋	1 31	22	16
1 6 23	18	25	1	2 14	22	17
1 10 7	19	26	2	2 58	23	18
1 13 51	20	27	3	3 43	24	19
1 17 35	21	28	3	4 27	25	20
1 21 20	22	29	4	5 12	25	21
1 25 6	23	♊	5	5 56	26	22
1 28 52	24	1	6	6 40	27	22
1 32 38	25	2	7	7 25	28	23
1 36 25	26	2	8	8 9	29	24
1 40 12	27	3	9	8 53	♍	25
1 44 0	28	4	10	9 38	1	26
1 47 48	29	5	10	10 24	1	27
1 51 37	30	6	11	11 8	2	28

Sidereal Time.	10 ♉	11 ♊	12 ♋	Ascen ♌	2 ♍	3 ♍
H. M. S.	°	°	°	° '	°	°
1 51 37	0	6	11	11 8	2	28
1 55 27	1	7	12	11 53	3	29
1 59 17	2	8	13	12 38	4	♎
2 3 8	3	9	14	13 22	5	1
2 6 59	4	10	15	14 8	5	2
2 10 51	5	11	15	14 53	6	3
2 14 44	6	12	16	15 39	7	4
2 18 37	7	13	17	16 24	8	4
2 22 31	8	14	18	17 10	9	5
2 26 25	9	15	19	17 56	10	6
2 30 20	10	16	20	18 41	10	7
2 34 16	11	17	20	19 27	11	8
2 38 13	12	18	21	20 14	12	9
2 42 10	13	19	22	21 0	13	10
2 46 8	14	19	23	21 47	14	11
2 50 7	15	20	24	22 33	15	12
2 54 7	16	21	25	23 20	16	13
2 58 7	17	22	25	24 7	17	14
3 2 8	18	23	26	24 54	17	15
3 6 9	19	24	27	25 42	18	16
3 10 12	20	25	28	26 29	19	17
3 14 15	21	26	29	27 17	20	18
3 18 19	22	27	♌	28 4	21	19
3 22 23	23	28	1	28 52	22	20
3 26 29	24	29	1	29 40	23	21
3 30 35	25	♋	2	0♍29	24	22
3 34 41	26	1	3	1 17	24	23
3 38 49	27	2	4	2 6	25	24
3 42 57	28	3	5	2 55	26	25
3 47 6	29	4	6	3 43	27	26
3 51 15	30	5	7	4 32	28	27

Sidereal Time.	10 ♊	11 ♋	12 ♌	Ascen ♍	2 ♍	3 ♎
H. M. S.	°	°	°	° '	°	°
3 51 15	0	5	7	4 32	28	27
3 55 25	1	6	8	5 22	29	28
3 59 36	2	6	8	6 10	♎	29
4 3 48	3	7	9	7 0	1	♏
4 8 0	4	8	10	7 49	2	1
4 12 13	5	9	11	8 40	3	2
4 16 26	6	10	12	9 30	4	3
4 20 40	7	11	13	10 19	4	4
4 24 55	8	12	14	11 10	5	5
4 29 10	9	13	15	12 0	6	6
4 33 26	10	14	16	12 51	7	7
4 37 42	11	15	16	13 41	8	8
4 41 59	12	16	17	14 32	9	9
4 46 16	13	17	18	15 23	10	10
4 50 34	14	18	19	16 14	11	11
4 54 52	15	19	20	17 5	12	12
4 59 10	16	20	21	17 56	13	13
5 3 29	17	21	22	18 47	14	14
5 7 49	18	22	23	19 39	15	15
5 12 9	19	23	24	20 30	16	16
5 16 29	20	24	25	21 22	17	17
5 20 49	21	25	25	22 13	18	18
5 25 9	22	26	26	23 5	18	19
5 29 30	23	27	27	23 57	19	20
5 33 51	24	28	28	24 49	20	21
5 38 12	25	29	29	25 40	21	22
5 42 34	26	♌	♍	26 32	22	22
5 46 55	27	1	1	27 25	23	23
5 51 17	28	2	2	28 16	24	24
5 55 38	29	3	3	29 8	25	25
6 0 0	30	4	4	30 0	26	26

Sidereal Time.	10 ♋	11 ♌	12 ♍	Ascen ♎	2 ♎	3 ♏
H. M. S.	°	°	°	° '	°	°
6 0 0	0	4	4	0 0	26	26
6 4 22	1	5	5	0 52	27	27
6 8 43	2	6	6	1 44	28	28
6 13 5	3	6	7	2 35	29	29
6 17 26	4	7	8	3 28	♏	♐
6 21 48	5	8	9	4 20	1	1
6 26 9	6	9	10	5 11	2	2
6 30 30	7	10	11	6 3	3	3
6 34 51	8	11	12	6 55	3	4
6 39 11	9	12	13	7 47	4	5
6 43 31	10	13	14	8 38	5	6
6 47 51	11	14	15	9 30	6	7
6 52 11	12	15	15	10 21	7	8
6 56 31	13	16	16	11 13	8	9
7 0 50	14	17	17	12 4	9	10
7 5 8	15	18	18	12 55	10	11
7 9 26	16	19	19	13 46	11	12
7 13 44	17	20	20	14 37	12	13
7 18 1	18	21	21	15 28	13	14
7 22 18	19	22	22	16 19	14	15
7 26 34	20	23	23	17 9	14	16
7 30 50	21	24	23	18 0	15	17
7 35 5	22	25	24	18 50	16	18
7 39 20	23	26	25	19 41	17	19
7 43 34	24	27	26	20 30	18	20
7 47 47	25	28	27	21 20	19	21
7 52 0	26	29	28	22 11	20	22
7 56 12	27	♍	29	23 0	21	23
8 0 24	28	1	♎	23 50	21	24
8 4 35	29	2	1	24 38	22	24
8 8 45	30	3	2	25 28	23	25

Sidereal Time.	10 ♌	11 ♍	12 ♎	Ascen ♎	2 ♏	3 ♐
H. M. S.	°	°	°	° '	°	°
8 8 45	0	3	2	25 28	23	25
8 12 54	1	4	3	26 17	24	26
8 17 3	2	5	4	27 5	25	27
8 21 11	3	6	5	27 54	26	28
8 25 19	4	7	6	28 43	27	29
8 29 26	5	8	7	29 31	28	♑
8 33 31	6	9	7	0♏20	28	1
8 37 37	7	10	8	1 8	29	2
8 41 41	8	11	9	1 56	♐	3
8 45 45	9	12	10	2 43	1	4
8 49 48	10	13	11	3 31	2	5
8 53 51	11	14	12	4 18	3	6
8 57 52	12	15	12	5 6	4	7
9 1 53	13	16	13	5 53	5	8
9 5 53	14	17	14	6 40	5	9
9 9 53	15	18	15	7 27	6	10
9 13 52	16	19	16	8 13	7	10
9 17 50	17	20	17	9 0	8	11
9 21 47	18	21	18	9 46	9	12
9 25 44	19	22	19	10 33	10	13
9 29 40	20	23	19	11 19	10	14
9 33 35	21	24	20	12 4	11	15
9 37 29	22	24	21	12 50	12	16
9 41 23	23	25	22	13 36	13	17
9 45 16	24	26	23	14 21	14	18
9 49 9	25	27	24	15 7	15	19
9 53 1	26	28	24	15 52	15	20
9 56 52	27	29	25	16 38	16	21
10 0 43	28	♎	26	17 22	17	22
10 4 33	29	1	27	18 7	18	23
10 8 23	30	2	28	18 52	19	24

Sidereal Time.	10 ♍	11 ♎	12 ♎	Ascen ♏	2 ♐	3 ♑
H. M. S.	°	°	°	° '	°	°
10 8 23	0	2	28	18 52	19	24
10 12 12	1	3	29	19 36	20	25
10 16 0	2	4	29	20 22	20	26
10 19 48	3	5	♏	21 7	21	27
10 23 35	4	6	1	21 51	22	28
10 27 22	5	7	1	22 35	23	28
10 31 8	6	7	2	23 20	24	29
10 34 54	7	8	3	24 4	25	♒
10 38 40	8	9	4	24 48	25	1
10 42 25	9	10	5	25 33	26	2
10 46 9	10	11	6	26 17	27	3
10 49 53	11	12	7	27 2	28	4
10 53 37	12	13	7	27 46	29	5
10 57 20	13	14	8	28 29	♑	6
11 1 3	14	15	9	29 14	1	7
11 4 46	15	16	10	29 57	1	8
11 8 28	16	17	11	0♐42	2	9
11 12 10	17	17	11	1 27	3	10
11 15 52	18	18	12	2 10	4	11
11 19 34	19	19	13	2 55	5	12
11 23 15	20	20	14	3 38	6	13
11 26 56	21	21	14	4 23	7	14
11 30 37	22	22	15	5 6	7	15
11 34 18	23	23	16	5 52	8	16
11 37 58	24	23	17	6 36	9	17
11 41 39	25	24	18	7 20	10	18
11 45 19	26	25	18	8 5	11	19
11 49 0	27	26	19	8 48	12	20
11 52 40	28	27	20	9 37	13	22
11 56 20	29	28	21	10 22	14	23
12 0 0	30	29	21	11 7	15	24

TABLES OF HOUSES FOR NEW YORK, *Latitude* 40º 43' N.

Sidereal Time.	10 ♎	11 ♎	12 ♏	Ascen ♐	2 ♑	3 ♒
H. M. S.	°	°	°	° '	°	°
12 0 0	0	29	21	11 7	15	24
12 3 40	1	♏	22	11 52	16	25
12 7 20	2	1	23	12 37	17	26
12 11 0	3	1	24	13 19	17	27
12 14 41	4	2	25	14 7	18	28
12 18 21	5	3	25	14 52	19	29
12 22 2	6	4	26	15 38	20	♓
12 25 42	7	5	27	16 23	21	1
12 29 23	8	6	28	17 11	22	2
12 33 4	9	6	28	17 58	23	3
12 36 45	10	7	29	18 45	24	4
12 40 26	11	8	♐	19 32	25	5
12 44 8	12	9	1	20 20	26	7
12 47 50	13	10	2	21 8	27	8
12 51 32	14	11	2	21 57	28	9
12 55 14	15	12	3	22 43	29	10
12 58 57	16	13	4	23 33	♒	11
13 2 40	17	13	5	24 22	1	12
13 6 23	18	14	6	25 11	2	13
13 10 7	19	15	7	26 1	3	15
13 13 51	20	16	7	26 51	5	16
13 17 35	21	17	8	27 40	6	17
13 21 20	22	18	9	28 32	7	18
13 25 6	23	19	10	29 23	8	19
13 28 52	24	19	10	0 ♑ 14	9	20
13 32 38	25	20	11	1 7	10	21
13 36 25	26	21	12	2 0	11	23
13 40 12	27	22	13	2 52	12	24
13 44 0	28	23	13	3 46	13	25
13 47 48	29	24	14	4 41	15	26
13 51 37	30	25	15	5 35	16	27

Sidereal Time.	10 ♏	11 ♏	12 ♐	Ascen ♑	2 ♒	3 ♓
H. M. S.	°	°	°	° '	°	°
13 51 37	0	25	15	5 35	16	27
13 55 27	1	25	16	6 30	17	29
13 59 17	2	26	17	7 27	18	♈
14 3 8	3	27	18	8 23	20	1
14 6 59	4	28	18	9 20	21	2
14 10 51	5	29	19	10 18	22	3
14 14 44	6	♐	20	11 16	23	5
14 18 37	7	1	21	12 15	24	6
14 22 31	8	2	22	13 15	26	7
14 26 25	9	2	23	14 16	27	8
14 30 20	10	3	24	15 17	28	9
14 34 16	11	4	24	16 19	♓	11
14 38 13	12	5	25	17 23	1	12
14 42 10	13	6	26	18 27	2	13
14 46 8	14	7	27	19 32	4	14
14 50 7	15	8	28	20 37	5	16
14 54 7	16	9	29	21 44	6	17
14 58 7	17	10	♑	22 51	8	18
15 2 8	18	10	1	23 59	9	19
15 6 9	19	11	2	25 9	11	20
15 10 12	20	12	3	26 19	12	22
15 14 15	21	13	4	27 31	14	23
15 18 19	22	14	5	28 43	15	24
15 22 23	23	15	6	29 57	16	25
15 26 29	24	16	6	1 ♒ 14	18	26
15 30 35	25	17	7	2 28	19	28
15 34 41	26	18	8	3 46	21	29
15 38 49	27	19	9	5 5	22	♉
15 42 57	28	20	10	6 25	24	1
15 47 6	29	21	11	7 46	25	3
15 51 15	30	21	13	9 8	27	4

Sidereal Time.	10 ♐	11 ♐	12 ♑	Ascen ♒	2 ♓	3 ♉
H. M. S.	°	°	°	° '	°	°
15 51 15	0	21	13	9 8	27	4
15 55 25	1	22	14	10 31	28	5
15 59 36	2	23	15	11 56	♈	6
16 3 48	3	24	16	13 23	1	7
16 8 0	4	25	17	14 50	3	9
16 12 13	5	26	18	16 9	4	10
16 16 26	6	27	19	17 50	6	11
16 20 40	7	28	20	19 22	7	12
16 24 55	8	29	21	20 56	9	13
16 29 10	9	♑	22	22 30	11	15
16 33 26	10	1	23	24 7	12	16
16 37 42	11	2	24	25 44	14	17
16 41 59	12	3	26	27 23	15	18
16 46 16	13	4	27	29 4	17	19
16 50 34	14	5	28	0 ♓ 45	18	20
16 54 52	15	6	29	2 27	20	22
16 59 10	16	7	♒	4 11	21	23
17 3 29	17	8	2	5 56	23	24
17 7 49	18	9	3	7 43	24	25
17 12 9	19	10	4	9 30	26	26
17 16 29	20	11	5	11 18	27	27
17 20 49	21	12	7	13 8	29	28
17 25 9	22	13	8	14 57	♉	♊
17 29 30	23	14	9	16 48	2	1
17 33 51	24	15	10	18 41	3	2
17 38 12	25	16	12	20 33	5	3
17 42 34	26	17	13	22 25	6	4
17 46 55	27	19	14	24 19	7	5
17 51 17	28	20	16	26 12	9	6
17 55 38	29	21	17	28 7	10	7
18 0 0	30	22	18	30 0	12	9

Sidereal Time.	10 ♑	11 ♑	12 ♒	Ascen ♈	2 ♉	3 ♊
H. M. S.	°	°	°	° '	°	°
18 0 0	0	22	18	0 0	12	9
18 4 22	1	23	20	1 53	13	10
18 8 43	2	24	21	3 48	14	11
18 13 5	3	25	23	5 41	16	12
18 17 26	4	26	24	7 35	17	13
18 21 48	5	27	25	9 27	18	14
18 26 9	6	28	27	11 19	20	15
18 30 30	7	29	28	13 12	21	16
18 34 51	8	♒	♓	15 3	22	17
18 39 11	9	2	1	16 52	23	18
18 43 31	10	3	3	18 42	25	19
18 47 51	11	4	4	20 30	26	20
18 52 11	12	5	5	22 17	27	21
18 56 31	13	6	7	24 4	29	22
19 0 50	14	7	9	25 49	♊	23
19 5 8	15	9	10	27 33	1	24
19 9 26	16	10	12	29 15	2	25
19 13 44	17	11	13	0 ♉ 56	3	26
19 18 1	18	12	15	2 37	4	27
19 22 18	19	13	16	4 16	6	28
19 26 34	20	14	18	5 53	7	29
19 30 50	21	16	19	7 30	8	♋
19 35 5	22	17	21	9 4	9	1
19 39 20	23	18	22	10 38	10	2
19 43 34	24	19	24	12 10	11	3
19 47 47	25	20	25	13 41	12	4
19 52 0	26	21	27	15 10	13	5
19 56 12	27	23	29	16 37	14	6
20 0 24	28	24	♈	18 4	15	7
20 4 35	29	25	2	19 29	16	8
20 8 45	30	26	3	20 52	17	9

Sidereal Time.	10 ♒	11 ♒	12 ♈	Ascen ♉	2 ♊	3 ♋
H. M. S.	°	°	°	° '	°	°
20 8 45	0	26	3	20 52	17	9
20 12 54	1	27	5	22 14	18	9
20 17 3	2	29	6	23 35	19	10
20 21 11	3	♓	8	24 55	20	11
20 25 19	4	1	9	26 14	21	12
20 29 26	5	2	11	27 32	22	13
20 33 31	6	3	12	28 46	23	14
20 37 37	7	5	14	0 ♊ 3	24	15
20 41 41	8	6	15	1 17	25	16
20 45 45	9	7	16	2 29	26	17
20 49 48	10	8	18	3 41	27	18
20 53 51	11	10	19	4 51	28	19
20 57 52	12	11	21	6 1	29	20
21 1 53	13	12	22	7 9	♋	20
21 5 53	14	13	24	8 16	1	21
21 9 53	15	14	25	9 23	2	22
21 13 52	16	16	26	10 30	3	23
21 17 50	17	17	28	11 33	4	24
21 21 47	18	18	29	12 37	5	25
21 25 44	19	19	♉	13 41	6	26
21 29 40	20	21	2	14 43	6	27
21 33 35	21	22	3	15 44	7	28
21 37 29	22	23	4	16 45	8	28
21 41 23	23	24	6	17 45	9	29
21 45 16	24	25	7	18 44	10	♌
21 49 9	25	27	8	19 42	11	1
21 53 1	26	28	9	20 40	12	2
21 56 52	27	29	11	21 37	12	3
22 0 43	28	♈	12	22 33	13	4
22 4 33	29	1	13	23 30	14	5
22 8 23	30	3	14	24 25	15	5

Sidereal Time.	10 ♓	11 ♈	12 ♉	Ascen ♊	2 ♋	3 ♌
H. M. S.	°	°	°	° '	°	°
22 8 23	0	3	14	24 25	15	5
22 12 12	1	4	15	25 19	16	6
22 16 0	2	5	17	26 14	17	7
22 19 48	3	6	18	27 8	17	8
22 23 35	4	7	19	28 0	18	9
22 27 22	5	8	20	28 53	19	10
22 31 8	6	10	21	29 46	20	11
22 34 54	7	11	22	0 ♋ 37	21	11
22 38 40	8	12	23	1 28	21	12
22 42 25	9	13	24	2 20	22	13
22 46 9	10	14	25	3 9	23	14
22 49 53	11	15	27	3 59	24	15
22 53 37	12	17	28	4 49	24	16
22 57 20	13	18	29	5 38	25	17
23 1 3	14	19	♊	6 27	26	17
23 4 46	15	20	1	7 17	27	18
23 8 28	16	21	2	8 3	28	19
23 12 10	17	22	3	8 52	28	20
23 15 52	18	23	4	9 40	29	21
23 19 34	19	24	5	10 28	♌	22
23 23 15	20	26	6	11 15	1	23
23 26 56	21	27	7	12 2	2	23
23 30 37	22	28	8	12 49	2	24
23 34 18	23	29	9	13 37	3	25
23 37 58	24	♉	10	14 22	4	26
23 41 39	25	1	11	15 8	5	27
23 45 19	26	2	12	15 53	5	28
23 49 0	27	3	12	16 41	6	29
23 52 40	28	4	13	17 23	7	29
23 56 20	29	5	14	18 8	8	♍
24 0 0	30	6	15	18 53	9	1

PROPORTIONAL LOGARITHMS FOR FINDING THE PLANETS' PLACES

Min	DEGREES OR HOURS																Min
	0	1	2	3	4	5	6	7	8	9	10	11	12	13	14	15	
0	3.1584	1.3802	1.0792	9031	7781	6812	6021	5351	4771	4260	3802	3388	3010	2663	2341	2041	**0**
1	3.1584	1.3730	1.0756	9007	7763	6798	6009	5341	4762	4252	3795	3382	3004	2657	2336	2036	**1**
2	2.8573	1.3660	1.0720	8983	7745	6784	5997	5330	4753	4244	3788	3375	2998	2652	2330	2032	**2**
3	2.6812	1.3590	1.0685	8959	7728	6769	5985	5320	4744	4236	3780	3368	2992	2646	2325	2027	**3**
4	2.5563	1.3522	1.0649	8935	7710	6755	5973	5310	4735	4228	3773	3362	2986	2640	2320	2022	**4**
5	2.4594	1.3454	1.0614	8912	7692	6741	5961	5300	4726	4220	3766	3355	2980	2635	2315	2017	**5**
6	2.3802	1.3388	1.0580	8888	7674	6726	5949	5289	4717	4212	3759	3349	2974	2629	2310	2012	**6**
7	2.3133	1.3323	1.0546	8865	7657	6712	5937	5279	4708	4204	3752	3342	2968	2624	2305	2008	**7**
8	2.2553	1.3258	1.0511	8842	7639	6698	5925	5269	4699	4196	3745	3336	2962	2618	2300	2003	**8**
9	2.2041	1.3195	1.0478	8819	7622	6684	5913	5259	4690	4188	3737	3329	2956	2613	2295	1998	**9**
10	2.1584	1.3133	1.0444	8796	7604	6670	5902	5249	4682	4180	3730	3323	2950	2607	2289	1993	**10**
11	2.1170	1.3071	1.0411	8773	7587	6656	5890	5239	4673	4172	3723	3316	2944	2602	2284	1988	**11**
12	2.0792	1.3010	1.0378	8751	7570	6642	5878	5229	4664	4164	3716	3310	2938	2596	2279	1984	**12**
13	2.0444	1.2950	1.0345	8728	7552	6628	5866	5219	4655	4156	3709	3303	2933	2591	2274	1979	**13**
14	2.0122	1.2891	1.0313	8706	7535	6614	5855	5209	4646	4148	3702	3297	2927	2585	2269	1974	**14**
15	1.9823	1.2833	1.0280	8683	7518	6600	5843	5199	4638	4141	3695	3291	2921	2580	2264	1969	**15**
16	1.9542	1.2775	1.0248	8661	7501	6587	5832	5189	4629	4133	3688	3284	2915	2574	2259	1965	**16**
17	1.9279	1.2719	1.0216	8639	7484	6573	5820	5179	4620	4125	3681	3278	2909	2569	2254	1960	**17**
18	1.9031	1.2663	1.0185	8617	7467	6559	5809	5169	4611	4117	3674	3271	2903	2564	2249	1955	**18**
19	1.8796	1.2607	1.0153	8595	7451	6546	5797	5159	4603	4109	3667	3265	2897	2558	2244	1950	**19**
20	1.8573	1.2553	1.0122	8573	7434	6532	5786	5149	4594	4102	3660	3258	2891	2553	2239	1946	**20**
21	1.8361	1.2499	1.0091	8552	7417	6519	5774	5139	4585	4094	3653	3252	2885	2547	2234	1941	**21**
22	1.8159	1.2445	1.0061	8530	7401	6505	5763	5129	4577	4086	3646	3246	2880	2542	2229	1936	**22**
23	1.7966	1.2393	1.0030	8509	7384	6492	5752	5120	4568	4079	3639	3239	2874	2536	2223	1932	**23**
24	1.7781	1.2341	1.0000	8487	7368	6478	5740	5110	4559	4071	3632	3233	2868	2531	2218	1927	**24**
25	1.7604	1.2289	0.9970	8466	7351	6465	5729	5100	4551	4063	3625	3227	2862	2526	2213	1922	**25**
26	1.7434	1.2239	0.9940	8445	7335	6451	5718	5090	4542	4055	3618	3220	2856	2520	2208	1917	**26**
27	1.7270	1.2188	0.9910	8424	7318	6438	5706	5081	4534	4048	3611	3214	2850	2515	2203	1913	**27**
28	1.7112	1.2139	0.9881	8403	7302	6425	5695	5071	4525	4040	3604	3208	2845	2509	2198	1908	**28**
29	1.6960	1.2090	0.9852	8382	7286	6412	5684	5061	4516	4032	3597	3201	2839	2504	2193	1903	**29**
30	1.6812	1.2041	0.9823	8361	7270	6398	5673	5051	4508	4025	3590	3195	2833	2499	2188	1899	**30**
31	1.6670	1.1993	0.9794	8341	7254	6385	5662	5042	4499	4017	3583	3189	2827	2493	2183	1894	**31**
32	1.6532	1.1946	0.9765	8320	7238	6372	5651	5032	4491	4010	3576	3183	2821	2488	2178	1889	**32**
33	1.6398	1.1899	0.9737	8300	7222	6359	5640	5023	4482	4002	3570	3176	2816	2483	2173	1885	**33**
34	1.6269	1.1852	0.9708	8279	7206	6346	5629	5013	4474	3994	3563	3170	2810	2477	2168	1880	**34**
35	1.6143	1.1806	0.9680	8259	7190	6333	5618	5003	4466	3987	3556	3164	2804	2472	2164	1875	**35**
36	1.6021	1.1761	0.9652	8239	7174	6320	5607	4994	4457	3979	3549	3157	2798	2467	2159	1871	**36**
37	1.5902	1.1716	0.9625	8219	7159	6307	5596	4984	4449	3972	3542	3151	2793	2461	2154	1866	**37**
38	1.5786	1.1671	0.9597	8199	7143	6294	5585	4975	4440	3964	3535	3145	2787	2456	2149	1862	**38**
39	1.5673	1.1627	0.9570	8179	7128	6282	5574	4965	4432	3957	3529	3139	2781	2451	2144	1857	**39**
40	1.5563	1.1584	0.9542	8159	7112	6269	5563	4956	4424	3949	3522	3133	2775	2445	2139	1852	**40**
41	1.5456	1.1540	0.9515	8140	7097	6256	5552	4947	4415	3942	3515	3126	2770	2440	2134	1848	**41**
42	1.5351	1.1498	0.9488	8120	7081	6243	5541	4937	4407	3934	3508	3120	2764	2435	2129	1843	**42**
43	1.5249	1.1455	0.9462	8101	7066	6231	5531	4928	4399	3927	3501	3114	2758	2430	2124	1838	**43**
44	1.5149	1.1413	0.9435	8081	7050	6218	5520	4918	4390	3919	3495	3108	2753	2424	2119	1834	**44**
45	1.5051	1.1372	0.9409	8062	7035	6205	5509	4909	4382	3912	3488	3102	2747	2419	2114	1829	**45**
46	1.4956	1.1331	0.9383	8043	7020	6193	5498	4900	4374	3905	3481	3096	2741	2414	2109	1825	**46**
47	1.4863	1.1290	0.9356	8023	7005	6180	5488	4890	4365	3897	3475	3089	2736	2409	2104	1820	**47**
48	1.4771	1.1249	0.9330	8004	6990	6168	5477	4881	4357	3890	3468	3083	2730	2403	2099	1816	**48**
49	1.4682	1.1209	0.9305	7985	6975	6155	5466	4872	4349	3882	3461	3077	2724	2398	2095	1811	**49**
50	1.4594	1.1170	0.9279	7966	6960	6143	5456	4863	4341	3875	3454	3071	2719	2393	2090	1806	**50**
51	1.4508	1.1130	0.9254	7947	6945	6131	5445	4853	4333	3868	3448	3065	2713	2388	2085	1802	**51**
52	1.4424	1.1091	0.9228	7929	6930	6118	5435	4844	4324	3860	3441	3059	2707	2382	2080	1797	**52**
53	1.4341	1.1053	0.9203	7910	6915	6106	5424	4835	4316	3853	3434	3053	2702	2377	2075	1793	**53**
54	1.4260	1.1015	0.9178	7891	6900	6094	5414	4826	4308	3846	3428	3047	2696	2372	2070	1788	**54**
55	1.4180	1.0977	0.9153	7873	6885	6081	5403	4817	4300	3838	3421	3041	2691	2367	2065	1784	**55**
56	1.4102	1.0939	0.9128	7854	6871	6069	5393	4808	4292	3831	3415	3034	2685	2362	2061	1779	**56**
57	1.4025	1.0902	0.9104	7836	6856	6057	5382	4798	4284	3824	3408	3028	2679	2356	2056	1774	**57**
58	1.3949	1.0865	0.9079	7818	6841	6045	5372	4789	4276	3817	3401	3022	2674	2351	2051	1770	**58**
59	1.3875	1.0828	0.9055	7800	6827	6033	5361	4780	4268	3809	3395	3016	2668	2346	2046	1765	**59**
	0	**1**	**2**	**3**	**4**	**5**	**6**	**7**	**8**	**9**	**10**	**11**	**12**	**13**	**14**	**15**	

RULE: – Add proportional log. of planet's daily motion to log. of time from noon, and the sum will be the log. of the motion required. Add this to planet's place at noon, if time be p.m., but subtract if a.m., and the sum will be planet's true place. If Retrograde, subtract for p.m., but add for a.m.

What is the Long. of ☽ December 27, 2002 at 2.15 p.m.?

☽'s daily motion – 14° 12'

Prop. Log. of 14° 12' 2279

Prop. Log. of 2h. 15m. 1.0280

☽'s motion in 2h. 15m. = 1° 20' or Log. 1.2559

☽'s Long. = 11° ♎ 49' + 1° 20' = 13° ♎ 09'

The Daily Motions of the Sun, Moon, Mercury, Venus and Mars will be found on pages 26 to 28.